First World War
and Army of Occupation
War Diary
France, Belgium and Germany

1 DIVISION
Divisional Troops
43 Brigade Royal Field Artillery
4 August 1914 - 30 November 1914

WO95/1250/2

The Naval & Military Press Ltd
www.nmarchive.com
Published in association with The National Archives

Published by

The Naval & Military Press Ltd

Unit 10 Ridgewood Industrial Park,

Uckfield, East Sussex,

TN22 5QE England

Tel: +44 (0) 1825 749494

www.naval-military-press.com

www.nmarchive.com

Contents

War Diary	Priez	10/09/1914	10/09/1914
War Diary	Coincy	11/09/1914	11/09/1914
War Diary	Bazoches	12/09/1914	12/09/1914
War Diary	Bourg	13/09/1914	13/09/1914
War Diary	Paissy	14/09/1914	15/09/1914
War Diary	Commin Fme.	16/09/1914	27/09/1914
War Diary	Commin Fe.	28/09/1914	04/10/1914
War Diary	Commin Fe	04/10/1914	07/10/1914
War Diary	Commin Fe.	07/10/1914	09/10/1914
War Diary	Commin Fe.	09/10/1914	10/10/1914
War Diary	Commin Fe.	11/10/1914	12/10/1914
War Diary	Commin Fe.	13/10/1914	14/10/1914
War Diary	Commin Fe.	14/10/1914	15/10/1914
War Diary	In train	16/10/1914	16/10/1914
War Diary	Commin Fe.	14/10/1914	15/10/1914
War Diary	In train	16/10/1914	16/10/1914
War Diary	St Omer	17/10/1914	21/10/1914
War Diary	Pilkem.	21/10/1914	22/10/1914
War Diary	Pilkem	22/10/1914	24/10/1914
War Diary	Pilkem	24/10/1914	26/10/1914
War Diary	Hooge	27/10/1914	30/10/1914
War Diary	Westhoek	31/10/1914	31/10/1914
War Diary	Hooge	27/10/1914	30/10/1914
War Diary	Westhoek	31/10/1914	31/10/1914
Heading	43rd Bde R.F.A. Vol IV. 1-30.11.14		
War Diary		01/11/1914	10/11/1914
War Diary	Hooge	10/11/1914	23/12/1914
War Diary	Sam	23/12/1914	30/12/1914
War Diary	Bethune.	23/12/1914	23/12/1914
War Diary	Beuvry	24/12/1914	01/01/1915
Heading	1st Division 43rd Brigade R.F.A. War Diary 1915 Jan-Dec		
Heading	1st Division Jany-Mch 1915 43rd Bde R F A. Vol V		
War Diary	Beuvry	01/01/1915	28/02/1915
War Diary	Pacaut	01/03/1915	07/03/1915
War Diary	Le Casan	07/03/1915	09/03/1915
Heading	Nerve Chapelle		
War Diary	Le Casan	10/03/1915	17/03/1915
War Diary	Laventie	18/03/1915	13/04/1915
War Diary	Riez Bailleul	14/04/1915	30/04/1915
Heading	1st Division Attached Indian Corps. 43rd Bde R.F.A. Vol VI		
War Diary		01/05/1915	30/05/1915
Heading	1st Division 43rd Bde R.F.A. Vol VII June.		
War Diary		31/05/1915	29/06/1915
Heading	1st Division 43rd Bde R.F.A. Vol VIII 29-6-31-7-15		
War Diary		29/06/1915	31/07/1915
Heading	1st Division 43rd Bde R F A. Vol IX August 15		
War Diary		01/08/1915	31/08/1915
Heading	Headquarters, 43rd Brigade, R.F.A. (1st Division) September 1915		
War Diary		01/09/1915	30/09/1915
Heading	1st Division 43rd Bde R.F.A. Oct to Nov. Vol XI		
War Diary		01/10/1915	30/11/1915
Heading	H.Q. 43rd Bde R.F.A. Dec Vol XII		
War Diary		01/12/1915	31/12/1915

Heading	1914-1916 1st Division Troops43rd Brigade R.F.A. Aug 1914-May 1916		
Heading	Gds Divn G. S. War Diary Appendices Jul 1917		
Heading	1st Division H.Q., 43rd Brigade R.F.A. Jan-May 1916		
Heading	H.Q. 43rd Brigade R.F.A. :: January 1916		
War Diary		01/01/1916	31/03/1916
Heading	43 Bde R F a Vol XVI		
War Diary		01/04/1916	30/04/1916
Miscellaneous	Officer i/c. Adjutant-General's Office at the Base.	22/05/1916	22/05/1916
War Diary		01/05/1916	22/05/1916
Heading	1st Division 40th Battery R.F.A. From 4th August To 30th Sept 1914		
Heading	40th Battery R F A XLII Bde 1st Division Vols I II 4.8.30.9		
War Diary	Deepcut.	04/08/1914	17/08/1914
War Diary	Boulogne	19/08/1914	19/08/1914
War Diary	Wassigny.	20/08/1914	20/08/1914
War Diary	Malassisse.	21/08/1914	21/08/1914
War Diary	Dompierre	22/08/1914	22/08/1914
War Diary	Croix Les Rouveroy.	23/08/1914	24/08/1914
War Diary	Feignies.	25/08/1914	25/08/1914
War Diary	Taisniers	26/08/1914	26/08/1914
War Diary	Oisy	27/08/1914	27/08/1914
War Diary	Bernot	28/08/1914	28/08/1914
War Diary	St. Gobin	29/08/1914	30/08/1914
War Diary	Pinon	31/08/1914	31/08/1914
War Diary	Laraperie (near Soissons)	01/09/1914	01/09/1914
War Diary	Marolles	02/09/1914	02/09/1914
War Diary	Meaux	03/09/1914	03/09/1914
War Diary	Le Grand Glairet	04/09/1914	04/09/1914
War Diary	Coulommiers.	05/09/1914	05/09/1914
War Diary	Rozny	06/09/1914	06/09/1914
War Diary	Voudnoy.	07/09/1914	07/09/1914
War Diary	Jouy-Sur-Morin.	08/09/1914	08/09/1914
War Diary	Hondevilliers	09/09/1914	09/09/1914
War Diary	Beaurepaire	10/09/1914	10/09/1914
War Diary	Rassy	11/11/1914	11/11/1914
War Diary	Coincy	12/11/1914	12/11/1914
War Diary	Bazouches	13/09/1914	13/09/1914
War Diary	Pargnan	14/09/1914	14/09/1914
War Diary	Mt. Faucon.	15/09/1914	17/09/1914
War Diary	Mt Gourtonne.	14/09/1914	30/09/1914
Heading	1st Division 57th Battery R.F.A. From 4th August To 30th Nov. 1914		
Heading	57th Battery R F A. 1st Division Vols I II VII 4.8-1.11.14		
War Diary	Deepcut.	04/08/1914	22/08/1914
War Diary	Rouveroy le Croux.	23/08/1914	28/08/1914
War Diary	St Gobain	29/08/1914	05/09/1914
War Diary	Rozoy	06/09/1914	06/09/1914
War Diary	Vaudoy.	07/09/1914	07/09/1914
War Diary	Choisy.	08/09/1914	08/09/1914
War Diary	Hondevilliers	09/09/1914	09/09/1914
War Diary	Beaurepair Farm.	10/09/1914	20/09/1914
War Diary	Paissy	21/09/1914	15/10/1914
War Diary	Bourg	15/10/1914	15/10/1914

War Diary	Muret	16/10/1914	16/10/1914
War Diary	Neuilly-Sur-Front.	16/10/1914	16/10/1914
War Diary	Saint Omer.	18/10/1914	18/10/1914
War Diary	Ballinchoue	19/10/1914	20/10/1914
War Diary	Poperinghe	21/10/1914	21/10/1914
War Diary	Pilkem	22/10/1914	22/10/1914
War Diary	1 Nil N.W. of Pilkem	23/10/1914	24/10/1914
War Diary	Ypres	25/10/1914	26/10/1914
War Diary	Gheluvelt	27/10/1914	29/10/1914
War Diary	Westhoek	30/10/1914	01/11/1914
Heading	57th Battn: R F A. 1st Division Vol IV. 1-30.11.14		
War Diary	Westhoek near Ypres	01/11/1914	01/11/1914
War Diary	Westhoek	01/11/1914	05/11/1914
War Diary	Halexbrouck	12/11/1914	12/11/1914
War Diary	Nr Vlamertigne	13/11/1914	13/11/1914
War Diary	Hooge	14/11/1914	15/11/1914
War Diary	Merris	23/11/1914	25/11/1914
War Diary	Estaires	26/11/1914	29/11/1914
War Diary	Bellewaarde (Hooge)	16/11/1914	16/11/1914
War Diary	Vlanertingne	17/11/1914	17/11/1914
War Diary	Merris	18/11/1914	22/11/1914
War Diary	Estaires	30/11/1914	30/11/1914

1st Division

43rd BDE. R.F.A.

From 5th August. To 31st Dec. 1914

Instructions regarding War Diaries and Intelligence Summaries are contained in F. S. Regs., Part II. and the Staff Manual respectively. Title pages will be prepared in manuscript.

WAR DIARY
or
~~INTELLIGENCE SUMMARY.~~ 43rd Bde R.F.A

(Erase heading not required.)

Army Form C. 2118.

Page (1)

Hour, Date, Place	Summary of Events and Information	Remarks and references to Appendices
6 pm. 5/8/14. DEEPCUT	Order to mobilise received 6 pm.	Elw
6th "	1st day of mobilisation. Capt Drought arrived to command Amm Column	Elw
7th "	LIEUT PRICE rejoined 30th battery having resigned R.H.A. to do so.	
	LIEUT. TURNER R.N.Z.A posted to AMM. COLUMN. CAPT. CHAMBERS to STAFF	
	CAPT. 1st D.A. replaced by CAPT. WOOLCOMBE ADAMS.	Elw
8th – 11th "	Progress normal.	
12th "	Progress normal. Major WHEELER 30th BTY reported "UNFIT".	Elw
13th "	Progress normal. MAJOR MACNAUGHTON joined 30th Bty	Elw.
14th. "	Mobilisation complete.	Elw
15th "	Route march as complete brigade	Elw
16th "	Entrained at FARNBOROUGH for SOUTHAMPTON start 11 am arrival 1 pm.	
	BDE HQ shipped on SS. TURCOMAN DOMINION LINE. Delay caused by	
	ship not being completely fitted for horses, and by necessity of	
	slinging majority of horses. S	Elw
8 am 17th	Ship left SOUTHAMPTON arrived off BOULOGNE 11 pm.	Elw
6 am. 18th	Unshipped at BOULOGNE	Elw

(9 29 6) W 2794 100,000 8/14 H W V Forms/C. 2118/11.

Instructions regarding War Diaries and Intelligence Summaries are contained in F. S. Regs., Part II. and the Staff Manual respectively. Title pages will be prepared in manuscript.

WAR DIARY
or
INTELLIGENCE SUMMARY.
(*Erase heading not required.*)

43rd Bde R.F.A.

Army Form C. 2118.

Page 1

Hour, Date, Place	Summary of Events and Information	Remarks and references to Appendices
6 pm. 5/8/14. DEEPCUT	Order to mobilise received 6 pm.	EAW
6th "	1st day of mobilisation. Capt Drought arrived to command Amm. Column	EAW
7th "	LIEUT. PRICE rejoined 30th battery having resigned R.H.A. to do so.	
	LIEUT. TURNER R.N.Z.A. posted to AMN. COLUMN. CAPT. CHAMBERS to Staff	
	CAPT. 1st D.A. replaced by CAPT. WOOLCOMBE ADAMS.	EAW
8th 11th "	Progress normal.	
12th "	Progress normal. Major WHEELER 30th Bty reported "UNFIT".	EAW
13th "	Progress normal. MAJOR MACNAUGHTON joined 30th Bty	EAW.
14th "	Mobilisation complete.	EAW
15th "	Route march as complete brigade	EAW
16th "	Entrained at FARNBOROUGH for SOUTHAMPTON start 4 am arrival 1 pm.	
	BDE HQ shipped on S.S. TURCOMAN. DOMINION LINE. Delay caused by	
	ship not being completely fitted for horses and by necessity of	
	slinging majority of horses.	EAW
8 am 17th	Ship left SOUTHAMPTON arrived at BOULOGNE 11 pm.	EAW
6 am. 18th	Unshipped at BOULOGNE	EAW

(9 29 6) W 2794 100,000 8/14 H W V Forms/C. 2118/11.

Instructions regarding War Diaries and Intelligence Summaries are contained in F. S. Regs., Part II. and the Staff Manual respectively. Title pages will be prepared in manuscript.

WAR DIARY
or
~~INTELLIGENCE SUMMARY~~. 43rd Bde. R.F.A.

(Erase heading not required.)

Army Form C. 2118.

Page (2)

Hour, Date, Place	Summary of Events and Information	Remarks and references to Appendices
3 pm 18. AUG. 1914 BOULOGNE	Brigade to rest camp 2 miles E of BOULOGNE	EWD
19 " " "	Brigade entrained at GARE DU NORD for WASSIGNY	EWD
20 LE NOUVION	BDE detrained at WASSIGNY to billets at MAL ASSISE, LE NOUVION	EWD
21 " DOMPIERRE	BDE marched with 1st DIV to billets at DOMPIERRE	EWD
22 " " ROUVEROY	Marched via MAUBEUGE across BELGIAN frontier at VIEUX RANG to ROUVEROY bivouac	EWD
23 " CROIX LES ROUVEROY	Preparing for defence – line HAULCHIEN – TEISSANT. All batteries in action.	
~~24~~ "	In evening advanced to position ½ mile SW of HAULCHIEN to try to neutralise German battery which was shelling our batteries in front of position. Range over 6000x, could not locate.	EWD
24th " CROIX LES ROUVEROY	Order for a movement in retreat southwards. 30th Bty fired at mass of hostile cavalry at 3000x. Effect apparently good. Marched back W of MAUBEUGE defences – to billets at GEIGNIES [F(?) see Diary of 40 Bty RFA]	EWD
25th " TAISNIÈRE	Marched to billets at TAISNIÈRE	EWD
26th " DISY.	Marched via MARBAIX – LE GRAND FAYT – FAYRIL – DISY billets	EWD.
27th " BERNOT	Marched via ETREUX – GUISE – to billets BERNOT. 30th Bty in action against hostile guns	EWD

(9 29 6) W 2794 100,000 8/14 H W V Forms/C. 2118/11.

Army Form C. 2118.

Instructions regarding War Diaries and Intelligence Summaries are contained in F. S. Regs., Part II. and the Staff Manual respectively. Title pages will be prepared in manuscript.

WAR DIARY
or
~~INTELLIGENCE SUMMARY~~. 43rd Bde. R.F.A.

(Erase heading not required.)

Page (2)

Hour, Date, Place	Summary of Events and Information	Remarks and references to Appendices
3 pm 18. Aug. 1914 BOULOGNE	Brigade to rest camp 2 miles E of BOULOGNE.	EAW.
19	Brigade entrained at GARE DU NORD for WASSIGNY	EAW
20 LE NOUVION	BDE detrained at WASSIGNY to billets at MAL ASSISE, LE NOUVION	EAW
21 DOMPIERRE	BDE marched with 1st DIV to billets at DOMPIERRE	EAW
22 " " ROUVEROY	Marched via MAUBEUGE across BELGIAN frontier at VIEUX RANG to ROUVEROY bivouac	EAW
23 " CROIX LES ROUVEROY	Preparing for defence – line HAULCHIN – PEISSANT. All batteries in action.	
~~24~~ "	In evening advanced to posit. ½ mile SW of HAULCHIN to try to neutralise German battery which was shelling our batteries in front of position. Range over 6000x could not locate	EAW
24th " CROIX LES ROUVEROY	Order for a movement in retirement southwards. 30th Bty fired at mass of hostile cavalry at 3000x. Effect apparently good. Marched back W of MAUBEUGE defences to billets at GEIGNIES	EAW.
25th " TAISNIÈRE	Marched to billets at TAISNIÈRE	EAW
26th " OISY.	Marched via MARBAIX – LE GRAND FAYT – FAVRIL – OISY billets	EAW.
27th " BERNOT	Marched via ÉTREUX – GUISE – to billets BERNOT. 30th Bty in action against hostile guns	EAW

Instructions regarding War Diaries and Intelligence Summaries are contained in F. S. Regs., Part II. and the Staff Manual respectively. Title pages will be prepared in manuscript.

WAR DIARY

or

~~INTELLIGENCE SUMMARY.~~

(Erase heading not required.) 43rd Bde. R.F.A. Page (3)

Army Form C. 2118.

Hour, Date, Place	Summary of Events and Information	Remarks and references to Appendices
28. AUG 1914 ST GOBAIN	March via ORIGNY to ST GOBAIN. 57TH fired a few rounds at cavalry.	
	Relieved in front line by new FRENCH arrivals.	EWW
29TH " " ST GOBAIN	Rest day.	EWW
30TH " " PINON	Marched to bivouac at PINON	EWW
31st " " REPERY	March to bivouac at REPERY.	EWW
1st SEP 1914 MAROLLES	March to bivouac at MAROLLES	EWW
2nd MEAUX	March to bivouac at MEAUX	EWW
3rd JOUARRE	March to bivouac at JOUARRE via LA FERTÉ SOUS JOUARRE. ~~[illegible]~~	EWW.
4TH " COULOMMIERS	March to bivouac ½ mile S of COULOMMIERS. All batteries in action during night 4TH – 5TH covering approaches to COULOMMIERS from NORTH, did not fire.	EWW
5TH " ROZOY EN BRIE	march to ROZOY EN BRIE billets.	EWW.
6TH " VAUDROY	commenced advance N+E to VAUDROY. 30TH & 57TH not action	EWW.
7TH " CHOISY	Advance to CHOISY.	EWW
8TH " HONDEVILLERS	Advance to HONDEVILLERS	EWW
9TH " BEAUREPAIRE	Recrossed MARNE without opposition. Bivouac at BEAUREPAIRE FERME	EWW

(9 29 6) W 2794 100,000 8/14 H W V Forms/C. 2118/11.

Instructions regarding War Diaries and Intelligence Summaries are contained in F. S. Regs., Part II. and the Staff Manual respectively. Title pages will be prepared in manuscript.

Army Form C. 2118.

WAR DIARY
or
~~INTELLIGENCE SUMMARY.~~
(Erase heading not required.)

4-3rd Bde. R.F.A. Page (3)

Hour, Date, Place	Summary of Events and Information	Remarks and references to Appendices
28. AUG 1914 ST GOBAIN	March via ORIGNY to ST GOBAIN. 57th fired a few rounds at cavalry.	
	Relieved in front line by new FRENCH arrivals.	BWD
29th " " ST GOBAIN	Rest day.	BWD
30th " PINON	Marched to bivouac at PINON	BWD
31st " REGERY	March to bivouac at REGERY.	BWD
1st SEP 1914 MAREILLES	March to bivouac at MAREILLES	BWD
2nd MEAUX	March to bivouac at MEAUX	BWD
3rd JOUARRE	March to bivouac at JOUARRE ~~near~~ LA FERTÉ SOUS JOUARRE. ~~[illegible]~~	BWD.
4th " COULOMMIERS	March to bivouac ½ mile S of COULOMMIERS. All batteries in action during night 4th – 5th covering approaches to COULOMMIERS from NORTH did not fire.	BWD
5th " ROZOY EN BRIE	March to ROZOY EN BRIE billets.	BWD.
6th " VAUDROY	Commenced advance N & E to VAUDROY. 55th & 57th not in action	BWD.
7th " CHOISY	Advance to CHOISY.	BWD
8th " HONDEVILLERS	Advance to HONDEVILLERS	BWD
9th " BEAUREPAIRE	Crossed MARNE without opposition. Bivouac at BEAUREPAIRE FERME	BWD

(9 29 6) W 2794 100,000 8/14 H W V Forms/C. 2118/11.

Army Form C. 2118.

Instructions regarding War Diaries and Intelligence Summaries are contained in F. S. Regs., Part II. and the Staff Manual respectively. Title pages will be prepared in manuscript.

WAR DIARY
or
~~INTELLIGENCE SUMMARY~~.
(*Erase heading not required.*)

43rd Bde. R.F.A. Page (4)

Hour, Date, Place	Summary of Events and Information	Remarks and references to Appendices
10TH SEP. 1914 PRIEZ	Had fight with flank guard of hostile column moving eastwards. All batteries engaged. Bivouac at PRIEZ. LIEUT HANDFORD 40TH Bty and four other ranks wounded. Expenditure of ammunition 270 Shrapnel 134 Lyddite.	EW
11TH COINCY	Marched to COINCY	EW
12TH BAZOCHES	Marched to BAZOCHES bivouac	EW
13TH ~~PAR~~ BOURG	Crossing of AISNE. 30TH Battery in action about 6pm just N.E of PARGNAN expended 12 shrapnel. 30TH Bty bivouac in action during night. 40TH Bty ½ mile S of ~~bivouac~~ PARGNAN. 57TH Bty, A.C. & HQ in action bivouac E of BOURG.	EW
14TH PAISSY	30TH & 57TH Btys in action just S of CHEMIN DES DAMES & due N of PAISSY. 40TH Bty in action near VENDRESSE. Expenditure of ammunition 247 Shrapnel 330 lyddite.	EW
15TH PAISSY	Battle continued. 30TH Bty in action N of PAISSY. 57TH & 40TH same positions. Major DESHON, 57TH BTY severely wounded, 1 Driver wounded. Expenditure of ammunition 769 Shrapnel 260 lyddite.	EW

(9 29 6) W 2794 100,000 8/14 H W V Forms/C. 2118/11.

Instructions regarding War Diaries and Intelligence Summaries are contained in F.S. Regs., Part II. and the Staff Manual respectively. Title pages will be prepared in manuscript.

WAR DIARY
or
INTELLIGENCE ~~SUMMARY~~.
(*Erase heading not required.*)

Army Form C. 2118.

43rd Bde. R.F.A. Page (4)

Hour, Date, Place		Summary of Events and Information	Remarks and references to Appendices
10th SEP. 1914	PRIEZ	Had fight with flank guard of hostile column moving eastwards. All batteries engaged. Bivouac at PRIEZ. LIEUT HANDFORD 40 Bty and four other ranks wounded. Expenditure of ammunition 270 Shrapnel 134 Lyddite.	E.a.w
11th	COINCY	Marched to COINCY	E.a.w
12th	BAZOCHES	Marched to BAZOCHES bivouac	E.a.w
13th	~~BAZ~~ BOURG	Crossing of AISNE. 20th Battery in action about 6 pm just N.E. of PARGNAN expended 12 Shrapnel. 20th Bty bivouac in action during night. 40th Bty ½ mile S of ~~[illegible]~~ PARGNAN. 57th Bty, A.C. & HQ in action bivouac E of BOURG.	E.a.w.
14th	PAISSY	20th & 57th Btys in action just S. of CHEMIN DES DAMES – due N of PAISSY. 40th Bty in action near VENDRESSE. Expenditure of ammunition 247 Shrapnel 330 Lyddite.	E.a.w
15th	PAISSY	Battle continued. 20th Bty in action N of PAISSY. 57th & 40th same positions. Major DESMAN, 57th Bty severely wounded, 1 Private wounded. Expenditure of ammunition 769 Shrapnel 26 [illegible] Lyddite.	E.a.w

(9 29 6) W 2794 100,000 8/14 H W V Forms/C. 2118/11.

Instructions regarding War Diaries and Intelligence Summaries are contained in F. S. Regs., Part II. and the Staff Manual respectively. Title pages will be prepared in manuscript.

WAR DIARY
or
~~INTELLIGENCE SUMMARY.~~
(Erase heading not required.) 43rd Bde R.F.A. page (5)

Army Form C. 2118.

Hour, Date, Place	Summary of Events and Information	Remarks and references to Appendices
16th COMMINENE	Battle continued. 30th Bty moved to position under N.E. end of COURTONNE ridge. 40th battery to position on COURTONNE ridge. 57th placed under orders of O.C. 26th BDE withdrew to position just N of PRISSY. Expenditure of ammunition 332 shrapnel 236 lyddite.	BW
17th COMMINENE.	Battle continued. Amm expended 202 shrapnel 177 lyddite	BW
18th "	do " 129 " 186 "	BW
19th do.	do do. 336 " 286 "	BW
20th "	do do 407 " 261 "	BW
" "	1 man killed 2 wounded.	
21st do.	Ammunition expended 287 shrapnel 223 lyddite, 1 man wounded	BW
22nd do.	" " 439 " 125 " 3 men + 1 interpreter wounded	BW
23rd do.	" " 444 " 145 " 2 men slightly wounded	BW
24th do.	" " 345 " 196 "	BW
25th do.	" " 307 " 235 " 1 man killed	BW
26th do.	" " 729 " 290 " 1 man killed 6 men wounded	BW
27th	" " 302 " 187 " 1 man slightly wounded	BW

Instructions regarding War Diaries and Intelligence Summaries are contained in F. S. Regs., Part II. and the Staff Manual respectively. Title pages will be prepared in manuscript.

WAR DIARY

or

~~INTELLIGENCE SUMMARY.~~

(Erase heading not required.) 43rd Bde R.F.A. page (5)

Army Form C. 2118.

Hour, Date, Place	Summary of Events and Information	Remarks and references to Appendices
16th COMMUN FME.	Battle continued. 30th Bty moved to position under N.E end of COURTONNE ridge. 40th battery to position on COURTONNE ridge. 57th placed under orders of O.C. 26th BDE with draws to position just N of PAISSY. Expenditure of ammunition 332 shrapnel 236 lyddite.	EAW.
17th COMMUN FME.	Battle continued. Amm. expended 302 shrapnel 177 lyddite	EAW
18th do	do 129 " 186 "	EAW
19th do.	do. do. 336 " 286 "	EAW
20th do	do do. 407 " 261 "	EAW
" "	1 man killed 2 wounded.	
21st. do.	Ammunition expended 237 shrapnel 225 lyddite, 1 man wounded	EAW
22nd do.	" " 439 " 125 " 3 men & 1 interpreter wounded	EAW.
23rd do	" " 444 " 145 " 2 men slightly wounded	EAW
24th do.	" " 345 " 176 "	EAW
25th do.	" " 307 " 235 " 1 man killed	EAW
26th do.	" " 729 " 290 " 1 man killed 6 men wounded	EAW
27th	" " 302 " 187 " 1 man slightly wounded	EAW

Instructions regarding War Diaries and Intelligence Summaries are contained in F. S. Regs., Part II. and the Staff Manual respectively. Title pages will be prepared in manuscript.

WAR DIARY
or
~~INTELLIGENCE SUMMARY.~~
(Erase heading not required.)

43rd Bde. R.F.A. page (6)

Army Form C. 2118.

Hour, Date, Place	Summary of Events and Information	Remarks and references to Appendices
28. SEP. 1914. COMMIN FE.	ammunition expended 442 shrapnel 257 lyddite.	EAW
29th " "	" " 124 " 99 "	EAW
30th " "	" " 135 " 107 " 1 man wounded	EAW
1st OCT 1914 "	Same position 40TH BTY shot chiefly at infantry digging in trenches. 30TH BTY intermittently at guns. Observation of fire by aeroplanes with wireless tried for the first time with 30TH BTY. Two targets observed. First target a hostile battery, range obtained in 6 rounds; second targets in 12 rounds. Ammunition expended 146 Shrapnel, 152 lyddite.	e EAW
2nd " " "	Fog in morning put a stop to bombardment on both sides. Amm expended 23 shrapnel 30 lyddite.	EAW
3rd " " "	Same positions intermittent shelling of enemy's guns during day.	
4 pm 3rd	40th Bty under heavy shrapnel fire from N. end of BEAULNE ridge. 1 Sgt killed, 3 men & 5 horses wounded.	EAW
7.30 am 4th	German battery opened with shrapnel on 40TH battery from direction of LA CREUTE. 30TH Bty replied without being able to locate battery	

Instructions regarding War Diaries and Intelligence Summaries are contained in F. S. Regs., Part II. and the Staff Manual respectively. Title pages will be prepared in manuscript.

WAR DIARY
or
~~INTELLIGENCE SUMMARY.~~
(*Erase heading not required.*)

Army Form C. 2118.

43rd Bde. R.F.A. page 6

Hour, Date, Place	Summary of Events and Information	Remarks and references to Appendices
28. SEP. 1914. COMMIN FE.	Ammunition expended 442 shrapnel 257 lyddite.	EAW
29th " "	" " 124 " 99 "	EAW
30th " "	" " 135 " 107 " 1 man wounded	EAW
1st OCT 1914 "	Same position 40th Bty shot chiefly at infantry digging in trenches. 30th Bty intermittently at guns. Observation of fire by aeroplane with wireless tried for the first time with 30th Bty. Two targets observed. First target a hostile battery, range obtained in 6 rounds, second targets in 12 rounds. Ammunition expended 146 Shrapnel, 152 lyddite.	a EAW
2nd "	Fog in morning put a stop to bombardment on both sides. Amm expended 23 shrapnel 30 lyddite	EAW
3rd " " "	Same positions intermittent shelling of enemy's guns during day.	
4 pm 3rd	40th Bty under heavy shrapnel fire from N. end of BEAULNE ridge 1 Sgt killed, 3 men & 5 horses wounded.	EAW.
7.30 am 4th	German battery opened with shrapnel on 40th battery from direction of LA CREUTE. 30th Bty replied without being able to locate battery	

(9 29 6) W 2794 100,000 8/14 H W V Forms/C. 2118/11.

Army Form C. 2118.

Instructions regarding War Diaries and Intelligence Summaries are contained in F. S. Regs., Part II. and the Staff Manual respectively. Title pages will be prepared in manuscript.

WAR DIARY
or
~~INTELLIGENCE SUMMARY.~~
(*Erase heading not required.*) 43rd Bde R.F.A. Page (7)

Hour, Date, Place	Summary of Events and Information	Remarks and references to Appendices
10 am 4th Oct 1914 COMMIN FE	40th Bty engaged German battery W of FACTORY ~~about~~ effect unknown.	
4 pm " "	40th Bty heavily shelled by 2 gun & one howitzer battery without result.	
4.15-4.30pm } 5.15-5.30pm }	General bombardment of German position	
	Expenditure of ammunition 177 shrapnel 220 lyddite	[illegible initials]
5th Oct. " "	30th & 40th batts engaged gun targets & trenches intermittently all day. Attempt at observation by wireless aeroplane, but light too bad. Forward observing officer sent to Hill SS of VENDRESSE unsatisfactory results though telephone communication established.	
5.15-5.30pm " " "	General bombardment of enemy's position. Amn expend. 80 Shr. 118 Lyd.	[illegible initials]
6th Oct " "	30th and 40th batteries in same position engaging guns & trenches. Hostile batteries very active in afternoon. +	
4 pm	Heavy bombardment of 1st Bde trenches.	
	Expenditure of ammunition 42 shrapnel 162 lyddite.	[illegible initials]
9 am. 7th Oct.	40th under shrapnel fire for about an hour.	

Instructions regarding War Diaries and Intelligence Summaries are contained in F. S. Regs., Part II. and the Staff Manual respectively. Title pages will be prepared in manuscript.

WAR DIARY
or
~~INTELLIGENCE SUMMARY.~~
(Erase heading not required.)

43rd Bde R.F.A. Page (7)

Army Form C. 2118.

Hour, Date, Place	Summary of Events and Information	Remarks and references to Appendices
10 am 4th Oct 1914 COMMIN TE	40th Bty engaged German battery W of FACTORY ~~about~~ effect unknown.	
4 pm " "	40th Bty heavily shelled by 2 gun + one howitzer battery without result.	
4.15–4.30pm } 5.15–5.30pm }	General bombardment of German position.	
	Expenditure of ammunition 177 shrapnel 220 lyddite	[illegible]
5th Oct " "	30th + 40th batts. engaged gun targets + trenches intermittently all day attempt at observation by wireless aeroplane but light too bad. Forward observing officer sent to hill 55 of VENDRESSE unsatisfactory results though telephone communication established.	
8.15–5.30pm " "	General bombardment of enemy's position. Amm expend. 80 Shr. 118 Lyd.	[illegible]
6th Oct " "	30th and 40th batteries in same position engaging guns + trenches. Hostile batteries very active in afternoon. +	
4 pm	Heavy bombardment of 1st Bde trenches.	
	Expenditure of ammunition 48 shrapnel 162 lyddite.	[illegible]
9 am. 7th Oct.	40th under shrapnel fire for about an hour.	

(9 29 6) W 2794 100,000 8/14 H W V Forms/C. 2118/11.

Instructions regarding War Diaries and Intelligence Summaries are contained in F. S. Regs., Part II. and the Staff Manual respectively. Title pages will be prepared in manuscript.

WAR DIARY

or

~~INTELLIGENCE SUMMARY.~~

(Erase heading not required.)

Army Form C. 2118.

43rd Bde R.F.A. Page (8)

Hour, Date, Place	Summary of Events and Information	Remarks and references to Appendices
12 noon. 7. OCT. 1914 COMMIN FE.	30th & 40th Brys on two gun targets each with wireless aeroplane. Very succesful results. Ammunition expended 130 shrapnel 247 lyddite. Casualties 1 Bombardier killed, 1 man wounded.	EAW
9 am 8th OCT. " "	German heavy howitzers very active firing about ⊕ of MOULINS. Chance shell fell near 40th battery.	
10-11 am. " " "	About 20 light howitzer shell fell behind near 40th Battery.	
11.30 am " " " "	30th & 40th Brys observation with wireless aeroplane. When aeroplane observing two targets in succession for one battery noted that sufficient time must be allowed to bring immediate	
4.15 pm 8th do	effective fire on to first target before turning on to second. Further wireless observation.	EAW.
	Ammunition expended 65 shrapnel 245 lyddite. Casualties, 1 man and 6 horses killed, 6 men and 10 horses wounded.	
9th OCT. do	Several German batteries changed position. Aeroplane reported 34 guns at MALYAL FE.	
3-3.20 pm 9th OCT do.	Combined firing by 30th Bry + 2nd DIV batteries on German batteries near	

Instructions regarding War Diaries and Intelligence Summaries are contained in F. S. Regs., Part II. and the Staff Manual respectively. Title pages will be prepared in manuscript.

Army Form C. 2118.

WAR DIARY
or
~~INTELLIGENCE~~ SUMMARY.
(Erase heading not required.)

43rd Bde R.F.A. Page (8)

Hour, Date, Place	Summary of Events and Information	Remarks and references to Appendices
12 noon. 7. Oct. 1914 CAMMIN FE.	30th & 40th Btys on two gun targets each with wireless aeroplane.	
	Very successful results. Ammunition expended 130 shrapnel	
	247 lyddite, Casualties 1 Bombardier killed, 1 man wounded.	[illegible]
9 am 8th Oct. " "	German heavy howitzers very active firing about 10 of MOULINS. Stray shell fell near 40th battery.	
10–11 am. " " "	About 20 light howitzer shell fell [illegible] near 40th Battery.	
11·30 am " " "	30th & 40th Btys. observation with wireless aeroplane. When aeroplane observing two targets in succession for one battery noted that sufficient time must be allowed to bring immediate	
4·15 pm 8th ↓ do	effective fire on to first target before turning on to second. Further wireless observation.	[illegible]
9	Ammunition expended. 65 shrapnel 245 lyddite. Casualties, 1 man and 6 horses killed, 6 men and 10 horses wounded.	
9th Oct. do	Several German batteries changed position. Aeroplane reported 34 guns at MALTAL FE.	
3–4 pm 9th Oct do.	Combined firing by 30th Bty & 2nd Div batteries on German batteries near	

(9 29 6) W 2794 100,000 8/14 H W V Forms/C. 2118/11.

Instructions regarding War Diaries and Intelligence Summaries are contained in F. S. Regs., Part II. and the Staff Manual respectively. Title pages will be prepared in manuscript.

WAR DIARY
or
~~INTELLIGENCE SUMMARY.~~
(Erase heading not required.)

Army Form C. 2118.

43rd Bde R.F.A. Page (9)

Hour, Date, Place	Summary of Events and Information	Remarks and references to Appendices
9th Oct. 1914 COMMIN FE.	COURTECON.	
4pm " " " "	combined firing with 2nd DIV batteries by 30th Bty on German batteries near MALVAL FE.	ews.
	Ammunition expended. 74 shrapnel 185 lyddite. 1 Driver slightly wounded.	
10th Oct. " " "	Mist in early morning delayed opening of fire.	
9.30 am " " " "	Two hostile batteries opened fire, one on hill about VENDRESSE, other	
10 am. " "	on MOULINS ridge, 40th replied and firing died down about 10 am	
11am " "	Several hostile batteries opened on 1st Bde trenches for a short time.	
12noon-1pm " " " "	General bombardment of hostile trenches & supports & approaches to position.	
9pm " " " "	Attack on 2nd Inf Bde. 30th & 40th Batteries fired on approaches to German position opposite 1st BDE in reply	Ew.
~~11th Oct~~ " "	Ammunition expended. 163 shrapnel 99 lyddite. Casualties 1 Sgt to hospital	
~~11th Oct.~~ "	~~Attack by French on right of 1st DIV~~.	
~~4.30-5am 11th Oct~~	~~All hostile artillery capable of bearing on French shelled by all batteries~~.	

(9 29 6) W 2794 100,000 8/14 H W V Forms/C. 2118/11.

Army Form C. 2118.

Instructions regarding War Diaries and Intelligence Summaries are contained in F. S. Regs., Part II. and the Staff Manual respectively. Title pages will be prepared in manuscript.

WAR DIARY
or
~~INTELLIGENCE SUMMARY.~~

(*Erase heading not required.*)

43rd Bde R.F.A. Page (9)

Hour, Date, Place	Summary of Events and Information	Remarks and references to Appendices
9th Oct. 1914 CONNIN FE.	COURTECON.	
4 pm " " " "	Combined firing with 2nd Div batteries of 30th Bty on German batteries near	
	MALVAL FE.	ecw.
	Ammunition expended. 74 Shrapnel 103 Lyddite. 1 Dr. was slightly wounded.	
10th Oct. " " "	Mist in early morning delayed opening of fire.	
9.30 am " " " " "	Two hostile batteries opened fire, one on hill above VENDRESSE, other	
10 am. " "	on MOULINS ridge. 40th replied and firing died down about 10 am	
11 am " "	Several hostile batteries opened on 1st Bde trenches for a short time.	
12 noon-1 pm. "	General bombardment of hostile trenches & supports & approaches	
	to position.	
9 pm " " " "	Attack on 2nd Inf Bde. 30th & 40th Batteries fired on approaches to	
	German position opposite 1st BDE. in reply.	ecw.
~~11th Oct.~~ " "	Ammunition expended. 163 Shrapnel 99 Lyddite. Casualties 1 Sgt to hospital	
~~11th Oct.~~ "	~~Attack by French on right of 1st DIV.~~	
4.30 ~~am.~~ ~~12th Oct~~	~~Old hostile artillery capable of bearing on French shelled by all~~	
	~~batteries.~~	

(9 29 6) W 2794 100,000 8/14 H W V Forms/C. 2118/11.

Instructions regarding War Diaries and Intelligence Summaries are contained in F. S. Regs., Part II. and the Staff Manual respectively. Title pages will be prepared in manuscript.

WAR DIARY
or
~~INTELLIGENCE SUMMARY.~~
(Erase heading not required.)

43rd Bde. R.F.A. Page 10

Army Form C. 2118.

Hour, Date, Place	Summary of Events and Information	Remarks and references to Appendices
~~6am~~. 11TH OCT, 1914 COMMIN FE.	German artillery fired on 1st Bde trenches for ¼ hour at dawn. During morning 40TH battery fired at hostile observation posts on CHEMIN DES DAMES. Hostile artillery quiet during morning.	
4.15pm 11TH Oct. "	Aeroplane observation 30TH & 40TH batteries, 2 targets each.	
	Expenditure of ammunition 115 shrapnel 196 Lyddite.	
12TH Oct. "	Attack by French on right of 1st DIV.	
4.30-5am " " " "	Enemy's artillery capable of bearing on French shelled by all batteries.	
6am. " " " "	French reported as having reached line of CHEMIN DES DAMES.	
10.15am " " " "	Hostile batteries again shelled preparatory to renewal of French attack.	
11am. " " " "	Renewal of bombardment by Germans of 1ST & 2nd Inf Bde trenches. 30TH replied on batteries near MALVAL FE. 40TH on battery W of factory.	
	During afternoon 30TH & 40TH Bty. observation stations fired on and telephone wires cut.	
	Expenditure of ammunition 300 shrapnel 327 Lyddite.	EAW

Instructions regarding War Diaries and Intelligence Summaries are contained in F. S. Regs., Part II. and the Staff Manual respectively. Title pages will be prepared in manuscript.

WAR DIARY
or
~~INTELLIGENCE SUMMARY.~~

(Erase heading not required.)

Army Form C. 2118.

43rd Bde. R.F.A. Page (10)

Hour, Date, Place	Summary of Events and Information	Remarks and references to Appendices
~~6am~~. 11th Oct. 1914 COMMIN FE.	German artillery fired on 1st Bde trenches for ¼ hour at dawn. During morning 40th battery fired at hostile observation posts on CHEMIN DES DAMES. Hostile artillery quiet during morning.	
4.15pm 11th Oct. "	Aeroplane observation 30th 40th batteries, 2 targets each.	EWO
	Expenditure of ammunition 112 shrapnel 116 lyddite.	
12th Oct. "	Attack by French on right of 1st DIV.	
4.30–5am " " " "	Enemy's artillery capable of bearing on French shelled by all batteries.	
6am. " " " "	French reported as having reached line of CHEMIN DES DAMES.	
10.15am " " "	Hostile batteries again shelled preparatory to renewal of French attack.	
11am. " " " "	Renewal of bombardment by Germans of 1st & 2nd Inf Bde trenches. 30th replied on batteries near CHALVAL FE. 40th on battery W of factory.	
	During afternoon 30th & 40th bty. observation stations fired on and telephone wires cut.	EWO
	Expenditure of ammunition 300 shrapnel 327 lyddite.	

Instructions regarding War Diaries and Intelligence Summaries are contained in F. S. Regs., Part II. and the Staff Manual respectively. Title pages will be prepared in manuscript.

WAR DIARY

or

~~INTELLIGENCE SUMMARY~~.

(Erase heading not required.)

43rd Bde. R.F.A. Page (11)

Army Form C. 2118.

Hour, Date, Place	Summary of Events and Information	Remarks and references to Appendices
~~13th~~ 13 OCT 1914 COMMIN FE.	During morning Germans fired bursts at long intervals on 1st & 2nd Inf Bde trenches. 30th replied on batteries at MALVAL FE, 40th on batteries S.E of CERNY. Enemy reported to have observation posts in FACTORY. Fire directed on this seemed to have good result in stopping hostile artillery fire.	EAW
7pm " "	40th Bty less 1 section moved to position S end of TERNUNE spur near VERNEUIL. Battery detached and under of O.C. 3rd Inf. Bde. Object of move to relieve 2nd DIV battery withdrawn. 1 section remained in position.	
	LIEUT TURNER, R.N.Z.A. posted from 48th Bde A.C. to 40th Bty. 2nd Lieuts. HUNT and WHITLAM posted to 43rd Bde A.C on promotion from 44th Bde R.F.A.	
	Expenditure of ammunition 49 shrapnel. 116 lyddite.	EAW
14th Oct 1914 " "	Same positions. Section 40th Bty on COURTONNE ridge chiefly fired at enemy's observation posts. 30th Bty at guns near MALVAL FE.	
8pm ~~att~~ " " "	Attack on 2nd Bde, 40th replied on battery N of TROXON.	

(9 29 6) W 2794 100,000 8/14 H W V Forms/C. 2118/11.

Instructions regarding War Diaries and Intelligence Summaries are contained in F.S. Regs., Part II. and the Staff Manual respectively. Title pages will be prepared in manuscript.

WAR DIARY
or
~~INTELLIGENCE~~ SUMMARY.
(*Erase heading not required.*)

43rd Bde. R.F.A. Page (11)

Army Form C. 2118.

Hour, Date, Place	Summary of Events and Information	Remarks and references to Appendices
~~13th~~ 13 Oct 1914 COMMIN FE.	During morning Germans fired bursts at long intervals on 1st & 2nd Inf Bde trenches. 30th replied on batteries at MALVAL FE. 40th on batteries S.E. of CERNY. Enemy reported to have observation posts in FACTORY, fire directed on this seemed to have good result in stopping hostile artillery fire.	BWO
7pm " "	40th Bty less 1 section moved to position S end of TROYON spur near VERNEUIL. Battery detached and under of O.C. 3rd Inf. Bde. Object of move to relieve 2nd DIV battery withdrawn. 1 section remained in position.	
	LIEUT TURNER, R.N.Z.A. posted from 43rd Bde A.C. to 40th Bty. 2nd Lieuts. HUNT and WHITLAM posted to 43rd Bde A.C. on promotion from 49th Bde R.F.A.	
	Expenditure of ammunition 47 shrapnel. 116 lyddite.	BWO
14th Oct 1914 " "	Same positions. Section 40th Bty on COURTONNE ridge chiefly fired at enemy's observation posts. 30th Bty at guns near MALVAL FE.	
8pm ~~13th~~ " "	Attack on 2nd Bde, 40th replied on battery N of TROYON.	

(9 29 6) W 2794 100,000 8/14 H W V Forms/C. 2118/11.

Instructions regarding War Diaries and Intelligence Summaries are contained in F. S. Regs., Part II. and the Staff Manual respectively. Title pages will be prepared in manuscript.

Army Form C. 2118.

WAR DIARY
or
~~INTELLIGENCE SUMMARY~~.
(Erase heading not required.)

43rd Bde R.F.A. Page (12)

Hour, Date, Place		Summary of Events and Information	Remarks and references to Appendices
11.40 pm.	14 OCT 1914, COMMIN FE.	Attack on 2nd Bde on BEAULNE ridge. 30th Bty replied on trenches on BEAULNE ridge.	
	15	LT. W. McC. Cowan slightly wounded. Major Madocks to hospital. Expenditure of ammunition 82 shrapnel 106 lyddite.	EW
	15th OCT.	Same positions during day engaging hostile guns.	
7 pm	" "	Brigade collected under E side of COURTONNE ridge.	
11 pm.	" "	Bde moved to BOURG and halted unable to move further owing to French infantry marching to relieve 1st Div being late.	EW.
2 am	16th OCT. Insttrain	Brigade clear of BOURG bridge. March via BRAINE to MURET (16 miles)	
8 am.	"	~~reached~~ MURET having picked up Bde A.C. 1 mile S of ~~in~~ BOURG.	
9.30 am	"	H.Q. + 30th Bty marched to NEUILLY ST FRONT (16 miles) to entrain	
1.15 pm	"	Due to arrive 12 noon but did not arrive till 1.15 pm owing to delay in BOURG. Bde entrained as follows:— H.Q. + 30th. 1.30pm train 3.51pm. 40th 3pm. train 6.51pm. 57th 6pm. 9.51pm. A.C. 9 pm. train 0.51 am 17. OCT.	EW.

(9 29 6) W 2794 100,000 8/14 H W V Forms/C. 2118/11.

Army Form C. 2118.

Instructions regarding War Diaries and Intelligence Summaries are contained in F. S. Regs., Part II. and the Staff Manual respectively. Title pages will be prepared in manuscript.

WAR DIARY
or
~~INTELLIGENCE~~ SUMMARY.
(*Erase heading not required.*)

43rd Bde R.F.A. Page (12)

Hour, Date, Place	Summary of Events and Information	Remarks and references to Appendices
11.40 pm. 14 OCT 1914 COMMIN FE.	Attack on 2nd Bde on BEAULNE ridge. 30th By replied on trenches on BEAULNE ridge.	
15'	LT. W. McC. Cowan slightly wounded. Major Madocks to hospital. Expenditure of ammunition 82 shrapnel 106 lyddite.	EAW
15th OCT.	Same positions during day engaging hostile guns.	
7 pm. " "	Brigade collected under E side of COURTONNE ridge.	
11 pm " "	Bde move to BOURG & halted unable to move further owing to French infantry marching to relieve 1st DIV. being late.	EAW.
2 am 16th OCT. Entrain	Brigade clear of BOURG bridge. March via BRAISNE to MURET (11 miles)	
8 am. "	reached MURET having picked up Bde A.C. 1 mile S of BOURG.	
9.30 am "	H.Q. & 30th Bty marched to NEUILLY ST FRONT (16 miles) to entrain.	
1.15 pm "	Due to arrive 12 noon but did not arrive till 1.15 pm owing to delay in BOURG. Bde entrained as follows:— H.Q. & 30th. 1.30 pm. train 3.51 pm. 40th 3 pm. train 6.51 pm. 57th 6 pm. 9.51 pm. A.C. 9 pm. train 0.51 am 17. OCT.	EAW.

(9 29 6) W 2794 100,000 8/14 H W V Forms/C. 2118/11.

Instructions regarding War Diaries and Intelligence Summaries are contained in F. S. Regs., Part II. and the Staff Manual respectively. Title pages will be prepared in manuscript.

WAR DIARY
or
~~INTELLIGENCE SUMMARY.~~

(*Erase heading not required.*) 43rd Bde. R.F.A. Page (13)

Army Form C. 2118.

Hour, Date, Place		Summary of Events and Information	Remarks and references to Appendices
	17th Oct. 1914 St OMER	In train Route NEUILLY ST FRONT – PARIS – AMIENS – ABBEVILLE – ETAPLES	
8pm		(Regulating Station) – BOULOGNE – CALAIS – St OMER: 1st train arrived	
		St OMER 8pm. having been delayed 8 hours by accident at	
		BOULOGNE.	
Night 17-18th Oct		Billeted H.Q. + 30th in barracks at St OMER. 40th Bty detrained	BW
		at HAZEBROUCK.	
	18th Oct	March to billets at BAYINCHOVE. (12½ miles)	
1.30pm	"	57th detrained at St OMER + marched to BAYINCHOVE.	
6.30pm	"	Bde A.C. arrived at St OMER	
9pm	"	Bde A.C. detrained – to billets in St OMER.	
	19th Oct.	Rest day Bde A.C. march to billets at St OMER.	BW
6am	20th Oct.	March to POPERINGHE.	BW Ref. Belgium. OSTEND 1/100000 a
5pm		To billets	
	21st Oct.	March – ELVERDINGE – BOESINGHE – PILKEM. Enemy encountered at	
		LANGEMARCK + driven back. 40th battery with advanced guard in	
		action 300x S. of LANGEMARCK station, with section detached	BW

Instructions regarding War Diaries and Intelligence Summaries are contained in F. S. Regs., Part II. and the Staff Manual respectively. Title pages will be prepared in manuscript.

WAR DIARY
or
INTELLIGENCE SUMMARY.
(Erase heading not required.)

43rd Bde. R.F.A. Page (13)

Army Form C. 2118.

Hour, Date, Place	Summary of Events and Information	Remarks and references to Appendices
17th Oct. 1914 ST OMER	In train Route NEUILLY ST FRONT – PARIS – AMIENS – ABBEVILLE – ETAPLES	
8pm	(Regulating Station) – BOULOGNE – CALAIS – ST OMER. 1st train arrived ST OMER 8pm, having been delayed 8 hours by accident at BOULOGNE.	
Night 17–18th Oct	Billeted H.Q. + 30th in barracks at ST OMER. 40th Bty detrained at HAZEBROUCK.	BW
18th Oct	March to billets at BAYINCHOVE. (12½ miles)	
1.30pm "	57th detrained at ST OMER + marched to BAYINCHOVE.	
6.30pm "	Bde A.C. arrived at ST OMER	
9pm "	Bde A.C. detrained – to billets in ST OMER.	
19th Oct.	Rest day. Bde A.C. march to billets at ST OMER.	BW
6am 20th Oct.	March to POPERINGHE.	Ref. Belgium. OSTEND 1/100000
5pm	To billets	
21st Oct.	March – ELVERDINGE – BOESINGHE – PILKEM. Enemy encountered at LANGEMARCK + driven back. 40th battery with advanced guard in action 300x S. of LANGEMARCK station, with section detached	BW

(9 29 6) W 2794 100,000 8/14 H W V Forms/C. 2118/11.

Instructions regarding War Diaries and Intelligence Summaries are contained in F. S. Regs., Part II. and the Staff Manual respectively. Title pages will be prepared in manuscript.

WAR DIARY
or
~~INTELLIGENCE~~ SUMMARY.
(*Erase heading not required.*)

Army Form C. 2118.

43rd Bde. R.F.A. Page (14)

Hour, Date, Place	Summary of Events and Information	Remarks and references to Appendices
21. OCT. 1914, PILKEM.	just N of station, supporting attack on line POELCAPELLE – POELCAPELLE STATION.	
11.30am.	Remainder of Brigade halted on ~~line~~ road BOESINGHE – LANGEMARCK with head ¼ mile E of PILKEM.	
5 pm.	1 section 30th battery sent ~~to~~ detached section 40th Bty & 57th Battery to position 1 mile N of PILKEM. Object 30th to assist in case of night attack. 57th to cover approaches. No firing during night.	
	57th Bty changed position during night owing to position being exposed.	
~~22nd Oct~~ 1914	Expenditure of ammunition 32 shrapnel 96 lyddite.	EWO
10 am 22nd Oct 1914 PILKEM	57th Bty changed position 1 mile N.W. of PILKEM to obtain better field of fire and cover ground SW of FORET D' HOULTHULST.	
	During morning 30th battery sent a second section to LANGEMARCK station, one section in reserve at PILKEM	EWO

Instructions regarding War Diaries and Intelligence Summaries are contained in F. S. Regs., Part II. and the Staff Manual respectively. Title pages will be prepared in manuscript.

WAR DIARY
or
INTELLIGENCE SUMMARY.
(Erase heading not required.)

43rd Bde. R.F.A. Page (14)

Army Form C. 2118.

Hour, Date, Place	Summary of Events and Information	Remarks and references to Appendices
21. OCT. 1914. PILKEM.	just N of station, supporting attack on line POELCAPELLE – POELCAPELLE STATION.	
11.30am.	Remainder of Brigade halted on ~~line~~ road BOESINGHE – LANGEMARCK with head ½ mile E of PILKEM.	
5 pm.	1 section 30th battery sent to detached section 30th Bty & 57th Battery to position 1 mile N of PILKEM. Object 30th to assist in case of night attack. 57th to cover approaches. No firing during night.	
	57th Bty changed position during night owing to position being exposed.	
	Expenditure of ammunition 32 shrapnel 96 Lyddite.	[initials]
~~22nd Oct 1914~~ 10 am 22nd Oct 1914 PILKEM	57th Bty changed position 1 mile N.W. of PILKEM to obtain better field of fire and cover ground. SW of FORET D' HOULTHULST.	
	During morning 30th battery sent a second section to LANGEMARCK station, one section in reserve at PILKEM	[initials]

Army Form C. 2118.

Instructions regarding War Diaries and Intelligence Summaries are contained in F. S. Regs., Part II. and the Staff Manual respectively. Title pages will be prepared in manuscript.

WAR DIARY
or
~~INTELLIGENCE SUMMARY.~~
(Erase heading not required.) 43rd Bde. R.F.A. Page (5)

Hour, Date, Place	Summary of Events and Information	Remarks and references to Appendices
22nd OCT 1914 PILKEM	40th battery detached section withdrawn & held in reserve near 40th Bty position. 57th Bty, 1 sec in reserve. Ammunition column at PILKEM.	
	Casualties 1 sgt. 1 gunner wounded Ammunition expended 131 Shrapnel 108 lyd.	
2 pm 22nd	57th Bty placed under orders of O C 26th Bde R.F.A	
2-30 pm	Attack on left of 1st BDE from BIXSCHOOTE. 57th under rifle	
4-30 pm.	fire about 4.30 pm. changed position moving ¼ mi. further South by order of Lt. Col Sharp.	
3 pm.	40th Bty puts under orders of O.C. 29th BDE.	EAW
23rd PILKEM	Action continued, same positions.	
6-9 am	30th & 40th batteries under heavy shell fire.	
	Expenditure of ammunition 337 Shrapnel 244 lyddite	
	Casualties. 2 Drivers killed, 2 cpls. 1 S.S. 1 Br. 8 men wounded.	EAW
24th.	Action continued. Same positions.	
11 am	Received order that 1st DIV. was to be relieved by the French. Col. Sharp's group consisting of 117th & 30th btys to be	

(9 29 6) W 2794 100,000 8/14 H W V Forms/C. 2118/11.

Army Form C. 2118.

WAR DIARY
or
~~INTELLIGENCE SUMMARY.~~

Instructions regarding War Diaries and Intelligence Summaries are contained in F. S. Regs., Part II. and the Staff Manual respectively. Title pages will be prepared in manuscript.

(*Erase heading not required.*) 43rd Bde. R.F.A. Page (5)

Hour, Date, Place	Summary of Events and Information	Remarks and references to Appendices
22nd OCT 1914 PILKEM	40TH battery detached section withdrawn & held in reserve near 40TH Bty position. 57TH Bty was in reserve. Ammunition column at PILKEM.	
	Casualties 1 Sgt. 1 gunner wounded. Ammunition expended 131 Shrapnel 108 Lydd.	
2 pm 22nd	57TH Bty placed under orders of O.C. 26th Bde R.F.A.	
2.30 pm	Attack on left of 1st BDE from BIXSCHOOTE. 57TH under heavy	
4.30 pm.	fire about 4.30 pm. changed position moving ¼ mi. further South by order of Lt. Col Sharp.	
3 pm.	40TH Bty. put under orders of O.C. 39th BDE.	RAW
23rd PILKEM	Action continued same positions.	
6–9 am	30TH & 40TH batteries under heavy shell fire.	
	Expenditure of ammunition 333 Shrapnel 214 Lyddite	
	Casualties. 2 Drivers killed. 1 Sgt. 1 Cpl. 1 Br. 8 men wounded.	RAW
24TH.	Action continued. Same positions.	
11 am	Received order that 1st DIV. was to be relieved by the French. Lt.Col. Sharp's group consisting of 117TH & 30TH btys to be	

Instructions regarding War Diaries and Intelligence Summaries are contained in F. S. Regs., Part II. and the Staff Manual respectively. Title pages will be prepared in manuscript.

Army Form C. 2118.

WAR DIARY
or
~~INTELLIGENCE~~ SUMMARY.
(Erase heading not required.)

43rd Bde R.F.A. Page (16)

Hour, Date, Place	Summary of Events and Information	Remarks and references to Appendices
24TH OCT. 1914 PILKEM	relieved ~~by the French Col. Ch. 43~~ by one French battery to be got into position by day light just S of wood 500x N of K in PILKEM.	
7.30pm	French battery did not arrive till 7.30 pm. Batteries of the brigade withdrawn from action about dusk by their respective group commanders. 30TH & 40TH batteries assembled at cross roads ½ mile E of PILKEM at 6pm. and marched via ST NEAN - ZILLYBEKE to billets 1 mile W of ZILLEBEKE. H.Q. 57TH & A.C. assembled ¼ mile W of PILKEM and marched to billets. amm. exp. 77 shrapnel 51 lyddite. LIEUT. MARSHALL wounded	[illegible]
25th OCT.	Rest day. 2LIEUT. RICHIE posted to 40TH Battery.	[illegible]
2am 26th OCT.	57TH bty. with advanced guard of 1st GDS BDE. marched 2am.	
6am	Remainder of Bde. rendezvous ZILLEBEKE 6am to Corps reserve with 3rd Inf Bde. marched to HOOGE. Afternoon 30th Battery under Lt Col. Carey's orders to position E of VELDHOEK. Ammunition expended 90 shrapnel 56 lyd.	[illegible]

(9 29 6) W 2794 100,000 8/14 H W V Forms/C. 2118/11.

Instructions regarding War Diaries and Intelligence Summaries are contained in F. S. Regs., Part II. and the Staff Manual respectively. Title pages will be prepared in manuscript.

WAR DIARY
or
INTELLIGENCE SUMMARY.
(*Erase heading not required.*)

Army Form C. 2118.

43rd Bde R.F.A. Page (16)

Hour, Date, Place	Summary of Events and Information	Remarks and references to Appendices
24th OCT. 1914 PILKEM	relieved by the ~~French Col~~ corps by one French battery to be got into position by daylight just S of wood 500x N of E in PILKEM.	
7.30 pm	French battery did not arrive till 7.30 pm. Batteries of the brigade withdrawn from action about dusk by their respective group commanders. 30th & 40th batteries assembled at cross roads ½ mile E of PILKEM at 6pm and marched via St JEAN–ZILLEBEKE to billets 1 mile W of ZILLEBEKE. H.Q. 57th & A.C. assembled ¼ mile W of PILKEM and marched to billets. amm. exp. 77 shrapnel 51 lyddite. LIEUT. MARSHALL wounded.	CAW
25th OCT.	Rest day. 2/LIEUT. RICHIE posted to 40th Battery.	CAW
2am 26th OCT.	57th Bty. with advanced guard of 1st GDS. BDE. marched 2am.	
6am	Remainder of Bde. rend[ezvous] from ZILLEBEKE 6am to Corps reserve with 3rd Inf Bde. marched to HOOGE.	
	Afternoon 30th Battery under Lt Col. Carey's orders to position E of VELDHOEK. Ammunition expended 90 shrapnel 58 lyd.	CAW

(9 29 6) W 2791 100,000 8/14 H W V Forms/C. 2118/11.

Army Form C. 2118.

Instructions regarding War Diaries and Intelligence Summaries are contained in F. S. Regs., Part II. and the Staff Manual respectively. Title pages will be prepared in manuscript.

WAR DIARY
or
~~INTELLIGENCE~~ SUMMARY.
(Erase heading not required.)

43rd Bde R.F.A. Page (17)

Hour, Date, Place	Summary of Events and Information	Remarks and references to Appendices
27TH OCT. 1914 HOOGE	30TH and 57TH batteries placed under orders of LT. COL SHARP. Objectives batteries E of GHELUVELT.	
	Ammunition expended 72 shrapnel 48 lyddite.	[illegible]
28th Oct "	Same positions Amm. expended. 189 shrapnel 103 lyddite.	[illegible]
29TH " "	do 294 shrapnel, 162 lyddite	[illegible]
30TH "	do 1 Br. killed 73 shrapnel 96 lyddite	[illegible]
31ST WESTHOEK	Hostile attack on GHELUVELT successful. 30TH and 57TH batteries withdrawn to positions SW of WESTHOEK, 1 section 57TH Bty. detached under orders of O.C. 2nd Inf. Bde. 1 mile S of HOOGE. At night one gun 57TH battery sent to position at cross roads just S of VELDHOEK to cover YPRES-MENIN road. 1 section 30TH Bty in action just E of HOOGE. Ammunition expended 272 shrapnel 181 lyddite. Casualties - 3 men slightly wounded.	[illegible]

(9 29 6) W 2794 100,000 8/14 H W V Forms/C. 2118/11.

Instructions regarding War Diaries and Intelligence Summaries are contained in F. S. Regs., Part II. and the Staff Manual respectively. Title pages will be prepared in manuscript.

WAR DIARY
or
~~INTELLIGENCE SUMMARY.~~
(Erase heading not required.)

43rd Bde R.F.A. Page (17)

Army Form C. 2118.

Hour, Date, Place	Summary of Events and Information	Remarks and references to Appendices
27TH OCT. 1914 HOOGE	30TH and 57TH batteries placed under orders of LT. COL SHARP. Objectives batteries E of GHELUVELT.	
	Ammunition expended 72 shrapnel 48 lyddite.	[illegible]
28th Oct "	Same positions Amm. expended. 189 shrapnel 103 lyddite.	[illegible]
29TH " "	do 294 shrapnel, 162 lyddite	[illegible]
30TH "	do. 1 Br. killed 73 shrapnel 96 lyddite	[illegible]
31ST WESTHOEK	Hostile attack on GHELUVELT successful. 30TH and 57TH batteries withdrawn to positions SW of WESTHOEK, 1 section 57TH btty. detached under orders of O.C. 2nd Inf. Bde. 1 mile S of HOOGE. At night one gun 57TH battery sent to position at cross roads just S of VELDHOEK to cover YPRES-MENIN road. 1 section 30TH Btty in action just E of HOOGE. Ammunition expended 272 shrapnel 101 lyddite. Casualties - 3 men slightly wounded.	[illegible]

(9 29 6) W 2794 100,000 8/14 H W V Forms/C. 2118/11.

1st Division

121/3971

43rd Bde R.F.A.

Vol IV. 1-30.11.14

Instructions regarding War Diaries and Intelligence Summaries are contained in F. S. Regs., Part II. and the Staff Manual respectively. Title pages will be prepared in manuscript.

WAR DIARY of 43rd BDE. R.F.A.

~~or~~

~~INTELLIGENCE~~ SUMMARY.

(*Erase heading not required.*)

Army Form C. 2118

Hour, Date, Place	Summary of Events and Information	Remarks and references to Appendices
NOV. 1st 1914	Batteries in same positions. Single gun of 57th Bty withdrawn at dawn and sent out again at dusk.	
	Ammunition expended 210 shrapnel 184 lyddite. Capt. Stack slightly wounded. Six men killed 4 men wounded.	EAW
2nd	30th Bty heavily shelled. Ammunition expended 302 shrapnel 80 lyddite Casualties 1 Br missing.	EAW
3rd	57th Bty sent one gun to position 300x W of VELHOEK to stay in position for local defence of infantry firing line with instructions only to fire in case of attack.	
	Ammunition expended 106 shrapnel 27 lyddite. Casualties 2 men wounded	EAW
5 am 4th	Owing to heavy shelling on 3rd 30th Bty changed position to position 200x N of YPRES-MENIN road and 300x E of HOOGE. 57th Bty to position just S.W of WESTHOEK. Change of position completed by 5 am. 57th Bty shelled during the day. Ammunition expended 99 shrapnel 44 lyddite	
	Casualties. 1 Cpl + 1 Gnr killed. 1 [illegible] + 2 Gnrs. wounded.	EAW

Instructions regarding War Diaries and Intelligence Summaries are contained in F. S. Regs., Part II. and the Staff Manual respectively. Title pages will be prepared in manuscript.

WAR DIARY ~~or INTELLIGENCE~~ SUMMARY. of 43rd Bde R.F.A.

(*Erase heading not required.*)

Army Form C. 2118.

Hour, Date, Place	Summary of Events and Information	Remarks and references to Appendices
Night 4th–5th NOV 1914.	During the night, 57th Bty withdrawn to reserve to billets 1 mile S of VLAMERTINGHE. One gun being left in position. W of VELDHOEK.	EAW
5th NOV.	30th Bty same position.	
3pm 5th	Owing to 2 btys. of brigade being detached Bde H.Q. to billets 1 mile S of VLAMERTINGHE.	EAW
	Ammunition expended 47 shrapnel 55 lyddite. Lieut Duncan wounded	
4am 6th NOV	57th Bty marched via HAZEBROUCK for St OMER under O.C. 26th Bde. ammunition expended 33 shrapnel 33 lyddite. Casualties – Lt. Lindsay wounded. 1 Br killed 1 Dr wounded.	EAW
7th NOV	Ammunition expended 46 shrapnel 42 lyddite	EAW
8th NOV	Action continued No change — — 73 — 103 —	EAW
9th NOV	Returns not available.	EAW
10th NOV.	Action continued no change. Gazette received promoting Capts. Woolcombe Adams, Robinson, and Longstaff ~~to be M~~ and Drought to be Majors. Lt Price & Rait Kerr to be capts. Ammunition expended 55 shrapnel 90 lyddite. Capt Rait Kerr killed.	EAW

Instructions regarding War Diaries and Intelligence Summaries are contained in F. S. Regs., Part II. and the Staff Manual respectively. Title pages will be prepared in manuscript.

WAR DIARY of 43rd Bde. R.F.A.

or

~~INTELLIGENCE SUMMARY.~~

(Erase heading not required.)

Army Form C. 2118.

Hour, Date, Place	Summary of Events and Information	Remarks and references to Appendices
10TH NOV 1914 HOOGE	40TH Bty to action ¼ mile N. W. of HOOGE from Corps reserve.	EW
11TH NOV	2Lt Abraham (S.R.) posted to 57TH bty. sent to take charge of single gun N. of YPRES-MENIN road.	
	Casualties 1 Dr. wounded	EW
12TH NOV 1914 HOOGE	Lt Abraham taken prisoner by Germans. Attack by Prussian Guard N of YPRES-MENIN road.	
	Casualties 1 Bt. 1 BSM 4 gunners 3 Drivers wounded.	EW
13TH NOV	57TH Bty to action ¼ mile N of HOOGE CHATEAU.	EW
14TH NOV	No change. 2Lt AIKENHEAD posted to 30TH Bty.	
	Ammunition expended 238 shrapnel 104 lyddite.	EW
15TH NOV	no change. Ammunition expended. 182 shrapnel 115 lyddite Casualties 2 Drs wounded	EW
16TH NOV	" " 172 shrapnel 159 lyddite.	EW
17TH NOV	" " 306 " 192 " Casualties 1 Cpl killed, 3 Cpls 2 Bdrs wounded.	EW
18TH NOV	57TH Bty had 1 section in position N of HOOGE CHATEAU, withdrawn after dark & marched to billets at VLAMERTINGHE.	EW EW

(9 29 6) W 2794 100,000 8/14 H W V Forms/C. 2118/11.

Instructions regarding War Diaries and Intelligence Summaries are contained in F. S. Regs., Part II. and the Staff Manual respectively. Title pages will be prepared in manuscript.

WAR DIARY of 43rd Bde. R.F.A. ~~or~~ ~~INTELLIGENCE~~ SUMMARY.

(*Erase heading not required.*)

Army Form C. 2118.

Hour, Date, Place	Summary of Events and Information	Remarks and references to Appendices
9 am 19th NOV 1914	57th Bty marched to MERRIS to billets,	
	30th Bty heavily shelled. Casualties 2Lt Hunt severely wounded,	
	died NOV 28th. B.S.M. Bull ~~slight~~ killed. 4 sergts wounded.	
	30th Bty moved by sections to position just W of HOOGE CHATEAU	
	change completed by 12 noon	EAW
~~5pm~~ 20th NOV 1914	1 secn 40th Bty, 30th Bty less 1 section, 1 section 57th Bty withdrawn	
	5.30pm and marched to billets at VLAMERTINGHE.	EAW
6am 21st NOV 1914	Remainder of Bde i.e. 2 sections 40th Bty, 1 secn. 30th Bty	
	withdrawn, marched to VLAMERTINGHE. Bde marched independently	
	by batteries via RENINGHELST, WESTOUTRE, LOCRE, BAILLEUL.	
	2Lieut Palmer posted to 57th Battery.	EAW
22nd NOV - 25th 1914	Bde resting and refitting.	EAW
26th NOV 1914	57th Bty transferred to 8th Division at LA GORGUE.	EAW
27th - 30th NOV 1914	Bde resting and refitting.	EAW

(9 29 6) W 2794 100,000 8/14 H W V Forms/C. 2118/11.

Instructions regarding War Diaries and Intelligence Summaries are contained in F. S. Regs., Part II. and the Staff Manual respectively. Title pages will be prepared in manuscript.

WAR DIARY OF 43RD BDE R.F.A.
or
~~INTELLIGENCE SUMMARY.~~
(Erase heading not required.)

Army Form C. 2118.

(1)

Hour, Date, Place	Summary of Events and Information	Remarks and references to Appendices
1st – 22nd Dec. 1914	Bde resting and refitting at MERRIS. During this period Major Woolcombe Adams from 40TH Bty to 114TH Bty. Capt. W.C.H. BELL from BASE to 40TH Bty (2ic). 2Lt. H.T. SELBY from 1st. D.A.C. to 30TH Bty. dt 1st DEC. Lt. J.M. ROWE R.A.M.C. took over medical officer vice Capt STACK. dt. 12TH.	Ref ST OMER 1/80000 Caw
8am 23rd Dec 1914	Colonel and Battery commanders proceeded by motor bus to take over positions from LAHORE DIV.	
9.30am " "	Brigade marched via MERVILLE to BETHUNE. Owing to late arrival of bus, positions could not be properly taken over this day. It was therefore decided that 40TH Bty should come into action before daylight 24TH in position previously occupied by 1 sec. 56th Bty. A 20 a 5.1 30TH Bty to put 1 section in action before daylight 24TH in position previously occupied by 1 sec 56th Bty	Ref ARRAS, LILLE 1/80000 BETHUNE. 1/40000 Ref. BETHUNE 1/40000

Instructions regarding War Diaries and Intelligence Summaries are contained in F. S. Regs., Part II. and the Staff Manual respectively. Title pages will be prepared in manuscript.

WAR DIARY of 43rd Bde R.F.A.
or
~~INTELLIGENCE~~ SUMMARY.
(*Erase heading not required.*)

Army Form C. 2118.

(3)

Hour, Date, Place	Summary of Events and Information	Remarks and references to Appendices
26th Dec 1914	No change. Expended 38 shrapnel 20 lyddite	EWW.
27th " "	" " " 66 " 12 "	EWW.
28th	" " " 45 " 53 "	EWW.
29th " "	Line held by 1st Div divided into 2 sections 30th Bty allotted to Northern, 40th Bty to Southern section. Orders received that all horses not actually required with the guns to be sent west of a line running N & S through BEUVRY, sanction obtained to leave 30th & 40th Bty horses in present positions until shelled, as all horses at present under cover from bad weather.	Ref. 1/40000 BETHUNE 1st ed.
	30th Bty no change.	
	Amm expended 109 Shrapnel 16 lyddite	EWW.
30th " "	No change 57 shrapnel 77 lyddite	EWW
~~31st~~		

(9 29 6) W4141—463 100,000 9/14 H W V Forms/C. 2118/10

Instructions regarding War Diaries and Intelligence Summaries are contained in F. S. Regs., Part II. and the Staff Manual respectively. Title pages will be prepared in manuscript.

WAR DIARY of 43rd BDE. R.F.A.
or
~~INTELLIGENCE SUMMARY.~~
(*Erase heading not required.*)

Army Form C. 2118.

(2)

Hour, Date, Place	Summary of Events and Information	Remarks and references to Appendices
23rd DEC. 1914. BETHUNE.	at F 5c 3.5. Battery commander to reconnoitre for a better position for battery as soon as it should be daylight.	
6pm " "	Bde. arrived at BETHUNE & billeted for the night.	EAW.
7am 24th DEC 1914 BEUVRY	Positions as stated above occupied. O.C. 30th could not find a better position for battery. Remainder of battery accordingly brought into same position.	Ref 1/40000 BETHUNE 1st Ed
	Bde HQ. F8c6.4.	
	Bde A.C. in E 4 d.	
	1 section 40th Bty placed under orders of O.C. 26th Bde.	
	Day occupied in registering targets.	
	Positions completely taken over by end of day.	EAW
25 " "	30th Bty engaged German trench opposite FESTUBERT.	
	Ammunition expended 27 shrapnel 16 lyddite	EAW.

Army Form C. 2118.

Instructions regarding War Diaries and Intelligence Summaries are contained in F. S. Regs., Part II. and the Staff Manual respectively. Title pages will be prepared in manuscript.

WAR DIARY of 43rd Bde R.F.A.
or
INTELLIGENCE SUMMARY.
(*Erase heading not required.*)

(4)

Hour, Date, Place	Summary of Events and Information	Remarks and references to Appendices
31st Dec 1914	K.R.R. shelled out of advanced post on railway A15d 10.9	Ref 1/40000 BETHUNE 1st ed.
3pm	40TH Bty shelled this post.	
10.30pm	40TH Bty shelled this post previous to attacks.	
3am 1st Jan 1915		
	Ammunition expended 141 shrapnel 120 lyddite	E.W.

(9 29 6) W4141—463 100,000 9/14 H W V Forms/C. 2118/10

43RD BRIGADE R.F.A.

WAR DIARY 1915

JAN-DEC

1st Division Jany - Mch 1915

121
6111

43rd Bde RFA.

Vol V. [~~Dec 1st 1914~~ Jan 1915 – ~~March 31st 1915~~]

Transferred to Indian Corps Feb. 19th 1915

Instructions regarding War Diaries and Intelligence Summaries are contained in F. S. Regs., Part II. and the Staff Manual respectively. Title pages will be prepared in manuscript.

WAR DIARY or INTELLIGENCE SUMMARY. of 43rd BDE RFA

(Erase heading not required.)

Army Form C. 2118.

(5)

Hour, Date, Place	Summary of Events and Information	Remarks and references to Appendices
1st Jan 1915 BEUVRY	Attacks by 2nd Bde during night failed. 40th Bty employed during day in shelling [illegible] post & Railway triangle to East of it	Ref 1/40000 BETHUNE. 1st ed.
	Ammunition expended 260 shrapnel 122 lyddite	[illegible]
	BQMS. W.F. KIDD 40th Bty promoted 2LT & proceeds to ENGLAND.	
2nd " " "	No change. Amm. 103 shrapnel 55 lyddite	[illegible]
3rd " " "	" " " 151 " 45 "	[illegible]
4th " " "	" " " 43 " 40 "	[illegible]
5th " " "	" " " 37 " 34 "	[illegible]
6th " " "	" " " 115 " 23 "	[illegible]
7th " " "	2LT H. PAGE posted to 30th Bty from 1st DAC. LT STEWART A.V.C. left for ENGLAND. Ammunition expended 60 shrapnel 19 lyddite	[illegible]
8th " " "	Capt T. H. BECKLEY from 16th Bde posted to BDE Amm Col. amm. expended 84 shrapnel + 35 lyddite	[illegible]
9th " " "	No change amm. 124 shrapnel 31 lyddite	[illegible]
10th " " "	Attack on observation post A15 d 10 9.	
11th 11.6 am	Short bombardment 3 rounds per gun – 40th Bty on	

(9 29 6) W4141—463 100,000 9/14 H W V Forms/C. 2118/10

Instructions regarding War Diaries and Intelligence Summaries are contained in F. S. Regs., Part II. and the Staff Manual respectively. Title pages will be prepared in manuscript.

WAR DIARY of 43rd BDE R.F.A. or INTELLIGENCE SUMMARY.

(*Erase heading not required.*)

Army Form C. 2118.

(6)

Hour, Date, Place	Summary of Events and Information	Remarks and references to Appendices
11–11.5am 10TH JAN. 1915	observation post – 30TH Bty on trenches on Northern bank of canal, north of post. After desultory fire on same targets,	Ref 1/40000 BETHUNE. 1st ed.
1.50pm – 2.5pm	heavy bombardment on same targets.	
2pm	Attack on observation post successful. 40TH Bty fired in front of advancing infantry.	
	2Lt N.W.W. FREER posted from 40TH Bty to RHA 2nd Ind CAV. DIV.	
	Major G.T.A. DROUGHT from Bde A.C. to 51ST Bty	
	Amm. expended 260 shrapnel 97 lyddite	EAW.
12 noon 11TH "	General bombardment on railway triangle at 12 noon. – Ammunition 145 shrapnel 40 lyddite	EAW
3.30pm 12TH " "	Observation post retaken by Germans	
	MAJOR W.R.N. MADOCKS proceeds to ENGLAND	
	ammunition expended 4 shrapnel 16 lyddite	EAW.
13TH	no change. Amm. 47 shrapnel 8 lyddite	EAW

Instructions regarding War Diaries and Intelligence Summaries are contained in F. S. Regs., Part II. and the Staff Manual respectively. Title pages will be prepared in manuscript.

WAR DIARY of 43rd BDE - R.F.A
or
~~INTELLIGENCE~~ SUMMARY.

(*Erase heading not required.*)

Army Form C. 2118.

(7)

Hour, Date, Place	Summary of Events and Information	Remarks and references to Appendices
14th JAN 1915. BEUVRY	2nd DIV took over line as far South as LE PLANTIN (incl) Task of 30th Bty transferred to support of 3rd BDE holding line from LE PLANTIN (excl) to canal, but to remain at call of Lt-Col Carey for support of 5th Inf Bde as far north as FESTUBERT	Ref 1/40000 BETHUNE. 1st ed.
	amm. expended 24 shrapnel 16 lyddite.	EAW
15 JAN 1915	30th Bty observation station transferred to GIVENCHY amm. expended 27 shrapnel 17 lyddite	EAW
16 " "	no change. Amm. expended 21 lyddite 2 shrapnel	EAW
17 " "	" " " " 6 " 9 "	EAW
18 " "	" " " " 18 " 9 "	EAW
19 " "	" " " " 4 " 41 "	EAW
20 " "	" " " " 22 " 16 "	EAW
21 " "	" " " " 99 " 360 "	EAW
22 " "	Increase in sniping noticed in GIVENCHY. 30th Bty fired on enemy's trenches in reply.	~~EAW~~
	Lt B.G.M. WATKIN from 1st D.A.C. posted to 40th Bty. Ammunition expended 1 shrapnel 20 lyddite	EAW
23 " "	no change, amm. " 26 " 19 "	EAW

(9 29 6) W4141—463 100,000 9/14 H W V Forms/C. 2118/10

Instructions regarding War Diaries and Intelligence Summaries are contained in F. S. Regs., Part II. and the Staff Manual respectively. Title pages will be prepared in manuscript.

WAR DIARY of 43rd BDE R.F.A.
or
~~INTELLIGENCE~~ SUMMARY.
(*Erase heading not required.*)

Army Form C. 2118.

(8)

Hour, Date, Place	Summary of Events and Information	Remarks and references to Appendices
24TH JAN 1915.	Increased activity on part of German artillery. 3 batteries registered on GIVENCHY. 30TH Bty replied on German trenches.	Ref 1/40000 BETHUNE. 1st ed.
	Ammunition expended 19 shrapnel 25 lyddite.	
25TH JAN. 1915.	German attack on CUINCHY and GIVENCHY. Work of 30TH Bty:—	
7.50 am	Germans shelled GIVENCHY and attacked. Communication between battery and O.P. station cut. Battery opened on German trenches in orchard N.E. of GIVENCHY (Sq a 6.5).	
8.15 am.	Telephone communication established to WINDY CORNER (S.8.c 3.8). Major MACNAUGHTON proceeded to GIVENCHY and found Germans had reached Church. The fire of 30TH Bty stopped German supports coming on.	
1 pm.	Local counter attacks had taken place and situation restored.	

(9 29 6) W4141—463 100,000 9/14 H W V Forms/C. 2118/10

Instructions regarding War Diaries and Intelligence Summaries are contained in F. S. Regs., Part II. and the Staff Manual respectively. Title pages will be prepared in manuscript.

Army Form C. 2118.

WAR DIARY of 43rd BDE R.F.A.
or
~~INTELLIGENCE~~ SUMMARY.
(*Erase heading not required.*)

(9)

Hour, Date, Place	Summary of Events and Information	Remarks and references to Appendices
25th JAN 1915.	Work of 40th Bty	
7am	German deserter reported that germans were going to attack ~~after~~ 7.15am.	Ref $\frac{1}{40000}$ BETHUNE 1st ed.
7.15 am " "	40th Bty opened fire on railway triangle (A 16 c)	
7.30 am	Germans attacked & took all trenches between railway and BETHUNE – LA BASSEE roads and advanced to hollow by railway embankment (A 15 d 1 9) where	
8 am	they were stopped by fire of 40th, 113th & 15 siege btys.	
11 am	Infantry reoccupied hollow	
12 noon	Line established 400x in front of CUINCHY brewery. Several counter attacks failed during remainder of day.	
	Amm. expended. 528 shrapnel 224 lyddite.	
	Casualties Lt B.G.N. WATKIN 40th Bty severely wounded (died of wounds about 28/1/15) 1 Sergeant 1 Bombr wounded.	BEW.
26th JAN 1915.	Quiet. In afternoon Germans reported massing in support trenches opposite GIVENCHY. 50th & 48th shelled them. Ammn expended 122 shrapnel 26 lyddite.	BEW.

(B 29 6) W4141—463 100,000 9/14 H W V Forms/C. 2118/10

Instructions regarding War Diaries and Intelligence Summaries are contained in F. S. Regs., Part II. and the Staff Manual respectively. Title pages will be prepared in manuscript.

WAR DIARY of 43rd BDE RFA
or
INTELLIGENCE SUMMARY.
(*Erase heading not required.*)

Army Form C. 2118.

(10)

Hour, Date, Place	Summary of Events and Information	Remarks and references to Appendices
27th JAN 1915	No change. Amm. expended 53 shrapnel 45 lyddite	Eaw
28th JAN "	" " " " 71 " 42 "	Eaw
9 am 29th JAN 1915.	German guns and minenwerfer shelled 4th Bde. trenches opposite CUINCHY and attack followed. Repulsed with heavy loss	Ref 1/40000 BETHUNE 1st Ed.
	Ammunition expended 106 shrapnel 98 lyddite 1 gunner wounded	Eaw
30th JAN "	No change Amm. expended 55 shrapnel 18 lyddite	Eaw
31st " "	" " " " 29 " 43 "	Eaw.
~~1st~~ J		

Instructions regarding War Diaries and Intelligence Summaries are contained in F. S. Regs., Part II. and the Staff Manual respectively. Title pages will be prepared in manuscript.

WAR DIARY of 43rd BDE R.F.A.
or
~~INTELLIGENCE~~ SUMMARY.
(Erase heading not required.)

Army Form C. 2118.

(11)

Hour, Date, Place	Summary of Events and Information	Remarks and references to Appendices
1st FEB 1915 BEUVRY	attack by 4th Bde on "Brickstacks".	Ref BETHUNE 1/40000 1st Ed & 36b
	40th Bty firing on trenches in front of Triangle	
	Major F. W. Robinson posted from 57th Bty to 130th Bty 27th DIV. 2Lt J.J. DONOGHUE posted to 40th Bty	
	Amm. expended 27 shrapnel 37 lyddite	EAW.
2nd FEB 1915	no change. Amm. expended 40 shrapnel 19 lyddite. 2Lt G.L.K. WISELY posted to 57th Bty.	EAW
2pm 3rd " "	Bde A.C. relieved by 44th Bde A.C. in BETHUNE, marched to billets at FERFAY. 44th Bde A.C. taken over supply of ammunition to 30th & 40th Bty.	
	ammunition expended 44 shrapnel 37 lyddite	EAW
4th do "	no change. Amm. expended 35 " 23 "	EAW
7am 5th " "	1 sec. 30th Bty relieved by 1 section 47th Bty. section marched to FERFAY.	
6pm	~~6pm~~ 2 sections 40th Bty relieved by 2 secs. 60th Bty sections to billets in BETHUNE.	EAW
	amm. expended 59 shrapnel 19 lyddite	

Instructions regarding War Diaries and Intelligence Summaries are contained in F. S. Regs., Part II. and the Staff Manual respectively. Title pages will be prepared in manuscript.

Army Form C. 2118.

WAR DIARY *or* INTELLIGENCE SUMMARY. of 43rd BDE. R.F.A.

(Erase heading not required.)

(12)

Hour, Date, Place	Summary of Events and Information	Remarks and references to Appendices
2pm 6TH FEB 1915	Bombardment of Brickstacks followed by attack by 4TH Bde 40TH Bty in support Ammunition expended 114 shrapnel 49 lyddite	EAW
7am 7TH FEB 1915.	1 sec. 40TH Bty relieved by 60TH Bty & whole Bty marched to LESTREM attached to 4TH Corps	Ref BETHUNE 1/40000 tinted. ARRAS 1/80000
3 pm 10 pm	~~2 sections 30TH Bty~~ relieved by 60TH Bty and marched to FERFAY arriving 10 pm	
10 am.	Bde. HQ to FERFAY.	EAW.
8TH – 17TH	Bde HQ & 30TH resting at FERFAY	EAW
16TH FEB	Capt A.G. CUNNINGHAM posted to 57TH Bty.	EAW
13TH FEB	2/LT P.J. MUIRHEAD posted to 40TH Bty 2LT. H. PHEAR posted to 30TH Bty	EAW.
8am 18TH FEB 1915	Order received that 43rd Bde is to be transferred to Indian Corps 57TH & 40TH Btys. will rejoin Bde	
1.30pm " "	30TH Bty march to L'ECLEME (V 2 3/2) to join MEERUT DIV 57TH Bty. to billets at LA BOHEME (R 28 a) under LAHORE DIV	EAW

(9 29 6) W 4141—463 100,000 9/14 H W V Forms/C. 2118/10

Instructions regarding War Diaries and Intelligence Summaries are contained in F. S. Regs., Part II. and the Staff Manual respectively. Title pages will be prepared in manuscript.

WAR DIARY of 43rd BDE, RFA Meerut
or
INTELLIGENCE SUMMARY. INDIAN CORPS. (13)
(Erase heading not required.)

Army Form C. 2118.

Hour, Date, Place	Summary of Events and Information	Remarks and references to Appendices
WITH INDIAN CORPS		
19th FEB 1915	Portion of Bde A.C. from FERFAY to L'ECLEME to join 30th Bty.	Ref BETHUNE 1/40000 first edition
	Bde HQ to billets at PACAUT under LAHORE DIV Q 23 C	
	30th Bty into action ½ mile S of RICHEBOURG ST VAAST – (R7 d 5.8) under MEERUT DIV.	
	40th Bty to billets at L'ECLEME.	
20th FEB 1915	No change	
	Bde A.C. (less 1 sec with 40th Bty at LES LOBES (R31 b 6.1)	EWD
21st FEB – 28 FEB	No change.	EWD
24 FEB.	Major E B MACNAUGHTON from 30th Bty to S.S. 1st Army	EWD

(9 29 6) W4141—463 100,000 9/14 H W V Forms/C. 2118/10

Instructions regarding War Diaries and Intelligence Summaries are contained in F. S. Regs., Part II. and the Staff Manual respectively. Title pages will be prepared in manuscript.

WAR DIARY of 43rd BDE R.F.A.
or
~~INTELLIGENCE~~ SUMMARY.
(*Erase heading not required.*)

Army Form C. 2118.

(14)

Hour, Date, Place	Summary of Events and Information	Remarks and references to Appendices
1st 2nd MARCH 1915. PACAUT	no change	Eaw.
	MAJOR P. SHEPPARD posted to 30th Bty	
3rd MARCH 1915	During day 57th Bty into action at S 8 a 1.4.	Eaw
4th MARCH 1915	Bde HQ to (X 9 b 7.4) LE CASAN.	Ref BETHUNE 1/40000 1st ed.
	40th Bty to action 400x S.W of RICHEBOURG ST WAAST. (S 1 d 6.3)	
	LT W.E. DUNCAN posted to 57th Bty	Eaw.
5th " "	Batteries registering. Bde HQ day station established at S 7 b 3.2	
	amm. expended 84 shrapnel 10 lyddite	Eaw.
6th " "	30th Bty registered redoubt S 10 b 6.1 and road junction S 11 a 7.8	
	Ammunition expended 22 shrapnel	Eaw
6.3am 7th " "	30th Bty registered German trenches near cross road in S 4 d	
7 am	30th Bty registered redoubt S 10 b 6.1.	

(9 29 6) W 4141—463 100,000 9/14 H W V Forms/C. 2118/10

Army Form C. 2118.

Instructions regarding War Diaries and Intelligence Summaries are contained in F. S. Regs., Part II. and the Staff Manual respectively. Title pages will be prepared in manuscript.

WAR DIARY of 43rd Bde R.F.A.
or
~~INTELLIGENCE~~ SUMMARY.
(*Erase heading not required.*)

(15)

Hour, Date, Place	Summary of Events and Information	Remarks and references to Appendices
7TH MARCH 1915 LE CASAN	30TH Bty fired by order of C.R.A on houses S5c 52 and set one on fire.	Ref BETHUNE 1/40000 first edition,
	40TH Bty registered German trenches at road junction S 5C and point on N.W face of BOIS DE BIEZ destroyed house in S 4 b.	
	57TH Bty registered trenches S11a, S5C & keep in S4 b 9.0.	
	Ammunition expended 64 shrapnel 53 lyddite	
8TH " "	Registration carried on by 3 Btys.	
	30TH Bty fired on trenches opposite cross roads in S4c in reply to heavy rifle fire during previous night.	
	30TH 45/Btys fired on houses overlooking these cross roads	
	Ammunition expended 19 shrapnel 21 lyddite.	EAW.
9TH " "	Registration checked.	
	Ammunition expended 105 shrapnel 31 lyddite	EAW.

(9 29 6) W4141—463 100,000 9/14 H W V Forms/C. 2118/10

Neuve Chapelle

Instructions regarding War Diaries and Intelligence Summaries are contained in F. S. Regs., Part II. and the Staff Manual respectively. Title pages will be prepared in manuscript.

Army Form C. 2118.

WAR DIARY of 43rd Bde R.F.A
or
INTELLIGENCE SUMMARY.
(Erase heading not required.)

(16)

Hour, Date, Place	Summary of Events and Information	Remarks and references to Appendices
10th MARCH 1915 LECASAN	Attack by 4th & Indian Corps on NEUVE CHAPELLE	Ref BETHUNE 1/40000 1st edition
	Task of Bde as follows:—	French plan No 5B92 1/5000
	Phase 1	~~attached marked A~~
7.30 am	30th Bty firing on redoubt South of C. (plan 1/5000)	
7.40 – 8.05 am	All 3 Btys firing on front German trenches opposite Indian attack. C to H at X fire 15 secs.	
8.05 am	Assault by GARHWAL BDE. Phase 2 commences	
	30th & 57th Btys. on trenches S11a 01 – S10b 9.5, S11a 2.8 S11a 2.9, S5c 4.1 and cross roads and houses at M	
	40th Bty redoubt S10b 62 and enemy's trenches in an area enclosed by ruckah just West of redoubt — ESTAIRES LA BASSEE road, front line of enemy's trenches and trench running SW to NE 150 yards S of redoubt at X fire 1 min.	
8.40 am	Report received that infantry had taken B.	
8.55 am	" " " " " " C+O	

(29 29 6) W4141—463 100,000 9/14 H W V Forms/C. 2118/10

Instructions regarding War Diaries and Intelligence Summaries are contained in F. S. Regs., Part II. and the Staff Manual respectively. Title pages will be prepared in manuscript.

WAR DIARY or ~~INTELLIGENCE SUMMARY~~ of 43rd Bde. R.F.A.

(Erase heading not required.)

Army Form C. 2118.

(17)

Hour, Date, Place		Summary of Events and Information	Remarks and references to Appendices
9.40am	10TH MARCH 1915	30TH Bty gave 5 mins burst of fire on LA BASSEE road (S11C 4 3)	Ref 1/40000 1st edition BETHUNE and 1/5000 French map ~~[illegible]~~
10.9 am		Report from GARHWAL BDE right flank not clear of enemy – asks for increased fire on K. 57TH ordered to comply.	
10.10am		30TH Bty 1 section on S 11C 3 8, 2 sections on redoubt S10 3 6.2 at slow rate of fire	
10.37am		Report received that GARHWAL BDE is on line NTP	
10.45 "		Infantry reported to be in possession of houses at M	
12.15 pm		Objectives of batteries as follows	
		30TH Bty – LA BASSEE road S11C 4 3	
		40TH " houses and road S5d	
		57TH S11 central	
12.25 pm		C.R.A. orders points K & L to be shelled. 57TH directed to do this.	
1.4 pm		GARHWAL BDE on line OPT	
[illegible] pm		Report received from forward observing officer that enemy	

1247 W 3299 200,000 (E) 8/14 J.B.C. & A. Forms/C. 2118/11.

Instructions regarding War Diaries and Intelligence Summaries are contained in F. S. Regs., Part II. and the Staff Manual respectively. Title pages will be prepared in manuscript.

WAR DIARY
or
INTELLIGENCE SUMMARY
of 43rd Bde R.F.A.

(Erase heading not required.)

Army Form C. 2118.

(18)

Hour, Date, Place	Summary of Events and Information	Remarks and references to Appendices
2pm 10th MARCH 1915	holding C. 57th turned 1 section on to L and 2 sections on to C	Ref 1/40000 BETHUNE
		T Trench plan 1/5000
3.15pm	GARHWAL BDE ask for guns shelling C to turn on 12 houses E of LA BASSEE road in 3.5.c. 57th Bty ordered to do this.	
6pm	Night lines for batteries ordered as follows	
	30th Bty on redoubt near A	
	57th on K	
	40th road junction S11d	
	Fire kept up throughout night rate of 2 rounds per hour.	
	Ammunition expended 286 Shrapnel 2550 lyddite	Exw.
	2 gunners wounded, 1 A.S.C driver killed	
11th MARCH 1915	Orders issued for attack to be continued at 7am objectives BOIS DE BIEZ and then line LA CLIQUETERIE FE (excl) to LIGNY LE GRAND (incl)	
7am	1st Phase 30th Bty on A	
	40th Bty on houses along road from S.3.c 8 5 to S.17.a 8 3 and on cross roads.	
	57th on redoubt 250x S.E. of A and S11c 0.8	

1247 W 3299 200,000 (E) 8/14 J.B.C. & A. Forms/C. 2118/11.

Instructions regarding War Diaries and Intelligence Summaries are contained in F. S. Regs., Part II. and the Staff Manual respectively. Title pages will be prepared in manuscript.

WAR DIARY
or
INTELLIGENCE SUMMARY
of 43rd BDE RFA.

(Erase heading not required.)

Army Form C. 2118.

(19)

Hour, Date, Place	Summary of Events and Information	Remarks and references to Appendices
11th MARCH 1915	2nd PHASE 35th Bty on LIGNY LE PETIT. 57th & 40th Btys as before	Ref BETHUNE 1/40000 and trench plan 1/5000
8.17 am	Report from 35th Bty of great activity about LA BASSEE road S17a 69. Gave them 5 mins burst of fire and returned to A	
8.5 am	57th Bty observed flashes S17a p o and engaged them and silenced them.	
	At this time light was very bad and observation difficult.	
9.20 am	Report received that infantry are being held up by machine gun fire from N W edge of BOIS DE BIEZ 40th Bty turned on to these machine guns	
9.43 am	Report from C.R.A. that 6 machine guns are supposed to be in neighborhood of A and holding up attack. 35th ordered to increase rate of fire on A	
10.27 am	Orders from BRA received to go steady with ammunition	
12.50 pm	Received message that 4th Corps expected to advance shortly alongside DEHRA DUN Bde.	
1.15 pm	Orders received that assault was about to take place	

Instructions regarding War Diaries and Intelligence Summaries are contained in F. S. Regs., Part II. and the Staff Manual respectively. Title pages will be prepared in manuscript.

WAR DIARY
or
INTELLIGENCE SUMMARY
of 43rd Bde R.F.A.

(Erase heading not required.)

Army Form C. 2118.

(20)

Hour, Date, Place	Summary of Events and Information	Remarks and references to Appendices
1.45pm 11TH MARCH 1915	and Phase 2 to be carried out.	Ref 1/40000 BETHUNE 1st edition and trench plan 1/5000
2.2pm	Message received that assault was taking place	
3.15pm	40TH Bty report that there is a trench about fig 5 in S5 [illegible] not marked on trench map, which is likely to hold infantry up.	
	40TH Bty engaged this trench successfully	
3.55pm	30TH Bty report that attack has not moved forward at all.	
	Night lines same as for 10TH — no firing carried out.	
6pm	Situation from forward officer at T — Infantry digging in on line P-T but 2/3 GURKHAS holding 200x NW of and parallel to R. DES LAYES. Company commander of 2/3rd reported Germans entrenched 300x SE of this.	
	GARHWALS reached M in morning but had to retire owing to lack of support on North. 4TH SEAFORTHS attempted attack on BOIS DE BIEZ but were held up by machine gun fire.	
	Ammunition expended 284 shrapnel 1056 Lyddite	[illegible]

1247 W 3299 200,000 (E) 8/14 J.B.C. & A. Forms/C. 2118/11.

Instructions regarding War Diaries and Intelligence Summaries are contained in F. S. Regs., Part II. and the Staff Manual respectively. Title pages will be prepared in manuscript.

WAR DIARY or INTELLIGENCE SUMMARY

of 43rd Bde R.F.A.

(Erase heading not required.)

Army Form C. 2118.

(21)

Hour, Date, Place	Summary of Events and Information	Remarks and references to Appendices
6.5am 12TH MARCH 1915	Germans attacked "crescent trench" (S10 3 4 6) and repulsed by BLACK WATCH	Ref. 1/40000 BETHUNE 1st ed. and 1/5000 trench plan
7.15am	situation quiet.	
7.25 "	Orders received to open steady fire on A and K at once. 30TH Bty on A — 57TH on K	
9.50am	Orders received for continuation of attack — 1st Brigade of Indian Corps — position from S6a 5.9 to S4a 6.7 at 11am.	
10.30am to 11 am	1st Phase 30TH Bty on A and redoubt 200yds SE. of A	
	57TH Bty on K and houses on LA BASSEE road near K.	
	40TH Bty on trenches between K and M and on houses on cross-roads S.17a.	
11am	2nd Phase 30TH & 40TH in observation on their tasks firing when necessary with great economy of ammunition	
	57TH Bty in observation	
9.50am	SEAFORTH'S report Germans digging and moving in considerable numbers on line S5c 5.5 to redoubt in S11a to point K and ask for fire on this — 40TH turn on to it	

Instructions regarding War Diaries and Intelligence Summaries are contained in F. S. Regs., Part II. and the Staff Manual respectively. Title pages will be prepared in manuscript.

WAR DIARY
or
INTELLIGENCE SUMMARY
of 43rd Bde R.F.A

(Erase heading not required.)

Army Form C. 2118.

(22)

Hour, Date, Place	Summary of Events and Information	Remarks and references to Appendices
10am – 12TH MARCH 1915	GARHWAL Bde reported within 15 yds of where trench crosses LA BASSEE road	Ref BETHUNE 1/40000 1st ed and trench plan 1/5000
10.15am	message received that advance is postponed from 10.30am to 12.30pm.	
10.35 am	Orders received to engage K and L where germans are massing for an attack.	
10.35am	Houses in S5c41 reported strongly held 30TH Bty engage them	
12.10 pm	Infantry report large number of enemy at M and on line 300x SE of L and B. 40TH Bty ordered to engage them	
12.23 pm.	40TH Bty ordered to include crossroads S17c to houses near them in task in phase I	
12.52 pm	Order received to increase rate of fire in vicinity of redoubt for 5 mins – (30TH Bty)	
2.5 pm.	3 battalions of Germans reported in BOIS DE BIEZ	

1247 W 3299 200,000 (E) 8/14 J.B.C. & A. Forms/C. 2118/11.

Instructions regarding War Diaries and Intelligence Summaries are contained in F. S. Regs., Part II. and the Staff Manual respectively. Title pages will be prepared in manuscript.

WAR DIARY
or
INTELLIGENCE SUMMARY
of 43rd BDE RFA

(Erase heading not required.)

Army Form C. 2118.

(23)

Hour, Date, Place	Summary of Events and Information	Remarks and references to Appendices
2.5pm 12th MARCH 1915	One section per battery ordered to turn on to eastern half of wood. At the same time especial care in watching right flank of attack.	BETHUNE 1/40000 1st Ed. Trench maps 1/5000
	Message received that GARHWAL BDE require support and enemy reinforced near B. 57th Bty ordered to deal with this if safe, but communication cut and support could not be given with safety.	
3pm	Order for all batteries to remain in observation	
3.30pm	40th Bty report no signs of infantry having reached edge of BOIS DE BIEZ, but Germans shelling M and road to South of M.	
4.45pm	Message received that GARHWAL BDE when it advances will do [illegible] trenches to the south of B.	
5.[illegible]pm	Orders received that all the operations would be	
5.50pm	repeated at 5.30pm, preliminary bombardment to last 15 mins instead of 30 mins	
	Attack did not succeed.	
6pm	Night lines ordered. 30th Bty on A and redoubt to S of it, 57th Bty on K and trenches to S of it 40th Bty	

1247 W 3299 200,000 (E) 8/14 J.B.C. & A. Forms/C. 2118/11.

Instructions regarding War Diaries and Intelligence Summaries are contained in F. S. Regs., Part II. and the Staff Manual respectively. Title pages will be prepared in manuscript.

WAR DIARY
or
~~INTELLIGENCE SUMMARY~~ of 43rd BDE RFA

(Erase heading not required.)

Army Form C. 2118.

(24)

Hour, Date, Place	Summary of Events and Information	Remarks and references to Appendices
6pm 12 MARCH 1915	covering Southern front of MEERUT DIV	Ref BETHUNE 1/40000, 1/5000 and 1/5000 trench plans
10.30pm–10.45pm	30TH & 57TH Btys opened on night lines	
	40TH Bty ordered by C.R.A not to fire	
9.50pm	Order to fire at night cancelled	
	ammunition expended 174 shrapnel 9 3.5 lyddite	EAW
13TH MARCH 1915	Operations suspended	
10.45am	Situation as follows —	
	BAREILLY BDE holding from Southern limit of Indian front to PORT ARTHUR inclusive	
	GARHWAL BDE from PORT ARTHUR exclusive to NEUVE CHAPELLE	
	DEHRA DUN BDE in support at RICHEBOURG ST VAAST	
	SIRHIND BDE in support at NEUVE CHAPELLE	
	2/3rd GURKHAS holding line T–P	
	LEICESTERS line P to Pirates road	
	1st SEAFORTHS from road through C to B	
	Enemy reported working in house in S11 c & b	
	Batteries in observation during day	
	ammunition expended 61 shrapnel 223 lyddite,	EAW

1247 W 3299 200,000 (E) 8/14 J.B.C. & A. Forms/C. 2118/11.

Instructions regarding War Diaries and Intelligence Summaries are contained in F. S. Regs., Part II. and the Staff Manual respectively. Title pages will be prepared in manuscript.

WAR DIARY
or
INTELLIGENCE SUMMARY
(Erase heading not required.)

~~43rd~~ 43rd BDE R.F.A.

Army Form C. 2118.

(25)

Hour, Date, Place	Summary of Events and Information	Remarks and references to Appendices
14TH MARCH 1915	NEUVE CHAPELLE and PORT ARTHUR heavily shelled. Amm expended 89 shrapnel 51 lyddite.	Ew. Ref BETHUNE $\frac{1}{40000}$ 1st Ed.
15TH MARCH 1915	No change. Amm expended 10 shrapnel 10 lyddite	Ew
16TH " "	40TH ~~B~~ 57TH Btys withdrawn at night going to billets at waggon lines.	
	30TH Bty remains in position under Indian Corps. Ammunition expended 5 shrapnel	Ew
17TH " "	Bde HQ 40TH 457TH Bty attached to 7TH DIV	
6.30pm.	40TH to action after dark at M 6 a 5.10	
	57TH Bty to M 5 b 2.0	
	Bde HQ to S 33 d 8.4	
	Bde A.C. ([illegible]) to R u d 10.8	
	Waggon lines to R 4 a 2.3.	Ew
	Organisation for offensive ordered. 3rd group consisting of 40TH 457TH Btys, 37TH Bde. [illegible] 1 Bty placed under orders of Lt Col. F.L. SMART 43rd Bde. R.F.A.	Ew.

1247 W 3299 200,000 (E) 8/14 J.B.C. & A. Forms/C. 2118/11.

Instructions regarding War Diaries and Intelligence Summaries are contained in F. S. Regs., Part II. and the Staff Manual respectively. Title pages will be prepared in manuscript.

WAR DIARY
or
INTELLIGENCE SUMMARY
of 43rd BDE R.F.A.

(Erase heading not required.)

Army Form C. 2118.

(26)

Hour, Date, Place	Summary of Events and Information	Remarks and references to Appendices
1pm 18th MARCH 1915 LAVENTIE	40th Bty checked lines & 57th Bty did not fire. Ammunition expended 16 shrapnel	Ref ~~Belts~~ 36 $\frac{1}{40000}$ 1st Ed. & trench map $\frac{1}{5000}$ 2789 a. EWD
19th " "	40th Bty did not fire.	
9.45 1015am	57th Bty registered brickfield N19c 60 and RUE D'ENFER (N 26 C). Ammunition expended 13 shrapnel	EWD
20th " " 11.30am to 12 noon	40th Bty registered house (298) trenches N13c 97 (321) (323) (326)	
10am	57th Bty trenches (317) to (320) Ammunition expended 42 shrapnel.	EWD
12 noon 21st " "	40th Bty registered FE. DELAVAL (N14a) and AUBERS 57th Bty did not fire. Amm. expended 13 shrapnel	EWD.
2.15-2.45pm 22nd " "	40th Bty registered ROUGES BANCS – ruined house N14 b 2.2 house (346) and (347)	
11.30am	57th Bty registered with aeroplane road junction N17a 2.3	

Instructions regarding War Diaries and Intelligence Summaries are contained in F. S. Regs., Part II. and the Staff Manual respectively. Title pages will be prepared in manuscript.

WAR DIARY
or
~~INTELLIGENCE SUMMARY~~
of 43rd BDE R.F.A.

(Erase heading not required.)

Army Form C. 2118.

(27)

Hour, Date, Place	Summary of Events and Information	Remarks and references to Appendices
3.20pm 22nd MARCH 1915	57TH Bty registered with aeroplane LARGIQUETERIE FE (T22 @ 6)	Ref 36 1/40000 & trench map 1/5000 2789 a
3.45pm	level crossing N32 c 2.1	
	amm expended 19 shrapnel 14 lyddite	ECW
23rd	40TH Bty did not fire	
10.30 am	57TH Bty registered ROUGES BANCS (N15 a)	
11 am	" " FE DELAVAL (N14 d)	
	amm expended 24 shrapnel	ECW
12 noon 24TH to 12.40pm	40 57TH bty registered (336) (334) (333) (331) (324)	
12.30pm	57TH bty " forward trench about (319) and 200x to N.E. also back trench about (327)	
	Ammunition expended 43 shrapnel	ECW
25TH	no targets engaged	ECW

1247 W 3299 200,000 (E) 8/14 J.B.C. & A. Forms/C. 2118/11.

Instructions regarding War Diaries and Intelligence Summaries are contained in F. S. Regs., Part II. and the Staff Manual respectively. Title pages will be prepared in manuscript.

WAR DIARY
or
INTELLIGENCE SUMMARY
of 43rd BDE R.F.A.

(Erase heading not required.)

Army Form C. 2118.

(28)

Hour, Date, Place	Summary of Events and Information	Remarks and references to Appendices
3-4 pm 26th MARCH 1915	40th Bty registered trench (332) to (334) and point (295)	Ref 36 1/40000 10th Ed & trench plan 1/5000 27.3.9a
	57th Bty did not fire	
	Ammunition expended 27 shrapnel	EWO
12 noon to 1 pm 27th MARCH 1915	40th Bty registered points on trenches between AUBERS and FROMELLES N27a1.3, N27b6.9, house on RUE DELAVAL N20b2.3 and redoubt 100x E of 299 Trench (321) to (303)	
	57th Bty registered redoubt 299 and cross trenches at (331)	
	Ammunition expended 1 lyddite 69 shrapnel	
28th MARCH 1915	118th Bde R.F.A CANADIAN DIV placed under orders of 3rd group.	EWO
3.30 to 5 pm	40th Bty registered german trenches in front of AUBERS N25b5.1, N26b2.1, N26a4.0, N26c7.7, N26c4.4, also german trench W of FROMELLES STATION (N22d6.7), LA PLOUICHE FE (N27d9.4).	
2.30 pm	57th Bty registered trenches N26a North of (216) to (228)	EWO
	Amm expended 49 shrapnel 3 lyddite	

Army Form C. 2118.

Instructions regarding War Diaries and Intelligence Summaries are contained in F. S. Regs., Part II. and the Staff Manual respectively. Title pages will be prepared in manuscript.

WAR DIARY
or
INTELLIGENCE SUMMARY
of 43rd BDE RFA.

(Erase heading not required.)

(29)

Hour, Date, Place	Summary of Events and Information	Remarks and references to Appendices
3pm 29th MARCH 1915	40th Bty registered Farm T2a 8 6 — Trenches N20a 6 5. Road N20a 6 5. Trench N20c 9 9.	Ref $\frac{1}{40000}$ 36 1st Ed. & trench map $\frac{1}{5000}$
2.30pm – 2.45pm	57th Bty registered trenches above (333) and orchard behind (299)	
	Ammunition expended 2 lyddite 57 shrapnel.	EAW
30th " " 31st " "	40th & 57th Btys did not fire.	EAW

1247 W 3299 200,000 (E) 8/14 J.B.C. & A. Forms/C. 2118/11.

Instructions regarding War Diaries and Intelligence Summaries are contained in F. S. Regs., Part II. and the Staff Manual respectively. Title pages will be prepared in manuscript.

WAR DIARY of 43rd Bde R.F.A.
or
~~INTELLIGENCE~~ SUMMARY
(Erase heading not required.)

Army Form C. 2118.

(30)

Hour, Date, Place	Summary of Events and Information	Remarks and references to Appendices
April 1st 1915	Hostile snipers and aeroplanes active — 118th Bde withdrawn from 3rd Group. Batteries did not fire	BETHUNE 1/40000
2nd 3rd	Batteries did not fire	
4th	43rd Bde returned to Indian Corps — 40th Bty to LAHORE DIV in action at CROIX BARBEE (M 32 b 4 8)	
8 pm	57th Bty & Bde HQ to billets at LES AMUSOIRES (P 17 b)	
	Batteries marched — Routes — 57th Bty & HQ NOUVEAU MONDE — ESTAIRES — [illegible] — [illegible] — CALONNE — LES AMUSOIRES —	
	40th Bty [illegible] via road junction M 9 a 6 1 — cross roads M 10 c 6 5 — road [illegible] M 9 a 6 [illegible] PONT DU HEM — road junc. M 21 a — M 22 b.	[illegible]
6th	Position of units of Bde on this day as follows	
	Bde HQ P 11 a 5 5 —	
	30th Bty P 23 10 0. (under MEERUT DIV)	
	57th Bty P 17 b	
	40th Bty M 32 b 4 8 (under LAHORE DIV)	
	Bde HQ [illegible] PONT RIQUEUL supplying 40th Bty — [illegible] at LES LOBES — [illegible] at P 17 b	[illegible]
6th – 12th	Resting.	
6 pm 10th	1 Sec 30th 1 Sec 57th Bty [illegible] M 32 d 8 3 [illegible] M 21 b 10 3	[illegible]

Instructions regarding War Diaries and Intelligence Summaries are contained in F. S. Regs., Part II. and the Staff Manual respectively. Title pages will be prepared in manuscript.

WAR DIARY of 43rd BDE R.F.A.
or
INTELLIGENCE SUMMARY
(Erase heading not required.)

Army Form C. 2118.

(31)

Hour, Date, Place	Summary of Events and Information	Remarks and references to Appendices
12 noon 14th April 1915 RIEZ BAILLEUL	Bde H Q to RIEZ BAILLEUL (M 7d 3.8) – Bde A C to LES LOBES	Ref BETHUNE [illegible]
6 pm	Remainder 30th & 57th Btys to positions as stated above.	Trench map 1/10000
	During day 30th Bty registered Distillery S 17a road junction S 11 a, house on LA BASSEE road about S 11 c 3.7 – trench S 10 [illegible]	Caw
	Ammunition expended 57 shrapnel	
15th April 1915	Batteries grouped with infantry brigades as follows.	
	Northern group 57th Bty with BAREILLY Bde.	
	Centre group 40th Bty with DEHRA DUN Bde	
	Southern group 30th Bty with GARHWAL Bde.	
12 noon	30th fired at trenches [illegible]	
1.30 pm.	Registered point (14)	Caw
11.15 am 16th April 1915	40th registered (53)	
12.30 pm	" " (69)	
1.40 pm	" fired on trench (130), (215), barricade on road near (133)	
3.30 pm	" " small parties Germans near (130)	Caw
5.30 am 17th April 1915	57th registered (110) fired at house (25) chimney of MOULIN DE PIETRE	Caw

1247 W 3299 200,000 (E) 8/14 J.B.C. & A. Forms/C. 2118/11.

Instructions regarding War Diaries and Intelligence Summaries are contained in F. S. Regs., Part II. and the Staff Manual respectively. Title pages will be prepared in manuscript.

WAR DIARY
or
INTELLIGENCE SUMMARY
of 43rd Bde R.F.A.

(Erase heading not required.)

Army Form C. 2118.

(32)

Hour, Date, Place	Summary of Events and Information	Remarks and references to Appendices
18th April 1915	57th Bty fired at (206) cross roads (201), house (203) house and trench (140), direct hit on machine gun (205) and house (113)	Bty [illegible] BETHUNE [illegible]
	ammunition expended [illegible]	[illegible]
4.30am 19th April	57th fired on Bty [illegible]	
8pm	registered (204) &	
2.10pm	MOULIN DE PIETRE.	[illegible]
5.30am 20th April 1915	57th fired at house (196)	
3.30pm	LES MOTTES FARM.	
5.30pm	registered (262)	
	ammunition expended 13 shrapnel 4 lyddite	
5.30am 21st	57th Bty fired at (203)	
3.30pm	registered (204) [illegible]	
5pm	registered (2[illegible])	[illegible]
22nd	57th Bty [illegible] on [illegible] (203)	
	ammunition expended [illegible] shrapnel 6 lyddite	[illegible]
	to [illegible]	[illegible]
24th	57th fired [illegible] lyddite at (2[illegible]) [illegible]	
	after dark 40th & 57th [illegible] wagon lines for the night. [illegible] ammunition 5 lyddite	[illegible]

Major R Longstaff to R.F.C. 1st Army as liaison officer.

1247 W 3299 200,000 (E) 8/14 J.B.C. & A. Forms/C. 2118/11.

Instructions regarding War Diaries and Intelligence Summaries are contained in F. S. Regs., Part II. and the Staff Manual respectively. Title pages will be prepared in manuscript.

WAR DIARY *or* INTELLIGENCE SUMMARY

(Erase heading not required.)

Army Form C. 2118.

(33)

Hour, Date, Place	Summary of Events and Information	Remarks and references to Appendices
8.30 am 25th APRIL 1915	Bde H.Q. 40th, 57th [illegible] Btys [illegible] location [illegible] to ROBECQUE as follows:–	Ref BETHUNE [illegible]
	Starting point crossroads 8.0 am – Route LA GORGUE, NEUF BERQUIN, BLEU, METEREN, BERTHEN.	Sheet 28 1/40000
3 pm	Bde reached BERTHEN – Orders received to march to [illegible] to bivouac for night	HAZEBROUCK 5A 1/100000
12 noon 26th April 1915	Batteries to action 57th to B23 C 5.5 – 40th to ST JEAN position in support of [illegible] infantry brigade of LAHORE DIV.	
	Ammunition column to VLAMERTINGHE – H 3 – 1.6	
	LAHORE DIV to attack on front from C17a to [illegible] C18 [illegible] following bombardment carried out.	
1.20 pm	Section fire [illegible] bombardment to cover deployment lasting 40 mins.	
2 pm	Fire turned on to [illegible] front [illegible] [illegible] at section fire [illegible]	
2.5 pm	Assault delivered [illegible] 57th turned on to [illegible]	
2.30 pm	Ordered to keep fire down to [illegible]	
2.50 pm	Reported that [illegible] [illegible]	
[illegible] pm	Ordered to turn fire back on to enemy's trenches at slow rate of fire	

1247 W 3299 200,000 (E) 8/14 J.B.C. & A. Forms/C. 2118/11.

Instructions regarding War Diaries and Intelligence Summaries are contained in F. S. Regs., Part II. and the Staff Manual respectively. Title pages will be prepared in manuscript.

WAR DIARY
or
INTELLIGENCE SUMMARY

(Erase heading not required.)

J 4 3rd Bde T.F.A.

Army Form C. 2118.

(34)

Hour, Date, Place	Summary of Events and Information	Remarks and references to Appendices
3.35pm 26th APRIL 1915	[illegible] Informed that attack had failed	Ref 28 $\frac{1}{40000}$
3.45pm	Ordered to stop firing at trench in C15	
4.07pm	Informed that 1 bn. JULLUNDER BDE in German trenches. Ordered to stop firing on German trenches. SIRHIND BDE sent up to help. French reported to have been driven back. [illegible] reported [illegible] C.11 a + d, also southern edge of wood in C10	
4.45pm	[illegible] fire [illegible] ordered [illegible] counter-attack delivered	
5pm	Ordered to stop firing until situation alters	
12.30pm 27th April 1915	Orders received for attack by French and [illegible] DIV. 33rd Bty bombardment of German trenches N.E. of hill 29 (C15 a)	
12.40pm–1.15pm	bombardment — [illegible] intensive bombardment	
1.15pm	Fire lifted to strong points in German lines — SIRHIND Bde assault. FEROZEPORE Bde advance under cover of bombardment to the [illegible] right of SIRHIND and assault 1.15pm	

1247 W 3299 200,000 (E) 8/14 J.B.C. & A. Forms/C. 2118/11.

Instructions regarding War Diaries and Intelligence Summaries are contained in F. S. Regs., Part II. and the Staff Manual respectively. Title pages will be prepared in manuscript.

WAR DIARY
or
INTELLIGENCE SUMMARY

(Erase heading not required.)

Army Form C. 2118.

(35)

Hour, Date, Place	Summary of Events and Information	Remarks and references to Appendices
1.15pm 27th APRIL 1915	57th ordered to shell strong point C16a [illegible]	Ref. Sheet 28 [illegible]
2.40pm	57th Bty firing section fire 5 mins	HAZEBROUCK [illegible]
3.51pm	French reported checked from farm C16a 7 8 and trenches running through that point E + W.	
4.40pm	SIRHIND BDE checked.	
5.20pm	French reported advancing on line [illegible] in C15c but make no progress	
5.15pm	57th open fire on enemy's front line trenches opposite LAHORE DIV (29 to [illegible])	
5.40pm	Intensive bombardment	
5.45pm	Infantry attack failed	
	ammunition expended 102 lyddite 23 shrapnel	[illegible]
28th April 1915	French attacks	
1.15pm – 2pm	57th Bty in support on German trench C15a 7 8 to C16a 2 5	
2pm – 2.10pm	57th on house C9c 2 2 with two sections — 1 section on eastern part of trenches	
2pm	French attack.	
6.55 – 7pm	57th on German 2nd line trenches C9a 3 6 to C4d 8 4 in support of French attack from BOESINGHE line and from [illegible] point at [illegible]	

1247 W 3299 200,000 (E) 8/14 J.B.C. & A. Forms/C. 2118/11.

Instructions regarding War Diaries and Intelligence Summaries are contained in F. S. Regs., Part II. and the Staff Manual respectively. Title pages will be prepared in manuscript.

WAR DIARY
or
INTELLIGENCE SUMMARY

(Erase heading not required.)

of 43rd Bde RFA

(36)

Army Form C. 2118.

Hour, Date, Place	Summary of Events and Information	Remarks and references to Appendices
28 April 1915	Night [illegible] – French from 29 to North of [illegible]	Rf 28 – 1/40000
	40th Bty withdrawn to [illegible] B 28 a. [illegible]	
	[illegible] position B 23 a. [illegible]	
	Ammunition expended 1224 Lyddite – 71 Shrapnel	
29th April 1915	French attacks [illegible]	
	40th Bty [illegible] [illegible] battery	
	connected by telephone to [illegible] 122nd Heavy	
	battery – B 21 c [illegible]	
[illegible]	57th Bty fired on [illegible] in [illegible] to	
	request from infantry and made good shooting.	
	Amm exp. 91 lyd. 43 shrapnel.	
30th April 1915	French attack on [illegible] point 29 [illegible]	
[illegible]	40th & 57th in support. Bombardment [illegible]	
	57th [illegible] about point 29	
	French report fire on point 29 very successful	
	[illegible] attack	
[illegible]	40th stop firing on wood [illegible]	
11.20am	[illegible] 57th fire continue [illegible] on point 29 [illegible] another	
11.30am	15 rounds.	
12.10pm	French report they have not progressed [illegible]	
	and request fire to be kept up on [illegible]	
	[illegible] [illegible] 57th [illegible]	

1247 W 3299 200,000 (E) 8/14 J.B.C. & A. Forms/C. 2118/11.

Instructions regarding War Diaries and Intelligence Summaries are contained in F. S. Regs., Part II. and the Staff Manual respectively. Title pages will be prepared in manuscript.

WAR DIARY *of 43rd Bde R.F.A.*
or
INTELLIGENCE SUMMARY.
(Erase heading not required.)

Army Form C. 2118.

(37)

Hour, Date, Place	Summary of Events and Information	Remarks and references to Appendices
1.15pm 30th April 1915	Reported that French [illegible] on PILCKEM–YPRES Road have got German trenches.	Ref. sheet 28 1/40000 and HAZEBROUCK 5A 1/100000
1.35pm	French advance confirmed by 30th Bty.	
2.10pm	Report from CRA that French have reached C8 central. Order to stop firing on point 29.	
2.18pm	German reinforcements reported coming into PILCKEM. Order to shell village and cross roads in C20 [illegible].	
2.35pm	Request from French General to shell PILCKEM heavily. B.R. batteries ordered to comply.	
3.11pm	Ordered to slow down rate of fire on PILCKEM.	
3.15pm	Stopped firing as situation not clear.	
5.15–5.30pm	PILCKEM shelled at request of French.	
4–4.10pm	Point 29 shelled by 57th at request of French.	
	Night [illegible] 57th on point 29.	
	Casualties – Lieut P. G. MUIRHEAD slightly wounded. 1 Gunner wounded.	
	Ammunition expended [illegible] lyddite 32 shrapnel.	[illegible]

1st Division

ATTACHED INDIAN CORPS.

121/6111

43rd Bde R.F.A.

Vol VI ~~April~~ May

Mr

A2

A/6

Instructions regarding War Diaries and Intelligence Summaries are contained in F. S. Regs., Part II. and the Staff Manual respectively. Title pages will be prepared in manuscript.

WAR DIARY *or* INTELLIGENCE SUMMARY. of 43rd Bde R.F.A.

(Erase heading not required.)

Army Form C. 2118.

(38)

Hour, Date, Place	Summary of Events and Information	Remarks and references to Appendices
1st May 1915	attack intended by French at 8.15 am did not take	Ref Sheet 28 1/40000
	place — 57th Bty fired on front 29 at intervals	and [illegible] BROEK 5a 1/10000
	40th Bty counter battery.	
3.50 – 4.15 pm	57th fired on PILCKEM	
	Night lines 57th on PILCKEM.	
	Bde A.C. moved to A 30 b 8 8.	
	Ammunition expended 298 lyddite	[illegible]
10.50 am 2nd May 1915	Order for batteries to be in observation	
2.20 pm	Information received that French expect attack from PILCKEM	
	57th ordered to fire a few rounds at PILCKEM	
6 pm	57th Bty heavily shelled.	
7.15 pm	57th Bty report our troops driven from trenches S.E. of	
	hill 29. by gas — no sign of Germans advancing —	
	Turned fire on to German trenches — 1 sec 40th — 1 sec	
8.30 pm	57th withdrawn and marched to OUTERDOM	
	Casualties 1 Bty [illegible] 2 gunners killed, 3 gunners wounded.	[illegible]
	Ammunition expended 94 lyddite	

(9 29 6) W 2794 100,000 8/14 H W V Forms/C. 2118/11

Instructions regarding War Diaries and Intelligence Summaries are contained in F. S. Regs., Part II. and the Staff Manual respectively. Title pages will be prepared in manuscript.

WAR DIARY *or* INTELLIGENCE SUMMARY. of 43rd Bde RFA

(Erase heading not required.)

Army Form C. 2118.

(39)

Hour, Date, Place	Summary of Events and Information	Remarks and references to Appendices
3rd May 1915	57th Bty changed position to B28d 2.0	Ref Sheet 28 1/40000
	Several German attempts to attack repulsed – all stopped	and HAZEBROUCK 5A 1/100000
	by gun fire – 57th shelled wood C16 b – C17a	
[illegible]pm	40th & 57th Btys withdrawn and marched via VLAMERTINGHE –	
	OUDERDOM – RENINGHELST – WESTOUTRE – MONT NOIR [illegible] – MONT DES CATS	
	to billets – Bde in billets by 5am	
	Ammunition expended 152 by [illegible]	[illegible]
4th May 1915.	Bde marched with LAHORE DIV ARTILLERY – Starting point	
[illegible]pm	Xroads ½ mile SE of METEREN at [illegible]pm via NOOTE BOOM	
	– DOULIEU – MERVILLE – LESTREM – billets near [illegible]. Bde	
	A.C. to M19 d 7.7.	
5th May 1915	Resting	Ref 36a 1/40000 3rd Edition
[illegible]pm	57th Bty to action M21 d 8.5	
	1 sec 40th Bty action M32 b 4.5.	
	30th bty at M32 b 6.4. Bde A.C. to R11a 9.1.	[illegible]
[illegible]	~~Ammunition expended~~	

(9 29 6) W2794 100,000 8/14 H W V Forms/C. 2118/11

Instructions regarding War Diaries and Intelligence Summaries are contained in F. S. Regs., Part II. and the Staff Manual respectively. Title pages will be prepared in manuscript.

WAR DIARY
or
INTELLIGENCE SUMMARY.
(*Erase heading not required.*)

of 43rd BDE R.F.A.

Army Form C. 2118.

(40)

Hour, Date, Place	Summary of Events and Information	Remarks and references to Appendices
6th May 1915	Battys registering — after dark remainder 40th Bty to action M 32 b 4 5.	Ref HAZEBROUCK 5A 1/100000
	Ammunition expended 2 lyddite 25 shrapnel	French Map 1/10000 Ew Sheet 36 1/20000
7 May 1915	Batteries registering.	
7.30pm	Operations ordered for 8th postponed.	
	Ammunition expended 70 lyddite 63 shrapnel.	Ew
	2Lt H.T. SELBY from 30th Bty to R.F.C.	
8 May 1915	Batteries registering ammunition expended 123 lyddite 129 sh.	Ew
9 May 1915	Attack by Indian Corps along ESTAIRES–LA BASSEE road	
5am	Wire cutting by 18pr batteries 43rd Bde in observation	
5.10–5.20am	30th Bty on front (58) 40th on (51a) – (53) – 57th on (54) and (54a)	
5.20am	Bombardment of front trench from (58) incl to (61) excl	
"	& from 50 yds right of (60) to S 10 d 3 9	
5.40am	40th Bty on 52 to (53) and houses (49) (53) (64) (43)	
	57th V9, V10 V10a – V7, V8 V12.	
	30th – V6 – V4a + V5a to LA TOURELLE Xroads.	

(9 29 6) W 2794 100,000 8/14 H W V Forms/C. 2118/11

Instructions regarding War Diaries and Intelligence Summaries are contained in F. S. Regs., Part II. and the Staff Manual respectively. Title pages will be prepared in manuscript.

WAR DIARY of 43rd Bde R.F.A.
or
INTELLIGENCE SUMMARY.
(Erase heading not required.)

Army Form C. 2118.

(41)

Hour, Date, Place	Summary of Events and Information	Remarks and references to Appendices
6am. 9-5-15.	Information received that attack is held up along whole front	Ref HAZEBROUCK 5a $\frac{1}{100000}$
	Batteries ordered to turn back on to front trench from	36² $\frac{1}{20000}$
6.10am – 6.20am	6.10 to 6.20 am	trench map $\frac{1}{10000}$.
6.25am	Order to bombard front trench 56 – 76 paying especial	
	attention to 59	
6.30am – 6.50am	Bombardment of front trench	
6.27am	57th ordered to pay especial attention to 59.	
7.36am	First bombardment of German trenches ordered	
7.45 8.10am	Bombardment.	
8.47am	Orders issued to batteries to re-register commencing	
9am	30th Bty registers.	
9.15am	57th Bty do.	
9.30 "	40th "	
9.40am	Orders received for reorganised attack. Bombardment etc	
	as in first attack, commencing 12 noon, assault 12.40pm	
	postponed to 2 pm assault 2.40 pm. postponed agai[n]	

(9 29 6) W 2794 100,000 8/14 H W V Forms/C. 2118/11

Army Form C. 2118.

Instructions regarding War Diaries and Intelligence Summaries are contained in F. S. Regs., Part II. and the Staff Manual respectively. Title pages will be prepared in manuscript.

WAR DIARY of 43rd BDE R.F.A.
or
INTELLIGENCE SUMMARY.
(*Erase heading not required.*)

(42)

Hour, Date, Place	Summary of Events and Information	Remarks and references to Appendices
9-5-15.	to 3.20pm assault 4pm.	Ref Sheet 5A HAZEBROUCK 1/100000
3.40pm - 4pm	Batteries firing on front trenches bombardment. All batteries communication cut during bombardment.	36 1/40000 Trench map 1/10000
	Attack failed.	
4.35pm	Batteries to observation.	
6.40pm	Night lines ordered — 57th from 140 to 130 — 40th from 130 to 51e — 30th 55 to V6.	
	Ammunition expended 1975 lyddite 261 shrapnel.	Enc
1.30am 10-5-15.	Batteries ordered to re-register as soon as it is light enough to do so	
11.10 am	Order received that operations are postponed. Batteries in observation ~~then~~	
	Ammunition expended 855 lyddite 69 shrapnel.	Enc
~~11-5-15~~	~~Batteries in observation~~	
	~~Ammunition expended~~	Enc
12.5.15	Batteries in observation	

(9 29 6) W2794 100,000 8/14 H W V Forms/C. 2118/11

Instructions regarding War Diaries and Intelligence Summaries are contained in F. S. Regs., Part II. and the Staff Manual respectively. Title pages will be prepared in manuscript.

WAR DIARY of 43rd Bde R.F.A.
or
~~INTELLIGENCE SUMMARY.~~
(Erase heading not required.)

Army Form C. 2118.

(43)

Hour, Date, Place	Summary of Events and Information	Remarks and references to Appendices
9 pm 11-5-15	Orders received not to fire during night except in case of attack.	Ref 36c $\frac{1}{20000}$ 3rd Ed.
10 pm 11-5-15	Received orders that Bde is now under orders of G.O.C. R.A. Meerut Div. — 30th Bty grouped with Southern group — 40th & 57th Btys. with Northern group.	dw
12.5.15	Ammunition expended 21 lyddite.	
13-5-15	Bde HQ to RIEZ BAILLEUL	
11 am	As a result of conference battys brought under orders of O.C. Bde and orders issued for a sustained and steady bombardment of enemy's front line trenches between V5 & V6. Bombardment to commence as soon as possible.	
5 pm	Bombardment commenced — light very bad. 30th registered and fired about 25 rounds on left hand	

(9 29 6) W 2794 100,000 8/14 H W V Forms/C. 2118/11

Army Form C. 2118.

Instructions regarding War Diaries and Intelligence Summaries are contained in F. S. Regs., Part II. and the Staff Manual respectively. Title pages will be prepared in manuscript.

WAR DIARY of 43rd Bde RFA
or
INTELLIGENCE SUMMARY.
(*Erase heading not required.*)

(44)

Hour, Date, Place	Summary of Events and Information	Remarks and references to Appendices
13-5-15	portion of trench	Ref 1/20000 36B 3rd Ed.
6 – 6.45pm	40 rounds per [illegible] fired on trenches.	& trench map 1/10000
	After dark batteries ordered to keep up fire	
	during night on portions of trench destroyed.	
	Rate 6 rounds per hour.	Amm exp. 12 noon – 12 noon
	Casualties 2Lt THEAK (attd. 30th Bty) wounded.	
	* Ammunition expended – nil.	[illegible]
14-5-15.	Bombardment at slow rate kept up during morning.	
2.30pm.	Order received that attack ordered for 1am 15.15.15 would	
	probably be postponed for 24 hours, in which case	
	ammunition allotted for bombardment would have to	
	be spread out over a further 24 hours. Batteries accordingly	
	ordered to stop firing till further orders.	
4pm	Batteries registered German 2nd line	
7.15pm	Order received that operations postponed for	
	24 hours.	

(9 29 6) W2794 100,000 8/14 H W V Forms/C. 2118/11

Instructions regarding War Diaries and Intelligence Summaries are contained in F. S. Regs., Part II. and the Staff Manual respectively. Title pages will be prepared in manuscript.

WAR DIARY of 43rd Bde R.F.A.
or
INTELLIGENCE SUMMARY.
(*Erase heading not required.*)

Army Form C. 2118.

(45)

Hour, Date, Place	Summary of Events and Information	Remarks and references to Appendices
15.5.15.	Batteries firing on german trenches at very slow rate – each battery for two hours at a time – Special target trench 310 c 8.9 to V6 and 2nd line trenches	Ref 36b 1/20000 3rd Ed. & trench map 1/10000
	3.15 pm 57th Bty report trench 54a 54 53 has been made much stronger – ~~For~~	
	From dusk till 11.25pm – btys on these trenches slow steady bombardment preparatory to attack by GARHWAL Bde. on front V5 – V6. Btys on 2nd line trenches with shrapnel and on trench running NNE from V6a	
6.~~30~~pm	~~6.30pm~~ 30th Bty engaged and breached trench running E from V6 towards W end of keep	
6.30 pm	Orders received & issued to 30th to shell trench between V6 & V3 obtained several direct hits	
11.25pm	Barrage formed batteries firing shrapnel on trenches and lyddite on points denoted by figures.	
	40th Bty covered way – V9a – V6a – to point 150x W	

(9 29 6) W2794 100,000 8/14 H W V Forms/C. 2118/11

Instructions regarding War Diaries and Intelligence Summaries are contained in F. S. Regs., Part II. and the Staff Manual respectively. Title pages will be prepared in manuscript.

WAR DIARY of 43rd BDE RFA
or
INTELLIGENCE SUMMARY.
(*Erase heading not required.*)

Army Form C. 2118.

(46)

Hour, Date, Place	Summary of Events and Information	Remarks and references to Appendices
15.5.15.	of V6c. 30th Bty on Keep	
	57th points 55, 56, 60, 59 & trench between these points	
11.30pm	Attack by GARHWAL Bde	
	ammunition expended 602 lyddite 193 shrapnel	EAD
	Casualty 2/Lt H. Somerville SMITH of 'B' Bty 113th Bde, attd. 30th Bty wounded.	
1.30am 16.5.15.	Information from 30th Bty that attack by 39th GARHWALIS had failed	
2am	Report from 30th Bty that GARHWAL Bde attack has failed.	
3am	Orders from C.R.A to bombard German 2nd line trench at quick rate from V6 to west till 3.12 am & then fire barrage as for 11.25 pm on 15th.	
3.45am	Report from 57th Bty that GARHWAL assault has again failed.	
5.18 am	Order to 3 batteries to go into observation	
7.5 am	30th Bty ordered to turn on to German 2nd line trench	

(9 29 6) W2794 100,000 8/14 H W V Forms/C. 2118/11

Instructions regarding War Diaries and Intelligence Summaries are contained in F. S. Regs., Part II. and the Staff Manual respectively. Title pages will be prepared in manuscript.

WAR DIARY of 43rd BDE R.F.A.
or
INTELLIGENCE SUMMARY.
(Erase heading not required.)

Army Form C. 2118.

(47)

Hour, Date, Place	Summary of Events and Information	Remarks and references to Appendices
5.55am. 16.5.15.	from V6 to V3 at very slow rate of fire.	Ref HAZEBROUCK 5a 1/100000
6 am	30th Bty report Germans moving along back trench from V6 to right and fire on them with effect.	+ 36c 1/20000 + trench map 1/10,000
6.40am	C.R.A. reports Germans massing from V6 towards our right. Order to watch for counter attack and form barrage. Tasks for barrage allotted as follows:— 30th + 40th to take on German front and 2nd line if Germans show signs of movement. 57th to watch "covered way".	
7.45am	Information from C.R.A. that our front trench is being cleared. Orders one battery to turn on to German front line at once.	
7.54 am	40th Bty ordered to do this.	
8.15 am	Information from CRA that 7th Div have reached LA QUINQUE RUE near (M5) + 2nd Div have reached V2.	
9 am	Batteries ordered to stop firing + go into observation.	

Instructions regarding War Diaries and Intelligence Summaries are contained in F. S. Regs., Part II. and the Staff Manual respectively. Title pages will be prepared in manuscript.

WAR DIARY of 43rd BDE RFA
or
INTELLIGENCE SUMMARY.
(*Erase heading not required.*)

Army Form C. 2118.

(48)

Hour, Date, Place	Summary of Events and Information	Remarks and references to Appendices
9.15 am 16–5–15	40th Bty report 7th Div holding line N9 to P10 & 6th Bde R1 – R3 – R7 and is advancing on Q7 and FE. DU BOIS 5th Bde right at R7.	Ref. HALEBROUCK 5a 1/100000 36c 1/20000 Trench map 1/10000
10.30 am	Order from C.R.A. to watch 2nd line trench V6 – V5 carefully as 2nd Div asking for assistance there	
10.50 am	CRA reports 2nd Div bombing parties moving East from V3 & V4.	
11.14 am	Order from CRA to stop firing at V6.	
11.20 am	57th Bty ordered to fire a few rounds at "Crossway" about V6a to help 2nd Div bombing parties.	
11.35 am	40th Bty ask for permission to fire at V6 as Observing Officer considers it requires attention – Permission given.	
	30th ask for permission to fire on S10c88 – Permission given.	
11.55 am	57th Bty ordered to turn on to communication trench running from S.W corner of heap to V5a.	
12 Noon	30th Bty report Germans going along back trench from V6 to right	

(9 29 6) W 2794 100,000 8/14 H W V Forms/C. 2118/11

Instructions regarding War Diaries and Intelligence Summaries are contained in F. S. Regs., Part II. and the Staff Manual respectively. Title pages will be prepared in manuscript.

WAR DIARY of 45th Bde RFA
or
INTELLIGENCE SUMMARY.
(Erase heading not required.)

Army Form C. 2118.

(43)

Hour, Date, Place	Summary of Events and Information	Remarks and references to Appendices
12.10 pm 16.5–15	and fire on them with effect	Ref HAZEBROUCK 5A 1/100000
12.10 pm	CRA reports machine gun 30x W of 56. 45th locate & engage it.	36c – 1/20000
12.25 pm	CRA reports our bombing parties nearing V6 from West. Batteries report they can see no signs of them	Trench map 1/10000.
1.30 pm	40th Bty ordered to cease firing on 56. 57th ordered to open fire on covered way from V6a towards V5 at very slow rate.	
2.25 pm	CRA reports CARNIVAL Bde about to reoccupy their front line trenches. Order not to fire on front line trenches any more.	
3.40 pm	CRA reports hostile movement at "distillery" batteries ordered to watch for opportunities.	
4.10 pm	Report from CRA that 7th Div hold line M5 – M6 – M8 – N12 and 2nd Div advancing North against P7 – P8 – P9 – P10.	
4.30 pm	Order from CRA that unless Observing Officers can see good targets, only to fire occasional rounds from	

Instructions regarding War Diaries and Intelligence Summaries are contained in F. S. Regs., Part II. and the Staff Manual respectively. Title pages will be prepared in manuscript.

WAR DIARY of 43rd Bde R.F.A.
or
~~INTELLIGENCE~~ SUMMARY.
(Erase heading not required.)

Army Form C. 2118.

(49)

Hour, Date, Place	Summary of Events and Information	Remarks and references to Appendices
		Ref
16-5-15	V6a to V6 + V5a.	HAZEBROUCK 5A 1/100.000
7.45 pm	Night lines ordered. Information that Germans are in	36c 1/20.000
	communication trench Q17 - Q18 - P19 - P20 - N25 - N23 -	trench map 1/10.000.
	Batteries of LAHORE DIV to fire in turn during night.	
	Each battery ordered to have one section on above	
	trench. Remainder of brigade as follows - 30TH zones	
	on 2nd line trench from V6 to ditch through V5.	
	40TH " " " 59 to V6.	
	57TH on "covered way" V9a to 150x W of V6a.	
	One round shrapnel to be fired from each gun at	
	stated times.	
10 pm	30TH Bty fire as ordered above.	
	Ammunition expended 667 lyddite 243 shrapnel.	EAW.
1 am 17-5-15	40TH Bty fired as above.	
2 am	57TH Bty. fired as above.	
6.25 am	Message from C.R.A. ordering to try and locate hostile batteries	

Instructions regarding War Diaries and Intelligence Summaries are contained in F. S. Regs., Part II. and the Staff Manual respectively. Title pages will be prepared in manuscript.

WAR DIARY of 43rd TSDE RFA

or

~~INTELLIGENCE SUMMARY.~~

(Erase heading not required.)

Army Form C. 2118.

(52)

Hour, Date, Place	Summary of Events and Information	Remarks and references to Appendices
17-5-15	and if possible engage them.	Ref HAZEBROUCK 5a 1/100000
9am	30th Bty engage and silence a battery.	36c 1/20000
10am	Report from CRA that 2nd Div about to attack up line Q14 FE DU BOIS – order for one battery to form barrage V6a to V6 and one battery V6a to V5e.	Trench map 1/10000.
10.50am	30th Bty report no Germans visible about V6.	
11.15am	Batteries opened fire as follows:–	
	30th Back trench V6 to V5.	
	40th V6 to 59.	
	57th Covered way V9e – V6e towards V6.	
	to cover advance of 2nd Div. Order to lift in case of advance. BAREILLY Bde to join up with 2nd Div if successful.	
~~1.20pm~~ 1.20pm	Report that BAREILLY Bde joining up with 2nd Div at V1 2nd Div not yet attacking.	
2.35pm	Order to stop firing for the present on German 2nd line trenches	

(9 29 6) W2794 100,000 8/14 H W V Forms/C. 2118/11

Instructions regarding War Diaries and Intelligence Summaries are contained in F. S. Regs., Part II. and the Staff Manual respectively. Title pages will be prepared in manuscript.

WAR DIARY of 43rd Bde R.F.A. ~~or~~ INTELLIGENCE SUMMARY.

(Erase heading not required.)

Army Form C. 2118.

(51)

Hour, Date, Place	Summary of Events and Information	Remarks and references to Appendices
2.35 pm 17-5-15	between V6 and V3, and at 1st & 2nd line trench	Ref. HAZEBROUCK 1/100000
	between 59 and V6	36c 1/20000
3.25 pm	Order to all batteries to fire 6 rounds per hour on barrage.	trench map 1/10000.
4.14 pm	Line reported as follows:- L2-L5-M6-M8-M9-LA QUINQUE RUE-P10. 22d DIV P10-Q7-Q8-R5-V1	
5.35 pm	Order received for night firing on barrage as for 11.25 pm 15-5-15.	
8-10 pm	all batteries firing barrage 20 rounds per hour.	
12 mn	burst of fire on barrage 2 rounds per gun.	
	Ammunition expended. 212 Lyddite 86 shrapnel.	
	1 Bombardier - 1 Gunner wounded.	BWD.
2am 18-5-15	Burst of fire on barrage 2 rounds per gun	
4am	do — do — do — do	
6am	do — do — do — do	
8am	do — do — do — do.	

(9 29 6) W 2794 100,000 8/14 H W V Forms/C. 2118/11

Instructions regarding War Diaries and Intelligence Summaries are contained in F. S. Regs., Part II. and the Staff Manual respectively. Title pages will be prepared in manuscript.

Army Form C. 2118.

WAR DIARY of 43rd BDE R.F.A.

~~or~~

~~INTELLIGENCE SUMMARY.~~

(*Erase heading not required.*)

(52)

Hour, Date, Place	Summary of Events and Information	Remarks and references to Appendices
8.35 am 18–5–15.	Report from CRA that 2nd Div ~~were~~ are going to attach at 9 am – Batteries on very slow barrage.	Ref HAZEBROUCK 5A 1/100000
		36B 1/20000
1.30 pm	30th & 40th Btys. ordered to register FE DU BOIS.	trench map 1/10000
2.10 pm	Information from CRA that 2nd Div attaching FE DU BOIS at 4.30 pm. Order for one battery to shell it at very slow rate, one battery to barrage on 'covered way'.	
	30th Bty on FE DU BOIS with lyddite – 40th on 'covered way'	
2.35 pm	CRA orders no more lyddite to be used today.	
	30th Bty ordered to turn off FE DU BOIS on to trench V6a – V5a.	
3.46 pm	Rate of fire ordered as follows:– ~~4p~~	
4 pm – 4.20 pm	Section fire 1 minute.	
4.20 pm – 4.30 pm	Section fire 30 secs.	
4.30 pm	Slow rate.	
7 pm	Batteries stop fire as there is no sign of German activity and no sign of attach.	

Army Form C. 2118.

Instructions regarding War Diaries and Intelligence Summaries are contained in F. S. Regs., Part II. and the Staff Manual respectively. Title pages will be prepared in manuscript.

WAR DIARY of 43rd Bde R.F.A.
~~or~~
INTELLIGENCE SUMMARY.
(Erase heading not required.)

(53)

Hour, Date, Place	Summary of Events and Information	Remarks and references to Appendices
8.45pm - 18-5-15	Night lines ordered - 30th Bty V6e - V5e - 40th Bty "Covered way" V9e - V6e towards V6 - 57th covered way 30th & 40th to fire 18 rounds per hour until further orders - 57th in observation.	Ref HAZEBROUCK 5A 1/100000 36a 1/20000 Trench maps 1/10000.
9pm.	30th & 57th Bty wagon lines & Bde Amm Cols. to R73 10.5. Ammunition expended. 9 lyddite 345 shrapnel.	caw.
5.47am 19-5-15.	Enemy reported bombing from V2 towards R6 - Order to increase rate of fire on barrage to section fire 5 mins. by 30th & 40th Btys.	
9.45am	Order to stop firing on barrage.	
10.45am	Order to 30th & 40th btys to continue on barrage at X fire 10 mins.	
11.30am	Order from C.R.A that night lines will be 1 Bty V6 to LA BASSEE road (incl) 1 Bty 63 to 59, 1 Bty 59 to R7 Allotted 57th Bty to LA BASSEE road - 40th 63-59 - 30th 59-R7.	
7pm.	Order to turn one battery on to "covered way" V9e-V6	

(9 29 6) W 2794 100,000 8/14 H W V Forms/C. 2118/11

Instructions regarding War Diaries and Intelligence Summaries are contained in F. S. Regs., Part II. and the Staff Manual respectively. Title pages will be prepared in manuscript.

WAR DIARY of 43rd BDE R.F.A. ~~or INTELLIGENCE~~ SUMMARY.

(*Erase heading not required.*)

Army Form C. 2118.

(54)

Hour, Date, Place	Summary of Events and Information	Remarks and references to Appendices
		Ref HAZEBROUCK 5A 1/100000
7pm 19-5-15	at slow rate rate from 12 mn to 4am	36 B 1/20000
10pm	Order for burst of fire at 12.5am 20-5-15	trench map 1/10000.
	Ammunition expended 552 shrapnel.	Caw.
12mn-4am 20-5-15.	40TH Bty on "covered way" 12 rounds per hour.	
12.5am	40TH Bty fired burst of 12 rounds on "covered way".	
10am	30TH Bty ordered to fire 30 rounds lyddite on V2 with occasional rounds shrapnel on trenches near it.	
	40TH Bty ordered to fire 30 rounds on "covered way" with some shrapnel as well	
11am	30TH registered V2 and commenced firing	
12.45pm	40TH Bty ordered to stop firing at "covered way".	
	30TH Bty ordered to fire another 20 rounds at V2.	
6.30pm	30TH Bty ordered to fire another 40 rounds at V2 and trenches round about it. Fire to be slow up to 7pm, quickening up between 7 & 8 pm.	
8pm.	30TH stop firing and go on to night lines as for 19TH.	

Instructions regarding War Diaries and Intelligence Summaries are contained in F. S. Regs., Part II. and the Staff Manual respectively. Title pages will be prepared in manuscript.

WAR DIARY of 43rd Bde R.F.A.

or

~~INTELLIGENCE SUMMARY.~~

(*Erase heading not required.*)

Army Form C. 2118.

(55)

Hour, Date, Place	Summary of Events and Information	Remarks and references to Appendices
8 pm 20-5-15.	40th 57th Btys. on night lines as for 19th	Ref HAZEBROUCK 5a 1/100000 36a 1/20000 trench map 1/10000.
	Capt. T.H. BECKLEY from 43rd Bde A.C. to 13th Bde. R.F.A.	
	Ammunition expended 30 lyddite 153 shrapnel	EAW.
11.45am 21-5-15.	Germans reported to be massing E of V2 – 30th Bty report they can see no signs of this	
1.40pm	30th Bty ordered to turn on to trench V2-R7-R8 to SW corner of FE DU BOIS also to shell small trench 150x E of V2 connecting main trenches – Rate of fire 15 rounds per hour – 90 rounds lyddite allowed.	
6.40pm.	Orders for bombardment received – Bombardment preparatory to attack by SIRHIND Bde on FE DU BOIS Orders for bombardment at intervals from 5-8.30pm – Owing to limit placed on use of lyddite (90 rounds for the day. 25 remaining at 6.30pm) bombardment could not be properly carried out.	
8.30pm – 11pm	30th Bty firing at 15 rounds per hour on trenches near V2.	

Instructions regarding War Diaries and Intelligence Summaries are contained in F. S. Regs., Part II. and the Staff Manual respectively. Title pages will be prepared in manuscript.

WAR DIARY of 43rd BDE R.F.A.
or
~~INTELLIGENCE~~ SUMMARY.
(Erase heading not required.)

Army Form C. 2118.

(56)

Hour, Date, Place	Summary of Events and Information	Remarks and references to Appendices
7pm 21-5-15.	Orders issued to 40th Bty for night [illegible] as for previous night – only to fire in case of attack.	Ref. 36b 1/20000 3rd Ed Trench map 1/10000
9pm	Message from C.R.A that attack will take place 1am 22nd	
10pm	Order to 30th Bty not to fire on FE DU BOIS and trenches near or on points R7, R8, Q15, Q16, after 12 mn.	
12 mn	30th Bty stops firing.	
	Ammunition expended 69 lyddite 72 shrapnel.	EAO
22-5-15	SIRHIND Bde attack failed.	
6.20am	30th Bty ordered to turn on to V2 – R7 – R8 with shrapnel to fire at quick rate for ½ hour, then slow down	
8.55am	30th Bty ordered to fire 15 rounds at V2 & connecting trenches V2 to V4.	
12.15pm.	30th Bty. they have done much damage to trenches round V2	
2pm	30th Bty. register trench V2 to R8.	
2.25pm	57th Bty detailed as counter battery to work with aeroplane (lamp signalling) – ordered to register FE DES TULOTTES & gun	

Army Form C. 2118.

Instructions regarding War Diaries and Intelligence Summaries are contained in F. S. Regs., Part II. and the Staff Manual respectively. Title pages will be prepared in manuscript.

WAR DIARY of 43rd Bde RFA
~~INTELLIGENCE~~ SUMMARY.

(Erase heading not required.)

(57)

Hour, Date, Place	Summary of Events and Information	Remarks and references to Appendices
2.25pm 22—5—15.	Allowed 24 rounds lyddite.	Ref 36 $\frac{1}{20000}$ 3rd Ed Trench map $\frac{1}{10000}$
6.30pm.	Aeroplane attempted to observe for 57TH but weather too thick	
7pm	57TH register FE DES TULOTTES by direct observation.	
7.5pm.	Order received not to fire after 7pm except in case of attack.	
9pm–12 mn	German guns very active shelling roads.	
	Ammunition expended 107 lyddite 110 shrapnel.	EAW.
7am. 23—5—15.	Waggon lines 30TH Bty, 57TH Bty and Bde A.C. return to former billets.	
9.15am	30TH wag ordered to watch V2 and not to fire except in case of hostile movement.	
11am	57TH Bty ordered to register road junction Q 12 and road junction just SW of Q 14 by aeroplane.	
12 noon	Aeroplane up for 57TH Bty — Bty could not read signals — no result.	

Instructions regarding War Diaries and Intelligence Summaries are contained in F. S. Regs., Part II. and the Staff Manual respectively. Title pages will be prepared in manuscript.

WAR DIARY of 43RD BDE. R.F.A.
or
~~INTELLIGENCE SUMMARY~~.
(Erase heading not required.)

Army Form C. 2118

(58)

Hour, Date, Place	Summary of Events and Information	Remarks and references to Appendices
6pm 23 – 5 – 15	Operation order from CRA LAHORE Div. – Div taking up front from 140 to orchard (excl) (S 10 c 10 8) MEERUT Div on right.	Ref 36 $\frac{1}{20000}$ 3rd Ed Trench maps $\frac{1}{10000}$
	57TH Bty to be under direct control of CRA ~~MEERUT~~ LAHORE.	
	40TH Bty to rest in present position.	
	30TH Bty under CRA MEERUT.	
6.25pm	Night lines ordered for 57TH Bty 140 to ORCHARD trench.	
	Ammunition expended 25 lyddite 21 shrapnel	EAW.
10 am 24 – 5 – 15	Bde HQ to RIEZ BAILLEUL	
	Ammunition expended 6 lyddite 22 shrapnel.	EAW
25 – 5 – 15	No change – amm. expended 3 lyddite 67 shrapnel	EAW
26 – 5 – 15	Batteries did not fire	EAW.
27 – 5 – 15	ammunition expended 2 lyddite 23 shrapnel	EAW.
28 – 5 – 15	" " 3 " 13 "	EAW.
29 – 5 – 15	Batteries did not fire.	EAW.
30 – 5 – 15	30TH Bty changed position S 1 d 3.1 under orders of CRA MEERUT Div. Batteries did not fire	EAW.

(9 29 6) W2794 100,000 8/14 H W V Forms/C. 2118/11

1st Division

121/6111

43rd Bde R.F.A.

Vol VII June.

Nil

Instructions regarding War Diaries and Intelligence Summaries are contained in F. S. Regs., Part II. and the Staff Manual respectively. Title pages will be prepared in manuscript.

WAR DIARY *or* ~~INTELLIGENCE SUMMARY.~~ of 43rd BDE. R.F.A.

(Erase heading not required.)

Army Form C. 2118.

(59)

Hour, Date, Place		Summary of Events and Information	Remarks and references to Appendices
	31-5-15.	57th Bty changed position to M 32 b 7.5. Batteries did not fire	EAW. Ref BETHUNE 1/40000 2nd Ed.
	1-6-15	30th & 57th Btys registering. Ammunition expended 97 shrapnel 2 lyddite	EAW. Trench map 1/10000
	2-6-15	" " " " " 19 " 3 "	EAW.
	3-6-15	" " " " 118 " 6 "	EAW.
3pm.	4-6-15	Order received that brigade would be attached to 7th Div	~~EAW~~
		Batteries did not fire	EAW.
8.30pm	5-6-15	Batteries moved to positions as under:—	
		30th Bty F 11 c 8.7	
		40th Bty F 10 b 10.5	
		57th Bty F 11 c 5.8.	
		Bde placed under orders of CANADIAN CRA.	
		Ammunition expended 49 shrapnel 3 lyddite	EAW.
6am	6-6-15	Bde A.C. to X 20 b 3.5	
10am		Bde HQ to X 14 c 6.3	
		Waggon lines as follows 30th & 40th Btys F 1 b 9.5, 57th X 14 c 6.3	EAW
		118th Bde CANADIAN DIV placed under orders of 43rd Bde for form.	

(9 29 6) W 2794 100,000 8/14 H W V Forms/C. 2118/11

Instructions regarding War Diaries and Intelligence Summaries are contained in F. S. Regs., Part II. and the Staff Manual respectively. Title pages will be prepared in manuscript.

WAR DIARY of 43rd BDE R.F.A.
or
~~INTELLIGENCE SUMMARY~~.
(Erase heading not required.)

Army Form C. 2118.

(60)

Hour, Date, Place	Summary of Events and Information	Remarks and references to Appendices
6_6_15	"CANADIAN HOWITZER GROUP"	Ref BETHUNE 40000 2nd Ed.
	Batteries registering. Ammunition expended 129 shrapnel 20 lyddite	ECW Trench map 10000
7-6-15	Btys. registering. " " 140 " 12 "	ECW
8-6-15	Btys registered as follows	
	30th, 40th, 57th L10 + brickfields	
	30th I9 H10	
	40th I9 I12 I17 I18, I19, H10	
	Intended operations postponed. Amm. expended 138 shrapnel 12 lyd.	ECW
9-6-15	Fresh orders for registration issued.	
	Btys. registered 30th H20 I20 H6 I15 — 40th Trench I10, I20 —	* ammunition expenditure 12 noon to 12 noon —
	I14 - I9 — 57th Trench I8, I9, I12 – Points I9 I12	
	*Ammunition expended nil	ECW
10-6-15.	*Btys did not fire ammunition expended 38 lyddite – 112 shrapnel	ECW.
	Major C.L.C HAMILTON posted to 43rd Bde	
11-6-15.	Batteries did not fire.	
12-6-15	" " " " Major C.L.C HAMILTON to 49th Div	ECW.

(9 29 6) W2794 100,000 8/14 H W V Forms/C. 2118/11

Instructions regarding War Diaries and Intelligence Summaries are contained in F. S. Regs., Part II. and the Staff Manual respectively. Title pages will be prepared in manuscript.

WAR DIARY of 43rd BDE R.F.A.
or
~~INTELLIGENCE~~ SUMMARY.
(Erase heading not required.)

Army Form C. 2118.

(61)

Hour, Date, Place	Summary of Events and Information	Remarks and references to Appendices
4pm 13 – 6 – 15	40th Bty report germans bombing heavily in front of LE PLANTIN.	Ref BETHUNE 1/40000 2nd Ed. Trench map 1/10000
	2LT H PAGE rejoined 30TH Bty.	
	Ammunition expended – 2 lyddite 9 shrapnel.	Ewo.
12 noon–1pm 14 – 6 – 15. 5pm – 6pm 8pm – 9pm.	30TH & 57TH Btys firing on communication trenches. difficulty experienced owing to high wind	
	Ammunition expended 4 lyddite 277 shrapnel	Ewo.
2.30 am 15 – 6 – 15	message from CDA that brigade will not be required to fire before 12 noon.	
7am	Communication established with & liaison officers sent to 21st Inf Bde HQ at WINDY CORNER – and 1st CAN. INF. BDE HQ at PONT FIXE.	
12 noon to 4pm.	25 rounds shrapnel per gun – 30TH Bty on front trench H4–H8 searching back 400 yds. – 40TH Bty I21 – H19 – 57TH Bty communication trench N of J16 – I18 – J19.	
4 – 5pm	10 rounds lyddite per gun on communication trenches	

(9 29 6) W 2794 100,000 8/14 H W V Forms/C. 2118/11

Instructions regarding War Diaries and Intelligence Summaries are contained in F. S. Regs., Part II. and the Staff Manual respectively. Title pages will be prepared in manuscript.

WAR DIARY of 43rd BDE R.F.A.
or
~~INTELLIGENCE SUMMARY~~.
(Erase heading not required.)

(62)

Army Form C. 2118.

Hour, Date, Place	Summary of Events and Information	Remarks and references to Appendices
4-5pm 15-5-15.	30TH Bty on H5-H2 and H6 to front trench	Ref. BETHUNE 1/40000 & 1/20000
	40TH " " I17-I14-I7 and I8-I2	& trench maps 1/5000
	57TH " " I12-I9-I4	
4.30pm	Bde A.C. report no more shrapnel available.	
5.30pm-6pm.	bombardment prior to assault by 4TH Corps —	
	Batteries on new trench parallel to and 50 yds W of I12	
	- J14 - J13 also trench I9 - I8 - I10 - I14 - H5 firing 30	
	rounds lyddite per gun.	
6pm	Assault by 4TH Corps.	
6 - 6.5pm.	batteries lift to form barrage on trenches in rear	
6.5 - 6.20pm	batteries lift again to form barrage on trenches	
	further to rear at very slow rate.	
6.15pm	51st Div reported to be in german trenches at K6 also	
6.15pm.	seen advancing from L8 to L10.	
6.20 - 6.50pm	Batteries lift to third barrage	
6.20pm.	51st Div reported in L10.	

Instructions regarding War Diaries and Intelligence Summaries are contained in F. S. Regs., Part II. and the Staff Manual respectively. Title pages will be prepared in manuscript.

WAR DIARY of 43rd BDE R.F.A.
or
~~INTELLIGENCE SUMMARY.~~
(*Erase heading not required.*)

Army Form C. 2118.

(63)

Hour, Date, Place	Summary of Events and Information	Remarks and references to Appendices
7.10pm 15-6-15	51st Div reported advancing to Z 2 and K 7	Ref BETHUNE 1/40000 2nd Ed
7.12pm	51st Div " in Z 2	Trench map 1/5000
6.50pm	Batteries lift to final barrage	
8 pm	Attack reported held up at H 3 and I 2 — Infantry holding H 2 and 100x left.	
8.10pm	WELSH Reg. reported in J 13.	
8.45pm	57th Bty ordered to turn on to J18-J19 at slow rate till 9.15pm one round per gun every 2 mins	
11.25pm	30th Bty ordered to fire one round every 2 mins on enemy's 1st & 2nd lines trenches N of lines H8-H1 but no further North than 250x South of H2 - to stop at 12.25 am.	
	During day a gun of 57th Bty burst owing to lyddite bursting in bore.	ECLO
12.35am. 16-6-15.	All batteries ordered to stop firing.	
3am.	Order for attack by 7th & Canadian Divs. received	
	43rd Bde to bombard commn trenches firing 1 round lyddite	

(9 29 6) W2794 100,000 8/14 H W V Forms/C. 2118/11

Instructions regarding War Diaries and Intelligence Summaries are contained in F. S. Regs., Part II. and the Staff Manual respectively. Title pages will be prepared in manuscript.

WAR DIARY of 43rd BDE RFA. or ~~INTELLIGENCE~~ SUMMARY.

(*Erase heading not required.*)

Army Form C. 2118.

(64)

Hour, Date, Place	Summary of Events and Information	Remarks and references to Appendices
3 am 16-6-15	per battery per min from 3.30am to 5.30am.	Ref BETHUNE 1/40000 2nd Ed & Trench map 1/10000
4 am	Attack postponed. Batteries ordered to stop firing and be ready to open fire at a moment's notice.	
9.10 am	Report received from Bde A.C. that there is no shrapnel in Park, DA.C or Bde A.C.	
9.40 am	Our infantry reported back in original line – Germans very busy about I2 and H13.	
12.15 pm	51st Div reported at L10 and K7.	
1.45 pm	Report received that we still hold L10 & K7.	
2 pm.	Order for attack by IV Corps received to assault same points as on previous day, assault at 4.45pm bombardment to commence 4.5pm.	
4.5 pm	bombardment commences.	
	30th Bty on comm'n trench H5 – H6 – front trench	
	40th Bty on " " I17 – I14 – front trench.	
	57th " " I9 – I3 – I4.	

Instructions regarding War Diaries and Intelligence Summaries are contained in F. S. Regs., Part II. and the Staff Manual respectively. Title pages will be prepared in manuscript.

WAR DIARY of 43rd BDE R.F.A.
or
~~INTELLIGENCE~~ ~~SUMMARY~~.
(Erase heading not required.)

Army Form C. 2118.

(65)

Hour, Date, Place	Summary of Events and Information	Remarks and references to Appendices
4.15 - 4.23pm 16-6-15	batteries stop firing.	Ref BETHUNE 1/40000 2nd Ed + Trench map 1/10000
4.23pm - 4.45pm	Continuation of bombardment and then lift. ammn. allowed for bombardment 100 rounds lyddite per gun - 20 rounds to be kept for emergency till after 7.30 pm.	
4.45pm	30th lift to bend of trench E of H1 for 100x towards H8 and H4 to front trench 100x S.W. of H4.	
	40th Bty to I17, I15, I11 and house just S of I11	
	57th Bty to 3rd line trench I11 - J16 + W end of Brickfield.	
5pm	Infantry reported to have captured I4 + moving towards I2 - Later reported at I8 and working towards I9.	
5.15 pm	Information from C.D.A that attack had failed on H2 and H3	
5.30pm	118th Bde report infantry bombed out of I2 to I4 + coming back.	

Instructions regarding War Diaries and Intelligence Summaries are contained in F. S. Regs., Part II. and the Staff Manual respectively. Title pages will be prepared in manuscript.

WAR DIARY of 43rd BDE. R.F.A.
or
~~INTELLIGENCE~~ SUMMARY.
(*Erase heading not required.*)

Army Form C. 2118.

(66)

Hour, Date, Place	Summary of Events and Information	Remarks and references to Appendices
8.50pm 16-6-15	57th bty observation station in GIVENCHY demolished & bty stops firing as observation impossible.	Ref BETHUNE 1/40000 3rd Ed + Trench map 1/10000
6.46pm	Some of our infantry reported in I2 – Germans seen in I4.	
8.38pm	Order from C.R.A. to stop firing and to go on to night lines firing 15 rounds per hour per bty.	
11.50pm	Orders for registration on 17th issued.	
	Ammunition expended 995 lyddite 445 shrapnel	
	1 Corporal 30th Battery killed	EAW.
R. 17-6-15	Order received fixing proportion of ammunition at 70 lyddite to 30 shrapnel.	
2.7am	Order to all batteries to stop firing.	
8-9am	Batteries registering on RUE D'OUVERT, zones allotted 30th Bty. L13 – J12 — 40th K7 – J19, 57th J12 – cross roads 100x SE of J18.	
11.14am	Message from CRA. that no special operation intended	

(9 29 6) W 2794 100,000 8/14 H W V Forms/C. 2118/11

Instructions regarding War Diaries and Intelligence Summaries are contained in F. S. Regs., Part II. and the Staff Manual respectively. Title pages will be prepared in manuscript.

Army Form C. 2118.

WAR DIARY of 43rd BDE R.F.A.
or
~~INTELLIGENCE~~ ~~SUMMARY~~.
(*Erase heading not required.*)

(67)

Hour, Date, Place	Summary of Events and Information	Remarks and references to Appendices
11.19am 17-6-15	for to-day. — Order to keep Germans from working	Ref BETHUNE 1/40000 2nd Ed & Trench map 1/5000
4.15pm	btys. registered trenches with aeroplane.	
7.12 pm	30th Bty report house at K8 is occupied ordered to fire a few rounds at it.	
	Ammunition expended 916 lyddite 19 shrapnel.	EEW
2.5am 18-6-15.	Attack ordered for 3.5am postponed for 2 hours	
6.5am.	bombardment ordered postponed for 24 hours.	
6.20am	Our infantry reported bombed out of L10.	
8.10 am.	Germans reported working at K8.	
11.10am.	57th Bty registering with aeroplane J19 J12.	
1.45pm	CDA order no fire on L13 – L11.	
2pm	Order from CDA to register trench K7-22-K6	
2.40pm	Bde ordered to stop firing and placed in reserve	
	Ammunition expended 45 lyddite 18 shrapnel.	EEW
[illegible]am 19-6-15.	30th Bty ordered to register L13.	

(9 29 6) W 2794 100,000 8/14 H W V Forms/C. 2118/11

Instructions regarding War Diaries and Intelligence Summaries are contained in F. S. Regs., Part II. and the Staff Manual respectively. Title pages will be prepared in manuscript.

WAR DIARY of 43rd Bde R.F.A.
or
~~INTELLIGENCE~~ SUMMARY.
(*Erase heading not required.*)

Army Form C. 2118.

(59)

Hour, Date, Place	Summary of Events and Information	Remarks and references to Appendices
1pm 19-6-15	30TH Bty ordered to register L10	Ref BETHUNE 1/40000
	Ammunition expended 41 shrapnel 23 lyddite	BWW + Trench map 1/10000
20-6-15	No change Batteries did not fire	BWW + 36b 1/40000
21-6-15	" "	BWW
22-6-15	Ammunition expended 1 lyddite	BWW
9pm 23-6-15	43rd Bde (less 57TH Bty + 1 sec. Bde A.C.) marched via BETHUNE to GOSNAY to join 1st DIV.	
	~~9pm~~ 57TH Bty + 1 sec Bde A.C. marched via LE HAMEL - ZELOBES - LESTREM - LA GORGUE to G21 a 6.4 to join 8TH Div.	BWW
3pm 24TH-6-15	Bde marched to FERFAY to rest billets.	BWW
25-28-6-15	Bde resting at FERFAY	BWW
29-6-15.	30TH Bty marched via CAUCHY - MARLES LES MINES - PLACE A BRUAY - LABUISSIERE - ~~to~~ billets at HESDIGNEUL move completed by 3pm.	
4pm	40TH Bty marched via CAUCHY - MARLES LES MINES -	

(9 29 6) W 2794 100,000 8/14 H W V Forms/C. 2118/11

1st Division

121/6231

43rd Bde R. F. A.

Vol VIII

29-6 - 31 - 7 - 15

Instructions regarding War Diaries and Intelligence Summaries are contained in F. S. Regs., Part II. and the Staff Manual respectively. Title pages will be prepared in manuscript.

WAR DIARY of 43rd BDE R.F.A. or INTELLIGENCE SUMMARY.

(Erase heading not required.)

Army Form C. 2118.

(67)

Hour, Date, Place	Summary of Events and Information	Remarks and references to Appendices
4 pm 29-6-15.	PLACE A BRUAY - LABUISSIERE - DROUVIN - NOEUX LES MINES - to action in VERMELLES	Ref 1/40000 36b & 36c.
	Bde A.C. to E 30 b 4.8	
	40th Bty waggon line at E 30 c 3.0.	
30-6-15	Bde HQ to SAILLY LABOURSE	
	40th Bty placed under orders of Lt-Col HINTON commanding arty of Sec Y.	CAW.
1-7-15	No change ammunition expended Shrapnel 14 Lyddite nil	CAW
2-7-15	" " " nil	CAW
3-7-15.	" " " nil.	CAW
8 am 4-7-15.	Germans shelled VERMELLES 40th Bty replied on HALLUCH.	
11 am	40th shelled AUCHY & PUITS 13	
12.45 am - 1.30 pm	40th bty shelled AUCHY in reply to shelling of NOYELLES.	
	Ammunition expended 64 shrapnel 6 Lyddite 2 gunners wounded	CAW.

Instructions regarding War Diaries and Intelligence Summaries are contained in F. S. Regs., Part II. and the Staff Manual respectively. Title pages will be prepared in manuscript.

WAR DIARY of 43rd BDE R.F.A.
or
~~INTELLIGENCE SUMMARY~~.
(Erase heading not required.)

Army Form C. 2118.

(70)

Hour, Date, Place		Summary of Events and Information	Remarks and references to Appendices
		(Temp) 2LT NICHOLL to Bde A.C.	EWO
	5-7-15.	No change Ammunition expended 18 shrapnel 9 lyddite	Ref 1/40000 36B & 36C
	6-7-15	" " " " 12 " nil	EWO
	7-7-15	" " " " 16 17 "	
11.20am 4.30pm 6pm 6.45pm	8-7-15	40TH Bty firing in retaliation on PUITS 13 and houses and trenches SW of HAISNES.	
11 am	8-7-15.	40 bty fired on trenches between HALLUCH cross roads and BOIS CARRE in retaliation for the shelling of our trenches.	
5pm		40TH bty fired on trenches E of points 34 & 41 Ammunition expended 33 shrapnel 12 lyddite	EWO.
	9-7-15.	40TH Bty fired as follows:–	
6 40am		on PUITS 13	
9 20am		on trenches at HALLUCH cross roads.	
10 30am		on PUITS 13	
11 55am		on HALLUCH cross roads.	
		Ammunition expended 36 shrapnel 15 lyddite	EWO.

Instructions regarding War Diaries and Intelligence Summaries are contained in F. S. Regs., Part II. and the Staff Manual respectively. Title pages will be prepared in manuscript.

WAR DIARY of 43rd BDE R.F.A.
or
INTELLIGENCE SUMMARY.
(Erase heading not required.)

Army Form C. 2118.

(11)

Hour, Date, Place	Summary of Events and Information	Remarks and references to Appendices
10 – 7 – 15	40th Bty did not fire	RWO.
10.15am 11 – 7 – 15.	40th Bty fired on trenches at HALLUCH X roads	
	Ammunition expended 13 shrapnel 1 Lyddite	RWO
7.40am 12 – 7 – 15	40th Bty fired on trenches at HALLUCH x roads	
	Ammn expended 17 shrapnel	RWO.
12 0pm. ~~12 – 7 – 15~~	fired on commn trenches E of 41	
3pm	30th Bty marched to F16 central to bivouac	?
8.30am 13 – 7 15	40th Bty fired on AUCHY. Ammn exp. 21 sh. 6 Lyd	
9.40. + 11.10am	on commn trenches in Southern half of G113	
2.30pm	on AUCHY and trenches S of HALLUCH road	
4pm	on BOIS CARRE	
	30th Bty preparing position at A20C 3.1	RWO
10.40am 14 – 7 – 15.	40th Bty fired on trenches S of BOIS CARRE	
11.5am	on trenches at HALLUCH cross roads	
12.5am	on PUITS 13.	
6pm	1st Gds. Bde take over sec Y 40th Bty under	

(9 29 6) W 2794 100,000 8/14 H W V Forms/C. 2118/11

Instructions regarding War Diaries and Intelligence Summaries are contained in F. S. Regs., Part II. and the Staff Manual respectively. Title pages will be prepared in manuscript.

WAR DIARY of 43rd Bde R.F.A.
or
~~INTELLIGENCE SUMMARY.~~
(Erase heading not required.)

Army Form C. 2118.

(13)

Hour, Date, Place	Summary of Events and Information	Remarks and references to Appendices
6pm 14-7-15	Sec. Arty Commander LT-COL ELTON.	Ref 1/40000 36B + 36C
	3rd Inf Bde take over Sec. Z 30TH bty under	
	Sec Arty. commander Lt. Col. ~~Elton~~ WARDROP.	also AUCHY-LENS
	Sect LE RUTOIRE – LOOS road (excl.) to AUCHY-	1/10000 1st ed. 11/5/15.
	VERMELLES road (incl)	
	Sec Z AUCHY-VERMELLES road (excl) to	
	LA BASSEE – BETHUNE road (excl)	
9pm	30TH Bty to action.	
	Ammn expended 37 shrapnel 2 lyddite	ELW.
10.15am 15-7-15	40TH Bty on commn trenches G11B	
4.15pm	on BOIS CARRÉ	
7pm	on front trench at HALLUCH x roads	
	Ammn expended 33 shrapnel 11 lyddite	ELW.
16-7-15	Exchange – LT. A.F.S. NAPIER to 40TH Bty to	
	perform duties of captain	
	Ammunition expended 61 shrapnel	ELW

(9 29 6) W2794 100,000 8/14 H W V Forms/C. 2118/11

Army Form C. 2118.

Instructions regarding War Diaries and Intelligence Summaries are contained in F. S. Regs., Part II. and the Staff Manual respectively. Title pages will be prepared in manuscript.

WAR DIARY of 43rd Bde R.F.A.
or
~~INTELLIGENCE~~ SUMMARY.

(Erase heading not required.)

(73)

Hour, Date, Place		Summary of Events and Information	Remarks and references to Appendices
			Ref 1/40000 36c + 36a + AUCHY-LENS map 1/10000 1st ed. 11/5/15.
11.30am	17-7-15	40th Bty fired on FLIITS 13.	
		Amm. expended 96 shrapnel 16 lyddite.	Eaw
6pm	18-7-15	40th Bty fired on AUCHY	
6.15pm	19-7-15	40th Bty fired on comm^n trenches G11b Amm exp. 1 lyd.	Eaw.
9pm	20-7-15.	1 sec. D Bty 73rd Bde. relieved 1 sec 40th Bde. & 1 sec C Bty	
		73rd Bde relieved 1 sec 30th Bty for purposes of instruction	
		Ammunition expended 46 shrapnel 4 lyddite	Eaw.
4.15-5pm	21-7-15	40th Bty fired on AUCHY	
		Ammunition expended 29 lyddite 38 shrapnel	Eaw
	22-7-15	No change Amm expended 115 lyddite 158 shrapnel	Eaw.
	23-7-15	" " " 24 " 29 "	Eaw
	24-7-15	" " " 49 " 4 "	Eaw.
	25-7-15	" " " 13 " 11 "	Eaw
	26-7-15	" " " 8 " 7 "	Eaw.
	27-7-15	" " " 27 " 23 "	Eaw
	28-7-15	" Btys did not fire.	Eaw

(9 29 6) W2794 100,000 8/14 H W V Forms/C. 2118/11

Instructions regarding War Diaries and Intelligence Summaries are contained in F. S. Regs., Part II. and the Staff Manual respectively. Title pages will be prepared in manuscript.

WAR DIARY of 43rd BDE. R.F.A.

or

~~INTELLIGENCE~~ SUMMARY.

(Erase heading not required.)

Army Form C. 2118.

(74)

Hour, Date, Place	Summary of Events and Information	Remarks and references to Appendices
		Ref 36c + 36c 1/100000 No 9 AUCHY-LENS 1/10000 1st ed.
29-7-15.	No change Ammunition expended 155 lyddite 35 shrapnel	[illegible]. dt 11/5/15.
30-7-15	" " " " 25 " 91 "	[illegible]
31-7-15	" " " " 11 " 67 "	[illegible]

(9 29 6) W2794 100,000 8/14 H W V Forms/C. 2118/11

1st Division

121
6802

43rd Bde RFA

Vol IX

August 15

Instructions regarding War Diaries and Intelligence Summaries are contained in F. S. Regs., Part II. and the Staff Manual respectively. Title pages will be prepared in manuscript.

WAR DIARY of 43rd BDE RFA
or
~~INTELLIGENCE~~ SUMMARY.
(*Erase heading not required.*)

Army Form C. 2118.

(75)

Hour, Date, Place	Summary of Events and Information	Remarks and references to Appendices
1-8-15	No change. Ammunition expended 22 lyddite 34 shrapnel	EAW
2-8-15	" " " 53 " 43 "	EAW
3-8-15	LT. E.H.P. JACKSON to 30th Bty as acting captain	EAW
	ammunition expended 15 lyddite 2 shrapnel	
4-8-15	" " 8 " 9 " no change	EAW
5-8-15	Capt LA EDDIS from adjt. to ENGLAND. LT EA WOODS from orderly officer to adjt. CAPT J.T. PRICE from 30th Bty to adjt 25th Bde	
	Sections of 15th Bn Btys withdrawn replaced by sections of 30th & 40th Btys	EAW
	Ammunition expended 3 lyddite 72 shrapnel	
6-8-15	No change – Amm. expended 22 shrapnel	EAW.
7-8-15	2LT A. PROBART JONES from ~~amm exp~~ 1st DAC to orderly officer (amm exp. 36 L 68 S)	EAW
8-8-15	2Lt NICHOLLS from 43rd Bde A.C. to 30th Bty	
	Amm expended 26 lyddite 30 shrapnel	EAW.
9-8-15	No change. Amm exp. 37 lyddite 2 shrapnel	EAW

(9 29 6) W 2794 100,000 8/14 H W V Forms/C. 2118/11

Instructions regarding War Diaries and Intelligence Summaries are contained in F. S. Regs., Part II. and the Staff Manual respectively. Title pages will be prepared in manuscript.

WAR DIARY of 43rd Bde R.F.A.
or
INTELLIGENCE SUMMARY.
(Erase heading not required.)

Army Form C. 2118.

(96)

Hour, Date, Place		Summary of Events and Information	Remarks and references to Appendices
	10-8-15	No change. Amm expended 3 lyddite 4 shrapnel	EWO
	11-8-15	Lt V.B. HOHLAND from 1st DAC to 30th Bty. Ammn expended	
		69 lyddite 12 shrapnel	EWO
1.30pm 5.30pm	12-8-15	German artillery especially active – VERMELLES shelled at with	
6.30pm 7.5pm		77 mm + 5.9". 40th Bty retaliated on BENIFONTAINE	
		and AUCHY – Amm exp 7 lyd. 1 shrapnel	EWO
	13-8-15	No change Amm exp 71 lyddite 15 shrapnel	EWO
	14-8-15	" " " " 61 " 12 "	EWO
	15-8-15	" " " " 10 "	EWO
	16-8-15	" " " 11 " 7 "	EWO
	17-8-15	" " " 60 " 25 "	EWO
	18-8-15	40th Bty fired on German mineshafts in 2nd Div area	
		near "railway triangle". Amm exp 48 lyddite 27 shrapnel	EWO
	19-8-15	No change " " 59 " 2 "	EWO
	20-8-15	" " " 58 " 29 "	EWO
	21-8-15	" " " 72 " 15 "	EWO

Instructions regarding War Diaries and Intelligence Summaries are contained in F. S. Regs., Part II. and the Staff Manual respectively. Title pages will be prepared in manuscript.

WAR DIARY of 43rd Bde R.F.A.
or
INTELLIGENCE SUMMARY.
(*Erase heading not required.*)

Army Form C. 2118.

(97)

Hour, Date, Place		Summary of Events and Information	Remarks and references to Appendices
	22-8-15	No change Amm exp 21 lyddite 30 shrapnel	EWO
	23-8-15	Major W.H. WYNTER from 30th Bty to bde major 7th D.A. (temp)	
		2Lt NICHOLLS to 30th Bty Ammn exp 20 lyd 29 shrap	EWO
	24-8-15	No change Ammn exp. 34 lyd. 45 shrapnel	EWO
	25-8-15	" " " " 68 " 22 "	EWO.
	26-8-15	" " " " 93 " 14 "	EWO.
	27-8-15	" " " " 68 " 21 "	EWO.
	28-8-15	" " " 75 " 8 "	EWO.
	29-8-15	——— " 47	
8pm	&	Night 29/30 30th Bty withdraws one section to Waggon line & relieved by one section from 9th Div.	EWO.
7-30pm	30-8-15	40th Bty 1 sec withdrawn to waggon line relieved by section 7th Div. Ammn expended 26 lyd. 7 S.	
7-30pm	31-8-15	Remainder of 30th Bty withdrawn to new waggon line under 15th Div at VERQUIN.	

(9 29 6) W 2794 100,000 8/14 H W V Forms/C. 2118/11

Instructions regarding War Diaries and Intelligence Summaries are contained in F. S. Regs., Part II. and the Staff Manual respectively. Title pages will be prepared in manuscript.

WAR DIARY of 43rd BDE RFA
or
~~INTELLIGENCE~~ SUMMARY.
(Erase heading not required.)

Army Form C. 2118.

(78)

Hour, Date, Place	Summary of Events and Information	Remarks and references to Appendices
4pm 31-8-15	Bde HQ to NOEUX LES MINES L13C57.	
7pm	Bde Amm Col to E26d51	
	Amm expended 35 lyddite 38 shrapnel	EAW

WAR DIARY

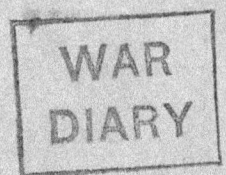

Headquarters,

43rd BRIGADE, R.F.A.

(1st Division)

S E P T E M B E R

1 9 1 5

Instructions regarding War Diaries and Intelligence Summaries are contained in F. S. Regs., Part II. and the Staff Manual respectively. Title pages will be prepared in manuscript.

WAR DIARY
or
~~INTELLIGENCE~~ SUMMARY.
(Erase heading not required.)

(79)

Hour, Date, Place	Summary of Events and Information	Remarks and references to Appendices
7 30 pm 1-9-15	40th Bty withdrew & came into action at L29b central to cover zone from BETHUNE-LENS road to double crassier of Fosse 11.	Ref 36c & 36 1/40000 and AUCHY-LENS 1/10000
	Ammn exp 3 lyddite 9 shrapnel.	E.W.
9 am 2-9-15	Bde HQ to LES BREBIS L35 a 3.5	
	Howitzer sub-group formed under 43rd Bde consisting of 40th Bty R.F.A., 24th Siege Bty R.G.A. & 21st London Bty. This group to be under 39th Bde group to be known as "MACNAGHTEN GROUP"	
	30th Bty under 15th Div Arty	E.W.
3-9-15	Batteries preparing positions. Telephonic communication established between 43rd Bde HQ and batteries of group and to MACNAGHTEN group. Battery line to observation stations laid	E.W.

(9 29 6) W2794 100,000 8/14 H W V Forms/C. 2118/11

Instructions regarding War Diaries and Intelligence Summaries are contained in F. S. Regs., Part II. and the Staff Manual respectively. Title pages will be prepared in manuscript.

WAR DIARY of 43rd Bde R.F.A.
or
INTELLIGENCE SUMMARY.
(Erase heading not required.)

Army Form C. 2118.

(80)

Hour, Date, Place	Summary of Events and Information	Remarks and references to Appendices
9 am 4–9–15	40th Btg commences registering for defensive line to cover front of 47th Div Northern Section from G 34 a 8 3 — M4A 1 3	
	Communication established by telephone between 40th Btg and Battn commander of W3 section	N.B ammunition expended is not given for 30th & 40th Btys at end of each day's record. When expenditure of other batteries is given it is stated which bty fired same
10 am	40th Btg completes registration for defensive line and commences defensive scheme.	
12 noon	Telephone comm established with Bde H.Q. at NOEUX LES MINES for communication with wagon lines and Bde A.C.	
9 pm	24th Siege Btg marched from NOEUX LES MINES to action at L 29 a 8 0. Amm exp 26 lydt 20 shrapnel	
6 AM 5–9–15.	24th Siege Btg in action. During day telephone communications completed. 2 lines laid to each battery position, one air one air and buried in exposed places. Testing station for 21st Btg	

WAR DIARY of 43rd (H) BDE RFA
or
INTELLIGENCE SUMMARY.
(Erase heading not required.)

Army Form C. 2118.

Instructions regarding War Diaries and Intelligence Summaries are contained in F. S. Regs., Part II. and the Staff Manual respectively. Title pages will be prepared in manuscript.

(8)

Hour, Date, Place	Summary of Events and Information	Remarks and references to Appendices
6-9-15	Line established at R5a 54 only to be used in case of fighting	
4.30pm-6pm	24th Siege Bty firing on group of houses M 35 c 2 5. Object to destroy houses and obtain [illegible] view of enclosure of houses at G 35 d 8.3. Shooting poor & object not attained.	
	40th Bty did not fire during day.	
	Ammon exp. 26 lyddite 20 shrapnel.	EAO
4 pm 6-9-15	24th Siege Bty registered M4a 8.9	
4.45pm-5.15pm	" " " " G 34 a 8.7	
9.40pm	21st London Bty to action	
10 pm	21st London Bty ordered not to fire till further orders.	
	40th Bty did not fire during day	
	Ammn expended 2 lyddite 6 shrapnel	EAO
9am 7-9-15	In retaliation for shelling of GRENAY 40th Bty [illegible]	

Instructions regarding War Diaries and Intelligence Summaries are contained in F. S. Regs., Part II. and the Staff Manual respectively. Title pages will be prepared in manuscript.

or

INTELLIGENCE SUMMARY.

(Erase heading not required.)

(82)

Hour, Date, Place	Summary of Events and Information	Remarks and references to Appendices
9am 7-9-15	retaliated on comm^n trench N of double crassier in M4a and registered keep on double crassier	
	24TH & 21ST Btys did not fire during day	
9.15pm	working party started work on new howitzer position for new battery at L24c2.8.	
	Capt J.T. PRICE from adjt 25th Bde to ~~adjt~~ Command 30TH Bty — Lt JACKSON from 30TH Bty to adjt 25th Bde. Amm^n exp 34 lyd. 37 shrap.	EAW
5pm 8-9-15	24TH Siege Bty registered G39c6.8.	
	40TH & 21ST btys did not fire.	
9.15pm	Working party of 21st London Bty started work on alternative position for 40TH Bty at M2 central to shoot on bearing 105° mag	
	2Lt DARDIER posted from 1st DAC to 43 Bde RA.	
	Amm^n exp. 11 lyddite 17 shrapnel.	EAW
9-9-15	Btys of group did not fire. Amm exp. 2 lyddite 58 shrapnel.	EAW.

(9 29 6) W2794 100,000 8/14 H W V Forms/C. 2118/11

Instructions regarding War Diaries and Intelligence Summaries are contained in F. S. Regs., Part II. and the Staff Manual respectively. Title pages will be prepared in manuscript.

or

~~INTELLIGENCE~~ SUMMARY.

(*Erase heading not required.*)

(83)

Hour, Date, Place	Summary of Events and Information	Remarks and references to Appendices
10-9-15	21st London Bty registered G 35c 2.5, M4a 6.4, G 34c 9 1 G 34 c 6.8, Fired 45 rounds of which 5 were blind. Delayed in shooting by 12 misfires due to faulty T-tubes.	
1pm	21st L. Bty took over defensive line from 40th Bty. Ammn expended Nil	EAW
11-9-15	24 Siege Bty registered 2nd line trench M4b 8.2 to M5d 2.6. 21st & 42nd did not fire. Ammn exp. 6 lyddite 7 shrapnel	EAW
4.25pm 12-9-15.	21st L. Bty in retaliation for German shooting registered G 35d 31. Preliminary orders received and issued for preliminary bombardment of 4 days and for day of assault. Orders issued to 40th Bty & C109 Bty. for supply of ammunition. To dump 108 rounds	

(9 29 6) W 2794 100,000 8/14 H W V Forms/C. 2118/11

Instructions regarding War Diaries and Intelligence Summaries are contained in F. S. Regs., Part II. and the Staff Manual respectively. Title pages will be prepared in manuscript.

or

~~INTELLIGENCE~~ SUMMARY.

(*Erase heading not required.*)

(84)

Hour, Date, Place	Summary of Events and Information	Remarks and references to Appendices
12 – 9 – 15	per gun at battery position and draw supply of 48 rounds per gun from Bde A.C + 44 per gun from D. A.C. to fill waggon lines up to 92 rounds per gun. At a date to be notified later a further 60 rounds per gun to be drawn (over establishment) to make allotment of ammunition as follows:–	
	At guns 108 rounds per gun.	
	" W.L. 108 " " "	
	" Bde A.C. 44 " " "	
	" D.A.C. Nil	
	Object, That batteries should only have to be supplied by night and not by day.	
9.30pm 12 – 9 – 15	C.109 bty 24th Div under orders of 43rd Bde group to action at M2 central.	
	Ammn expended 39 lyddite	EAW.

Instructions regarding War Diaries and Intelligence Summaries are contained in F. S. Regs., Part II. and the Staff Manual respectively. Title pages will be prepared in manuscript.

or

~~INTELLIGENCE~~ SUMMARY.

(*Erase heading not required.*)

[illegible] BDE RFA

(65)

Hour, Date, Place	Summary of Events and Information	Remarks and references to Appendices
3pm 13-9-15	C109 Bty registered trench junction M5a 2.6 with 4 guns and M4 a 8.8 with 2 guns.	
	Message received that extra allowance of 60 rounds per gun would not be replaced when expended. That expenditure of ammn during bombardment would be 80 rounds per gun for 4.5" hows and 90 for 5" and 6".	
4.55pm	40th Bty ordered to put 12 rounds lyddite into German trenches between G34 a 8.2 and G34 c 6.8 between 6pm and 7pm and to fire 2 rounds per hour at them during night. Object to prevent Germans interfering with working parties at Sap 18. (G34a 2.2)	
7.35pm	40th ordered to stop firing but to recommence at 2.15 am.	
	Ammn expended 56 lyddite.	E.W.

Instructions regarding War Diaries and Intelligence Summaries are contained in F. S. Regs., Part II. and the Staff Manual respectively. Title pages will be prepared in manuscript.

or

INTELLIGENCE SUMMARY.

(*Erase heading not required.*)

(86)

Hour, Date, Place	Summary of Events and Information	Remarks and references to Appendices
12 noon 14-9-15	21st London registered new trench G34d34 to G34d32 Orders received that advanced waggon lines are to be established in L19c consisting of one waggon per gun. Ammunition to be supplied from Bde. A.C's to this advanced echelon Difficulties experienced — C109 Bty on attachment to 1st Div brought no proportion of DAC with them and so became 20 rounds short (expended) and 44 per gun short (in DAC) ~~24th Div~~ Arrangements for communication ordered — Orderlies to be kept at various signal offices and messages to be sent through signals to ~~[illegible]~~ A.C's & W. Lines Ammn. exp. 66 lyddite 4 shrapnel.	[illegible]
9.15 am 15-9-15.	21st London Bty registered in retaliation trench G34b21 — G34c98	

(9 29 6) W2794 100,000 8/14 H W V Forms/C. 2118/11

Instructions regarding War Diaries and Intelligence Summaries are contained in F. S. Regs., Part II. and the Staff Manual respectively. Title pages will be prepared in manuscript.

or

~~INTELLIGENCE~~ SUMMARY.

(*Erase heading not required.*)

(87)

Hour, Date, Place	Summary of Events and Information	Remarks and references to Appendices
5.10pm 15-9-15	21st London registered G35a6.1 in retaliation	
5.35pm	" " M5a2.6 in retaliation	
	Ammn expended 65 lyddite	EAW.
3.40pm 16-9-15.	21st London Bty registered trench junction M4d8.8	
11 pm	Orders issued for redistribution of ammunition in echelons as follows:—	
	For 4.5" how. At guns 108 rds per gun.	
	Advanced WL 48 " " "	
	Gun limbers 12 " "	
	Bde A C 32 " "	
	1st line waggons empty	
	D.A.C empty.	
	For 5" how. At guns 92 50lb shell per gun	
	84 40lbs " " "	
	Gun limber 16 40 " " "	
	Advanced WL 12 40 " " " "	
	Other echelons empty.	
	Ammn expended 60 lyddite	EAW.

(9 29 6) W2794 100,000 8/14 H W V Forms/C. 2118/11

Instructions regarding War Diaries and Intelligence Summaries are contained in F. S. Regs., Part II. and the Staff Manual respectively. Title pages will be prepared in manuscript.

or

~~INTELLIGENCE~~ SUMMARY.

(Erase heading not required.)

(88)

Hour, Date, Place	Summary of Events and Information	Remarks and references to Appendices
10.5am 17-9-15	21st London retaliated on G 34 d 3.2.	
4.5pm	— — — on trench at G 35 d 6.1	
5.44pm	— — on G 34 d 5.7 (old mill) and on new trench in G 35 d	
11.40pm	— fired on new trench in G 35 d at request of infantry	
	Ammn expended nil.	EWW
9.24am 18-9-15	21st London Bty retaliated on G 34 c 9.1	
4.45pm	— — G 35 c 2.5.	
	Ammn expended 39 lyddite	EWW
5.22pm 19-9-15	21st London Bty retaliated on G 35 a 8.8 and G 34 d 5.8.	
6.30pm	— — — G 34 c 2.2	
	Arrangements for communication with W.L's & A.C's completed for 40th, C109, & 21st London Btys.	
	Ammn expended 24 lyddite	EWW.

(9 29 6) W 2794 100,000 8/14 H W V Forms/C. 2118/11

Instructions regarding War Diaries and Intelligence Summaries are contained in F. S. Regs., Part II. and the Staff Manual respectively. Title pages will be prepared in manuscript.

or

INTELLIGENCE SUMMARY.

(*Erase heading not required.*)

(89)

Hour, Date, Place	Summary of Events and Information	Remarks and references to Appendices
2.15pm – 3.15pm 20 — 9 — 15	24th Siege Bty fired 15 HE on new trench M5b8.2 – M5d2.3	Ref 36c & 36 1/40000 NW.
2.45pm – 4.15pm	21st London Bty fired on same target	and 36c NW Sheet 3 & part of 1
21 – 9 – 15	1st day of Bombardment. Action of batteries as follows	and 36c SW.1.
10am – 1pm	40th Bty on communication trenches M4a 4.4 and M4a 9.8 – M5a 2.6 and 2nd line trench M5a2.6 – M4d9.8 Observation difficult but results satisfactory used 138 HE.	
10.am – 1.30pm	21st London Bty on trench G35c 5.1 – G35a6.3 & on 2nd line trench from LENS – LABASSEE road to N end of LOOS cemetery Effect very good used 60 HE	
10am – 12 noon	C/109 Bty. trenches M5a2.6 – M5a6.8 effect good – used 76 HE & 4 shrap. M4a6.2 – M4d2.9 effect good used 80 HE	
9am – 10am	24th Siege Bty on Redoubt at M4d 3.9 good effect used 20 HE	
10am – 11am	redoubt at M4a 4.2 shooting erratic used 20 HE.	
11.30am – 2.30pm	front trench G34c10.1 – G34a7.1 some hits mostly over used 74 HE	
~~9.30am~~ 1.30pm – 5.30pm	21st London Bty G35c5.1 – G35a6.3 effect good used 80 rds HE	

(9 29 6) W2794 100,000 8/14 H W V Forms/C. 2118/11

Instructions regarding War Diaries and Intelligence Summaries are contained in F. S. Regs., Part II. and the Staff Manual respectively. Title pages will be prepared in manuscript.

or

INTELLIGENCE SUMMARY.

(Erase heading not required.)

(90)

Hour, Date, Place	Summary of Events and Information	Remarks and references to Appendices
1pm – 5.30pm 21-9-15	21st London Bty on houses at G34c10.8, G34b6.1, G34d5.8 G34b1.2. shooting erratic and not very effective 20 rounds	
3pm – 5.30pm	H.E. at each. Trench G34b1.2 – G34b5.5 Effect good used 70 HE	
3pm	24th Siege Bty 5 rounds at 2nd line trench in G34d	
3pm – 6pm	Trench M4a 8.9 – M4a 8.3 used 40 rounds HE.	
3.30pm – 6pm	C109 Bty on Enclosure in G34d – several houses hit used 80 HE	
	40th bty experienced large number of blinds during day nearly 25% using fuze 44 & chiefly those made by B.S.C	
	21st London Bty and 24th Seige Bty did not get through allowance of ammn at targets in time allowed during afternoon, were given extra time as shown above	[illegible]
	Ammn expe by 30th & 40th Btys. 629 lyddite.	
22-9-15.	2nd Day of Bombardment. Action of Batteries as follows:–	
7.55am – 8.6am	Demonstration as follows:–	

(9 29 6) W 2794 100,000 8/14 H W V Forms/C. 2118/11

Instructions regarding War Diaries and Intelligence Summaries are contained in F. S. Regs., Part II. and the Staff Manual respectively. Title pages will be prepared in manuscript.

~~INTELLIGENCE~~ SUMMARY.

(*Erase heading not required.*)

(91)

Hour, Date, Place	Summary of Events and Information	Remarks and references to Appendices
7.55am-8am 22-9-15	24th Siege Bty - Front Trench M4. a 1.3. - G 34 c 10.1	Ref 36b + 36c 1/40000
	21st Lndn Bty - Front Trench G34 c 10.1 - G 34 a 8.2.	and 36c NW Sheet 3 + part
	c/109 Bty - Support Trench M4 a 8.2 - G 34 c 10.1.	of 1 and 36c SW. 1.
	40th Bty - Support Trench in G 34 d.	
8 am - 8.3 am	24th Siege Bty 2nd Line G 35 a 6.3. - M4 d 8.8.	
	21st Lndn Bty G 35 c 5.1. - G 35 a 6.3.	
	c/109 Bty M5 a 2.6 - G 35 c 5.1	
	40th Bty M4 d 8.8. - M5 a 2.6.	
8.3am - 8.6am	Same as from 7.55 am - 8. am	
	Rate of fire:- 6" Howitzers Bty fire ~~[illegible]~~ 1 min	
	5" Howitzers Bty fire 30 secs	
	4.5" Howitzers Bty fire 20 secs	
8.30 am - 2 pm.	40th Bty - Trench M4 a 44 - M4 d 8.8. 2nd line trench M5 a. 2.6. - M.4 a 88	
	Good Effect used 263 H.E.	
3.15pm - 4.15p.m.	Communication Trench M5 a 1.4 to M5 c 2.5	

Instructions regarding War Diaries and Intelligence Summaries are contained in F. S. Regs., Part II. and the Staff Manual respectively. Title pages will be prepared in manuscript.

or
~~INTELLIGENCE~~ SUMMARY.
(Erase heading not required.)

(92)

Hour, Date, Place	Summary of Events and Information	Remarks and references to Appendices
22-9-15	and Railway M5c 8.2 – M6 c. 3.7 Good Effect used 28 H.E	Ref 36b + 36c 1/40000 and 36c N.W. Sheet 3 and part of 1 + 36c S.W. 1.
9.3 am	C/109 Bty on M5a 2.6 – 6.8 effect very good. Used 20 H.E.	
12.30 p.m.		
3 p.m.	G36c to M6a 3.9. used 60 H E	
	M5b 8.2 + M5b 8.2 – M6a 66 – M5d 8.10 good effect used 100 H.E.	
8.30 am – 10.30 am	21st Lndn Bty Trench G 35c 5.1. – G35a 6.3 Effect fairly good used 80 H.E.	
11. a.m – 2 p.m.	Enclosure at ~~[illegible]~~ G35 d 5.3. good effect used 100 H.E. destroyed	
3 p.m – 5 p.m.	G 35 c 7.5 – G35 d 6.1 good effect used 73 H.E.	
9 am – 10 am	24th Siege Bty Redoubt at M4 d 3.9. used 20 HE good effect.	
10 am – 11 am.	Redoubt M4a 4.2. used 17 H.E.	

Instructions regarding War Diaries and Intelligence Summaries are contained in F. S. Regs., Part II. and the Staff Manual respectively. Title pages will be prepared in manuscript.

~~WAR DIARY~~ or INTELLIGENCE ~~SUMMARY~~.

(Erase heading not required.)

(93)

Hour, Date, Place	Summary of Events and Information	Remarks and references to Appendices
		Ref. 36b + 36c 1/40000 and 36c NW Sheet 3 and part of 1 + 36c S.W. 1. V.B.J.
11.30 - 2 pm. 22-9-15	Trench G 34 d used 102 HE	
2.30 - 5 pm.	Trench M4 C 8.7 - M4 a 0.3. many hits. used 100 HE	
	ammunition Expended by 30th + 40th Btys 825 L	
23-9-15	Third Day of Bombardment.	
6 am. - 1 p.m	Two guns of the 24th Siege Bty placed at the disposal of the 15 D.A.	
9. am - 10.30 am	40th Bty M4 a 10.8 - M5 c 2.6. fair effect used 100 H.E.	
11.55 am.	Houses at G35 c 2.5. used 72 H.E.	
3.15 p.m.	New Trench in M5 d. used 59 H.E.	
9 am - 11.15 am.	C/109 Bty Trench M5 a 2.6. - M5 a 6.8. used 80 H.E.	
2 pm - 4 pm.	House at M6 C 1.9. used 20 H.E. 10 direct hits	
	House at M6 c 2.7. used 20 H.E.	
	W. end of DOUBLE CRASSIER used 72 HE.	
9 am - 11 am.	21st Lndn Bty Trench G 34 b 1.2. - 5.5. used 80 H.E.	
11 am - 12.45 p.m.	Trench G35 C 5.1. - G35 a 6.3. used 74 HE	
12.45 p.m - 1.55 p.m.	Houses at G 34 d 7.8. - G 34 d 2.1. - G35 c 8.7 used 42 H.E. 14 direct hits	

(9 29 6) W2794 100,000 8/14 H W V Forms/C. 2118/11

Instructions regarding War Diaries and Intelligence Summaries are contained in F. S. Regs., Part II. and the Staff Manual respectively. Title pages will be prepared in manuscript.

or

~~INTELLIGENCE~~ ~~SUMMARY~~.

(Erase heading not required.)

(94)

Hour, Date, Place	Summary of Events and Information	Remarks and references to Appendices
1.55 pm – 3 p.m. 23-9-15	Houses at G36c 2.4. used 42 H.E.	Ref 36b + 36c 1/40000
7.30 p.m – 1.35 am (24-9-15)	G34 b 1.2. – 5.5. G 35 c 5.0. – a 6.3. used 44 H.E.	and 36c N.W. sheet 3
8.30 am – 9.30 am	24th Siege Bty. ~~[illegible]~~ Redoubt on DOUBLE CRASSIER M4 a 42 used 20 H.E.	and part of 1 + 36c S.W.1.
10.15 am – 11 am	Redoubt on DOUBLE CRASSIER M4 d 3.9. used 20 H.E.	
11.30 am – 2.30 p.m.	Front Line Trench M4 a 1.3. – M4 a 6.4 used 50 H.E.	
3 p.m – 5 p.m.	Trench G34 c 10.1. – G34 a 8.2. used 100 H.E.	
	Ammunition Expended by 30th + 40th Btys 885 LYD 29 SHRAP	
	4th Day of Bombardment.	(initials)
6am – 12 noon 24-9-15	One Section of 24th Siege Bty placed at the disposal of the 15th D.A.	
8 am – 11 am.	40th Bty Communication Trench M4 a 4.4. – M4 a 88 observation difficult owing to bad light used 120 H.E.	

(9 29 6) W 2794 100,000 8/14 H W V Forms/C. 2118/11

Instructions regarding War Diaries and Intelligence Summaries are contained in F. S. Regs., Part II. and the Staff Manual respectively. Title pages will be prepared in manuscript.

or

INTELLIGENCE SUMMARY.

(Erase heading not required.)

95

Hour, Date, Place	Summary of Events and Information	Remarks and references to Appendices
24 – 9 – 15	Fired also on M4 a 9.8 – M5 a. 2.6 and 2nd	Ref 36b + 36c 1/40000
	line Trench M5 a 2.6. – M4 a 4.4.	and 36c N W Sheet 3
11 am – 1.30 p.m.	Communication Trench M4 b 10.4 – M5 c 5.2.	and part of 1 + 36c S.W. 1.
	used 80 H.E.	
1.40 p.m – 2.6 p.m. } 2.20 p.m – 3. p.m. }	New Trench M5 b 8.0. – M5 d 4.5. used 48 H.E.	
9 am – 12 noon	C/109 Bty Trench M5 a. 2.6. – M5 a 6.8 ~~used~~ used 60 HE	
11 am – 11.30 am	M5 b 8.8 used 20 HE	
1.55 p.m – 2.6 p.m.	Trenches in M10a used 80 HE	
3 – 3.48 p.m.	M4 b 8.2. used 25 HE	
4 pm – 5 p.m.	Trenches at foot of DOUBLE CRASSIER	
	21st Lndn Bty used 40 HE	
8 am – 9.45 am	Houses in G34 b and G34 d used 60 HE	
10 am – 1 p.m	Houses G85 c and G85 d used 100 HE	
2 pm – 3 p.m	Trench G34 b 2.1 – G34 b 5.5.	
3 p.m – 3.30 p.m.	Railway cutting M6 b 3.8 – M6 d 9.9. used 15 HE	

Instructions regarding War Diaries and Intelligence Summaries are contained in F. S. Regs., Part II. and the Staff Manual respectively. Title pages will be prepared in manuscript.

~~WAR DIARY~~ or INTELLIGENCE SUMMARY.

(Erase heading not required.)

(96)

Hour, Date, Place	Summary of Events and Information	Remarks and references to Appendices
1·55 - 2·6 p.m. 24 - 9 - 15	Demonstration	Ref 36b + 36c 1/40000 and 36c NW Sheet 3 and part of 1 + 36c S.W. 1.
1·55 p.m - 2 p.m	M4 c 5.2. - M4 c 3·9. used 11. HE	
2 p.m - 2·3 p.m.	M4 d 7.4 - M10 b 5.8. used 6 HE	
2·3 pm - 2·6 pm.	M4 c 5.2 - M4 c 3·9. used 5 HE	
9·20 am - 10 am	24th Siege BTY Redoubt M4 a 44 used 10 HE	
10·20 - 11 am	Redoubt M4 d 2·9 used 10 HE	
11 pm - 12·20 pm.	Trench G34 c 8.5. - G34 c 82 used 47 HE	
12·20 pm - 1 pm	Trench M4 a 7·9 - G34 c 8·5 used 28 HE	
1 pm - 1·50 pm	G34 c 77 - G34 c 7.10 used 33 HE	
1·50 pm - 3 pm	G34 c 7-10 - G34 a 8.2. used 44 HE	
3 pm - 5 pm	M4 a 1.3. - M4 a 4.4. - M4 c 7·9 used 90 HE	
3 p.m.	40th Battery Wagon Line moved to G35 a 3·8	
	Ammunition expended by 30th & 40th Batteries 960 LYD 25 SHR	V. B. H.
25 - 9 - 15	Day of Assault	
5·50 am - 6·30 am	24th Siege Bty on 2nd line Trench from G35 a 0·3 - M4 d 88	

(9 29 6) W2794 100,000 8/14 H W V Forms/C. 2118/11

Instructions regarding War Diaries and Intelligence Summaries are contained in F. S. Regs., Part II. and the Staff Manual respectively. Title pages will be prepared in manuscript.

WAR DIARY of 40th Bde R.F.A.
or
~~INTELLIGENCE~~ SUMMARY.
(Erase heading not required.)

(97)

Hour, Date, Place	Summary of Events and Information	Remarks and references to Appendices
5.50am - 6.30am 25-9-15	21st London Bty - Communication Trench from G 35 c 7.5. and G 35 c 9.7 to G 35 d 6.1. and 2nd line Trench from G 35 a 6.3 (including cemetery) to G 35 c 5.1 (road inclusive)	Ref 36b + 36c 1/40000 and 36c NW sheet 3 and part of 1 + 36c S.W.1.
	40th Bty - Barrage from point M 5 c 5.1 to M 6 c 3.7.	
	C/109 Bty - 2nd line Trench from M 4 d 88 to G 35 c 5.1 (road exclusive), and communication Trench from M 4 b 10.4 to M 5 c 1.5	
6.30am.	INFANTRY ASSAULT.	
6.30am - 6.40am	24th Siege Bty - East of LOOS CRASSIER from G 36 a 5.2 - G 36 c 8.6	
	21st London Bty - Communication Trench from G 36 c 7.5 and G 35 c. 9.7 to G 35 c 6.3. (including cemetery) ~~and~~ to G 35 c 5.1 (road inclusive)	
	40th Bty - Barrage from pt M 5 c 5.1 to pt M 5 c 3.7.	
	C/109 Bty - 2nd Line Trench from M 4 d 8.6 - G 35 c. 5.1	

Instructions regarding War Diaries and Intelligence Summaries are contained in F. S. Regs., Part II. and the Staff Manual respectively. Title pages will be prepared in manuscript.

or
~~INTELLIGENCE SUMMARY.~~
(Erase heading not required.)

(98)

Hour, Date, Place	Summary of Events and Information	Remarks and references to Appendices
25-9-15	(road exclusive) and communication Trench from M4 b 10.4 to M5 c 1.5.	Ref 36b + 36c 1/40000 and 36c N.W. Sheet 3 and part of 1 + 36c S.W. 1.
6.40 am - 7.5 am	24th Siege Bty on East of LOOS CRASSIER from G36 c 5.2. - G36 c 8.6.	
	21st Lndn Bty 1 section House at G35 d 7.8 and G35 d 10.9 and 1 Section Houses on enclosure in G35 d.	
	40th Bty Barrage from pt M5 c 5.1 to point M6 c 3.7	
	C/109 Bty System of Trenches between enclosures in G35 d and wood in M5 b + M6a.	
	Wood in M6a	
	Sunken road from G36 c 3.3 to M6 a 6.8.	
7.5 am - 7.20 am	24th Siege Bty Barrage from pt M6 c 3.7 to M6 d 9.8.	
	21st London Bty New Trench running S.W. from M5 b 8.0.	
	40th Bty Barrage from M5 c 5.1 to M6 c 3.7.	
	C/109 Bty. Wood in M5 b and M6a and Trenches	

Instructions regarding War Diaries and Intelligence Summaries are contained in F. S. Regs., Part II. and the Staff Manual respectively. Title pages will be prepared in manuscript.

WAR DIARY
or
INTELLIGENCE SUMMARY.
(*Erase heading not required.*)

(99)

Hour, Date, Place	Summary of Events and Information	Remarks and references to Appendices
25 - 9 - 15	therein	Ref 36b + 36c 1/40000 and ~~part~~ 36c N W Sheet 3 and part of 1 + 36c S.W.1.
7.20. am onwards	24th Siege Bty Barrage from M 6c 3.7 to M 6 d. 9.8	
	21st London Bty Trenches in Southern half of M 6c.	
	40th Bty Barrage from pt M6c 3.7 to M 5d 5.3.	
	C/109 Bty Barrage from pt M 5.b 5.3 to M 6c 3.7.	
7.20 am	Reported that 47th Division had taken front line trenches opposite W.3 Section.	
7.55 am.	21st London Report that 47th Div have taken LOOS cemetery	
	24th Siege Bty report that the infantry have taken German 2nd Line in M 5a.	
11.25 am.	24th Siege Bty placed under the orders of the 15th D.A.	
12.30 p.m.	C/109 Bty warned to be ready to join their Division at short notice.	
1.5. p.m.	24th Siege Bty placed under the orders of the 43rd Bde R.F.A.	
2.5 p.m.	C/109 Bty warned to turn fire on to DYNAMITIÈRE	

(8.29 6) W 4141—463 100,000 9/14 H W V Forms/C. 2118/10

Instructions regarding War Diaries and Intelligence Summaries are contained in F. S. Regs., Part II. and the Staff Manual respectively. Title pages will be prepared in manuscript.

WAR DIARY
or
INTELLIGENCE SUMMARY.
(Erase heading not required.)

(100)

Hour, Date, Place	Summary of Events and Information	Remarks and references to Appendices
25 - 9 - 15	in N 1 b, 2 mins intense followed by steady fire.	Ref 36b + 36c 1/40000 and 36c N.W. Sheet 3 and part of 1 + 36c S.W. 1
2.45 p.m.	C/109 Bty ordered to turn on to DYNAMITIÈRE, also to fire about square N 1 a to meet German counter attack.	
3 p.m.	43rd Bde H.Q take over MACNAGHTEN group, consisting of 25th Bde, 1 section of 15th London Bty, 16th London Bty, 40th Bty, 21st London Bty, C 109 Bty, 24th Siege Bty.	
5.50 p.m.	Night Lines ordered as follows:—	
	15th London Bty in Fosse 7 — on railway from M 11 a 4.9. — M 5 c 10.3.	
8.35 p.m.	25th Bde:— 113 Bty M 6 d 0.7 to M 6 c 0.5.	
	114 Bty N 1 c 0.9 to M 6 d 0.7.	
	115 Bty DYNAMITIÈRE to N 1 c 0.9.	
	40th Bty + C/109 Bty M 6 c 1.5. to PUITS 11.	
	Occasional Rounds to be fired during the night	
11.15 am	30th Bty advanced + took up a position between	

Instructions regarding War Diaries and Intelligence Summaries are contained in F. S. Regs., Part II. and the Staff Manual respectively. Title pages will be prepared in manuscript.

WAR DIARY or INTELLIGENCE SUMMARY.

(Erase heading not required.)

(101)

Hour, Date, Place	Summary of Events and Information	Remarks and references to Appendices
25-9-15	BOIS CARÉE and LA HAIE at G17 b 2.7½ and laid out lines on HULLUCH. Ammunition expended by 30th + 40th Btys LYD 703 SHRAP 16	Ref 36b + 36c 1/40000 and 36c NW Sheet 3 and part of 1 and 36c S.W. 1. C.B.H.
6.a.m 26-9-15	Orders issued for fire in support of an attack by the 15th Division on Hill 70 Bombardment to commence at 8 a.m. Group to Barrage from 8.30 am. as follows:- 114 Bty DYNAMITIÈRE and trenches in N1b70 - N1d49 115 Bty Barrage N1c49 - M6d07 113 Bty M6d07 - M5d 0.2. 15prs. M5c 10.2 - M5c 4.0. 40th Bty in observation on PUITS 11 and the East end of the DOUBLE CRASSIER.	
7.34 am	22nd London Bty at G32 d 6.6. placed under MACNAGHTEN Group	
7.40 am	Order to start Barrage at once, attack to commence at 8.15 am.	
7.45 am.	24th Siege ordered to fire at once on Machine Gun emplacement at M5c 5.0.	

Instructions regarding War Diaries and Intelligence Summaries are contained in F. S. Regs., Part II. and the Staff Manual respectively. Title pages will be prepared in manuscript.

WAR DIARY or INTELLIGENCE SUMMARY.

(Erase heading not required.)

(102)

Hour, Date, Place	Summary of Events and Information	Remarks and references to Appendices
9.25 am 26-9-15.	15th Division on Hill 70 reported enfiladed from PUITS 11. 22nd London Bty ordered to open fire on it at 2 rounds per minute.	Ref 36b + 36c 1/40000 and 36c NW sheet 3 and part of 1 + 36c S.W. 1.
10.40 am.	20th London Regiment report 11th Corps seen retiring from North of LOOS for no apparent reason	
11.5 am.	114th Bty confirm this report.	
11.30 am.	22nd London report infantry held up at about H31d 2.6 by machine gun at H31d22. They are ordered to engage the machine gun but not to reduce the rate of fire on the Barrage	
12.45 p.m.	22nd London Bty report team bolted from Machine Gun	
12.30 p.m.	114th Bty ordered to give 10 minutes intense fire on the reverse slopes of Hill 70	
1.22 p.m.	22nd London Bty firing on the Copse in M6a.	
2 p.m.	113th Bty report infantry held up by a Trench along the East side of the LENS – LA BASSÉE road from H25d 2.3 to H31d 3.9.	
2.10 p.m	22nd London Bty ordered to slow down the Barrage	

(9 29 6) W4141—463 100,000 9/14 H W V Forms/C. 2118/10

Instructions regarding War Diaries and Intelligence Summaries are contained in F. S. Regs., Part II. and the Staff Manual respectively. Title pages will be prepared in manuscript.

WAR DIARY
or
~~INTELLIGENCE SUMMARY.~~
(Erase heading not required.)

(103)

Hour, Date, Place	Summary of Events and Information	Remarks and references to Appendices
26-9-15.	to one round per minute and turn one section on to the Northern side of the Redoubt on Hill 70.	Ref 36b + 36c 1/40000 and 36c N.W. Sheet 3 and part of 1 + 36c S.W. 1.
2.50 p.m.	15th London Bty ordered to turn on to the redoubt H 31 central to H 31 b 3.1 at one round per minute per gun to prevent the Germans from improving the redoubt	
2.25 pm.	15th London Bty report 4 guns in action in North MAROC.	
3.40 pm.	22nd London Bty stop firing owing to shortage of T-tubes	
6.50 pm.	Night Lines ordered as follows:— Occasional rounds to be fired during the night 40th Bty M 6 c 0.5 – M 5 d 3.3. 24th Siege PUITS 12, level crossing, M 6 c 3.7. PUITS 11 25th Bde G 36 d 5.4 – M 6 c 0.6. The remaining Batteries to rest—	
	LT. W. M. NICHOLLS (30th) Killed. 2 Sergts 2 Cpls, 2 Bdrs 3 gunners + 3 drivers of the 30th wounded	
	2/Lt ~~[illegible]~~ L. H. DARDIER posted from 43rd Bde A.C. to 30th Bty	
	Ammunition Expended by 30th + 40th 655 LYD 15 SHRAP	V.B.H.

(9 29 6) W 4141—463 100,000 9/14 H W V Forms/C. 2118/10

Instructions regarding War Diaries and Intelligence Summaries are contained in F. S. Regs., Part II. and the Staff Manual respectively. Title pages will be prepared in manuscript.

WAR DIARY or INTELLIGENCE SUMMARY.

(Erase heading not required.)

(104)

Hour, Date, Place	Summary of Events and Information	Remarks and references to Appendices
3.10. am. 27-9-15	Captain Fairbank 113th Bty is ordered to take over temporary command of the 117th Bty.	Ref 36b + 36c 1/40000 and 36c NW sheet 3 and part of 1 + 36c S.W. 1.
8 - 10.30 am	40th Bty fire on copse in M 6 a.	
9.20 am	141 Infantry Bde report that the 40th Bty fire is very good and effective	
10 am - 10.30 am	22nd London Bty Register the copse in M6a	
10.30 am - 11 am.	Bty fire 15" on same copse	
11 am.	One salvo as signal to Infantry that firing has ceased 67 rds used H.E.	
11.20 am	114th Bty between H31d 5.5 - H31d 3.9. used 30 H.E.	
1 P.M. - 3.45 P.M.	22nd London Bty Bombard copse in M6a 1 round 1 minute.	
3.45 p.m. - 5 p.m.	Barrage ordered as follows:— 40th Bty on Copse in M6a 24th Siege PUITS 12, level crossing M6c 3.7. PUITS 11 25th Bde G 36 d 5.4 - M6c 0.6 (50% H.E.) 22nd London DYNAMITIÈRE to N2 a 6.6. paying special attention to where this line crosses the LENS-LA BASSÉE Rd 21st London Bty M6 c 0.6. — M5d 3.3.	

Instructions regarding War Diaries and Intelligence Summaries are contained in F. S. Regs., Part II. and the Staff Manual respectively. Title pages will be prepared in manuscript.

WAR DIARY or ~~INTELLIGENCE~~ SUMMARY.

(Erase heading not required.)

(105)

Hour, Date, Place		Summary of Events and Information	Remarks and references to Appendices
8. p.m.	27-9-15.	Night lines — Barrage to begin at 8 P.M the same as last night, at the following rate 40th Bty 5 rds per ~~minute~~ hour 24th Siege 4 rds per ~~minute~~ hour 25th Bde 10 rds per hour The remaining Batteries to rest Ammunition Expended by the 30th + 40th Btys 1030 LYD 120 SHRAP	Ref 36b + 36c 1/40000 and 36c NW Sheet 3 and part of 1 + 36c S.W.1 } V.B.H
10.10 am.	28-9-15	40th Bty Destroy houses at M6 c 1.9. supposed to harbour machine guns.	
10.15 am.		16th London Bty ordered to register so as to be prepared to establish a Barrage from M5 C 54 to M6 c 3.6.	
10.30 am.		One Section of the 40th Bty ordered to move up to their new Position in M2 central.	
11 am.		22nd London Bty R.F.A. fired 3 rounds gun fire on LENS – LA BASSÉE Road on reported enemy cavalry	
3.40 p.m.		1 section of the 40th Bty in action + registered at M2 central	

(9 29 6) W4141—463 100,000 9/14 H W V Forms/C. 2118/10

Instructions regarding War Diaries and Intelligence Summaries are contained in F. S. Regs., Part II. and the Staff Manual respectively. Title pages will be prepared in manuscript.

WAR DIARY of 43rd Bde R.F.A.
or
~~INTELLIGENCE SUMMARY.~~
(Erase heading not required.)

(106)

Hour, Date, Place	Summary of Events and Information	Remarks and references to Appendices
7.15.p.m 28-9-15	2nd Section of the 40th Bty ordered to be in their New Position by 7 a.m. on the 29th	Ref 36B + 36C 1/40000 and 36C N.W. sheet 3 and part of 1 + 36C S.W. 1.
8 p.m	Night Lines ordered the same as last night. Rate of Fire:- 18 pdrs 20 H.E. per Battery per Hour 15 pdrs 15 Shrap per Battery per Hour Howitzers. Occasional rounds during the night economising ammunition. ammunition expended by 30th + 40th Btys 181 LYD 31 SHRAP	U.B.H.
9.30 am 29-9-15	40th Bty has a second section at M2 central ready to shoot.	
9.35 am.	All Batteries ordered on to their night lines to watch for opportunities to fire.	
8 p.m.	Night Lines the same as last night.	
10.10 p.m.	The 47th Division warned to be prepared to hand over the Division Area to the French. ammunition fired by 30th + 40th Btys 24 LYD 10 SHRAP	U.B.H.
10.18 am. 30-9-15	40th Bty fire on railway between M6B 5.5. – M6D 8.8 and M6c 3.7, on reported enemy troops.	
	25th Bde 40th Bty 22nd London Bty + 24th Siege Bty	

Instructions regarding War Diaries and Intelligence Summaries are contained in F. S. Regs., Part II. and the Staff Manual respectively. Title pages will be prepared in manuscript.

WAR DIARY of 45th Bde R.F.A.
or
~~INTELLIGENCE~~ SUMMARY.
(Erase heading not required.)

(107)

Hour, Date, Place	Summary of Events and Information	Remarks and references to Appendices
30-9-15	ordered to make arrangements to cover a zone from S.W. end of HULLUCH to the DYNAMITIÈRE in N16, arrangements to be completed by 6 am tomorrow, preparatory to an attack on HULLUCH by the 11th Corps.	Ref 36b + 36c $\frac{1}{40000}$ and 36c NW sheet 3 and part of 1 + 36c S.W. 1.
8 p.m	Night Lines ordered the same as last night. Firing only to be carried out in case of urgent necessity.	
	30th Bty had one telephonist wounded	
	Ammunition Expended by 30th + 40th Btys 11 LYD 6 SHRAP	U.B.H.

(9 29 6) W4141—463 100,000 9/14 H W V Forms/C. 2118/10

1st Division

43rd Bde R.F.A.

30. & 40 How's

Oct & Nov.

Vol XI

121
7717

Instructions regarding War Diaries and Intelligence Summaries are contained in F. S. Regs., Part II. and the Staff Manual respectively. Title pages will be prepared in manuscript.

WAR DIARY of 43rd Bde R.F.A.
or
~~INTELLIGENCE~~ SUMMARY.
(Erase heading not required.)

Army Form C. 2118.

(110)

Hour, Date, Place	Summary of Events and Information	Remarks and references to Appendices
12.50 am 1-10-15.	Enemy reported active South of copse M6a, all batteries ordered to put a few rounds on night lines, the activity thereupon ceased	36b + 36c ~~and~~ 1/40000 and 36c NW 3 & part of 1 and 36c S.W. 1.
10.30 am	The enemy start shelling the copse in M6a, retaliation promptly carried out by the 25th Bde on the railway trenches opposite	
11.40 AM – 12.30 AM	25th Bde & 40th Battery fire into Railway trenches in response to urgent call from infantry in copse at M6a who report that they are being heavily shelled	
1.15 PM	The 25th Bde receive orders to withdraw one gun per Battery in order to allow the French to register, the guns withdrawn to keep in the vicinity of MAZINGARBE	
1.15 PM.	Test concentration on attack on Railway N1c18 as follows 40th Battery 1 rnd on Puits 12. 22nd London. 1 rd on DYNAMITIÈRE. 113 Battery M6c37 – M6d37. 114. " M6d37 — N1c08. 115 " N1c08 — DYNAMITIÈRE	

Instructions regarding War Diaries and Intelligence Summaries are contained in F. S. Regs., Part II. and the Staff Manual respectively. Title pages will be prepared in manuscript.

WAR DIARY of 43rd Bde RFA
or
~~INTELLIGENCE~~ SUMMARY.
(*Erase heading not required.*)

(111)

Army Form C. 2118.

Hour, Date, Place	Summary of Events and Information	Remarks and references to Appendices
1—10—15	24th How 22nd London + 40th Bat ordered to register following	36c + 36e 1/40000.
5.50 PM	points	and 36c NW3 + part of 1/10,000 and 36c SW1.
	Hulluch, trenches Puits 13 — H 14 d 4.2. Redoubt H 20 d 2.0	
	East end of Bois Hugo	
	Night lines ordered as follows.	
	25th Bde RFA 1 Bty M6C37 — M6d 3.7	
	2 Btys H1C08 — H1b 0.1	
	To fire only at request of French infantry	
	40th Battery M6 c central	54 Hyd
7 PM	The section of the 16th London ceases to be in MACNAGHTEN GROUP and is withdrawn to their wagon line at Les Brebis L35a, this order also applies to the section of the 15th London Bty in position at Fosse 7	14 Sh.
		O.N.

Instructions regarding War Diaries and Intelligence Summaries are contained in F. S. Regs., Part II. and the Staff Manual respectively. Title pages will be prepared in manuscript.

WAR DIARY of 43rd Bde R.F.A.
or
~~INTELLIGENCE~~ SUMMARY.
(*Erase heading not required.*)

(112)

Army Form C. 2118.

Hour, Date, Place	Summary of Events and Information	Remarks and references to Appendices
2.10.15	Batteries ordered to register on the following points as being the most probable ones for them to be told to fire on in the forthcoming operations.	36b + 36c 1/40,000 and 36c NW3 and part of 1 and 36c SW1 1/10,000.
	24th Siege Bty Keep in H 20d	
	23rd Siege Bty 1 section on Puits 14 Bis	
	1 section on Flames H 31 b.39.	
	40th Battery Eastern half of Bois Hugo. trenches from H26c.3.9 to H26c.2.9.	
	21st Battery Western half of Bois Hugo. from H25d 0.7 — H26c2.9	
	22nd Battery Wood enclosed by area H25d 2.1 — H31 B2.7 — H26c4.3 — H26c.5.2.	
10.45 AM	24th Siege Battery registered Bois Hugo.	
11.30 AM	Trenches H14c 10.2 and trench running towards Puits 13 Bis.	
3.30 PM	Puits 13 Bis.	

(9 29 6) W4141—463 100,000 9/14 H W V Forms/C. 2118/10

Instructions regarding War Diaries and Intelligence Summaries are contained in F. S. Regs., Part II. and the Staff Manual respectively. Title pages will be prepared in manuscript.

WAR DIARY of 43rd Bde RFA
or
~~INTELLIGENCE~~ SUMMARY.
(*Erase heading not required.*)

(113)

Army Form C. 2118.

Hour, Date, Place	Summary of Events and Information	Remarks and references to Appendices
2.10.15	25th Bde orders to withdraw their Bde as soon as it is dark and bivouac in H16b.	36b + c 1/40,000. and 36c N.W.3 and part of 1 and 36c S.W.1. 1/10,000.
	Ammunition expended by 30 & 40th Btes. 17 Lyd and 3 Sh.	GPJ.
3.10.15	Targets for bombardment 3rd 4th & 5th commencing 12 noon 3rd. Programme as follows.	
	23rd Siege Railway H25c.5.5. to H26c7.4 and trench running South of Puits 14 Bis.	
	24th Siege System of trenches North of Wood 4 & 5.	
	21st London Search east half of Wood 6.	
	22 London Search West half of Wood 6.	
	40th Battery Search inside Wood 4 & 5 and buildings in Puits 14 Bis.	
1 PM.	The Macnaghten Group will in future be called the Sharp Group.	
4.15 PM.	Orders from 4th Corps Artillery says that 24th Siege Battery	

Instructions regarding War Diaries and Intelligence Summaries are contained in F. S. Regs., Part II. and the Staff Manual respectively. Title pages will be prepared in manuscript.

WAR DIARY
or
INTELLIGENCE SUMMARY.

(*Erase heading not required.*)

Of 43rd Bde R.F.A.

(114)

Army Form C. 2118.

Hour, Date, Place	Summary of Events and Information	Remarks and references to Appendices
3.10.15.	Will come under the orders C.R.A 15th DA and will be prepared to fire from Points 14 Bis to HULLUCH	36b+c 1/40,000. 36c NW3 and part of 1. 36c SW1 1/10,000.
5.30 PM.	orders that the Artillery preparation for 3rd to 5th was postponed	
6.10 PM.	message from 40th Battery saying that they had stopped firing at 5.45 PM but had expended 215 rounds lyddite from 12 noon up to that time.	
6.45 PM.	Night lines M6c 2.6 to M6d 3.7 particular attention to communication trenches M6c and M6d, no firing unless orders from 47th DA.	
7. PM	Owing to the 24th Siege Bty being placed under orders of 15th DA, the following reallotment of tasks has become necessary 21st London trenches running south from Wood 5 not to shoot further south than H 31b 1.7. 22 London Wood 6.	

(9 29 6) W4141—463 100,000 9/14 H W V Forms/C. 2118/10

Army Form C. 2118.

Instructions regarding War Diaries and Intelligence Summaries are contained in F. S. Regs., Part II. and the Staff Manual respectively. Title pages will be prepared in manuscript.

WAR DIARY of 43rd Bde RFA
or
INTELLIGENCE SUMMARY.
(*Erase heading not required.*)

(115)

Hour, Date, Place	Summary of Events and Information	Remarks and references to Appendices
3. 10. 15.	23rd Siege 1 Section Trenches North of Woods 4 & 5 and if necessary North edge of Woods 4 & 5.	36C + C 1/40,000.
	1 Section railway south of Woods 4 & 5 from H 25d 1.6 to H 26c.7.4.	36c NW3 and part of 1 + 36c SW1 1/10,000.
	40th Batty. No change	
	Until further orders batteries will only carry out any registration necessary to be able to carry out above tasks, this registration will be carried out as soon as possible.	
	Ammunition expended by 30th & 40th 329 Lyddite	GRJ.
4. 10. 15		
3.10 PM.	21st London Batty fired 20 rounds into CITÉ ST PIERRE.	
7.45 PM.	Night lines the same as last night same arrangements for firing	
	Ammunition expended by 30th & 40th 28 Lyddite.	
	LT. L.H. DARDIER killed + LT C.A. ROBERTS wounded	

(9 29 6) W4141—463 100,000 9/14 H W V Forms/C. 2118/10

Instructions regarding War Diaries and Intelligence Summaries are contained in F. S. Regs., Part II. and the Staff Manual respectively. Title pages will be prepared in manuscript.

WAR DIARY
or
~~INTELLIGENCE~~ SUMMARY.
(*Erase heading not required.*)

of 43rd Bde RFA

(116)

Army Form C. 2118.

Hour, Date, Place	Summary of Events and Information	Remarks and references to Appendices
5.10.15.	40th Battery will occupy on night 5/6 position recently vacated by the 5th Siege R.G.A. near Fosse 7 and will come under orders of 1st DA Group.	36C + c 1/40,000.
		36c NW3 and part of 1 + 36c SW1 1/10,000.
	Lt Colonel F. L. Sharpe will resume command of the 43rd Bde RFA. from night 5/6.	
	43rd Brigade Headquarters will be at L24c10.6 in GRENAY line trenches from 5 PM today.	
	40th Battery zone as follows CITÉ ST ELIE – Puits 14 Bis (both inclusive) covering 1st Infantry Brigade	
	Ammunition expended nil	
	1 Driver 30th Battery wounded.	o.N.

Army Form C. 2118.

Instructions regarding War Diaries and Intelligence Summaries are contained in F. S. Regs., Part II. and the Staff Manual respectively. Title pages will be prepared in manuscript.

WAR DIARY or ~~INTELLIGENCE SUMMARY.~~ of 43rd Bde RFA

(*Erase heading not required.*)

(117)

Hour, Date, Place	Summary of Events and Information	Remarks and references to Appendices
6 – 10 – 15.	Useful points for 40th Battery to register on in ST. ELIE. H1d, 1.2, mine buildings, water tower	36b + 36c 1/40,000
	In HULLUCH Houses near H13d 2.8, telephone exchange H13b 8.0. HQ at H13 d 4.0 and H14c 4.4, houses H14b 9.4, also any crossroads in both places.	36c NW 3 and part of I. + 36 c SW I 1/10,000.
	1st Division will tonight take over line of 12th Division.	
	40th Battery will cover line held by London Scottish H19a 8.0 – H19a.17.	
	30th Battery will cover line held by 1st Gloucesters + 1st Camerons. H19a.17 – G18b 66.	
	30th Battery night lines trench Puits 13 Bis to H13d 2.5. with two sections one gun H13b 7.0 one gun H13b 4.0.	
	40th. Battery one section of Puits 14 Bis one section North edge of BOIS HUGO where trenches leave wood one section redoubt in H20d.	

(9 29 6) W4141—463 100,000 9/14 H W V Forms/C. 2118/10

Instructions regarding War Diaries and Intelligence Summaries are contained in F. S. Regs., Part II. and the Staff Manual respectively. Title pages will be prepared in manuscript.

WAR DIARY of 43rd Bde RFA
or
~~INTELLIGENCE~~ SUMMARY.
(Erase heading not required.)

(118)

Army Form C. 2118.

Hour, Date, Place	Summary of Events and Information	Remarks and references to Appendices
6-10-15	Lt Lely & Lt Stewart posted to 30th Battery from 1st DAC	
	Ammunition expended Lyddite. 29. Shrapnel. 3.	a.P.I.
7-10-15. 5.10 PM	<u>30th Battery</u> night lines cross roads H17 c.5.2 trench junctions at points H13b 1.9., H13b 0.5., H13a 9.4 road junction H13b 2.2.	36b + 36c 1/40,000. 36c NW3 and part of I 36c SW I 1/10,000.
	<u>40th Battery</u> night lines H13d 2.5, H13d 7.4, H14c22, H13d 9.3 PUITS 14 BIS and redoubt in H20d.	
9.45 PM	The line of the German trench is reported to run, H26a 0.2 H19d4.0, H19 a.8.0, H19a 66, H13c 4.2, H13a 4.2, H13 a.44.	
	For purposes of night firing, night is to be considered to be from 6PM - 6AM	
	Lt Mugleston posted to AC from 1st DAC	
	Ammunition expended Lyddite 20 6 Shrapnel	

Instructions regarding War Diaries and Intelligence Summaries are contained in F. S. Regs., Part II. and the Staff Manual respectively. Title pages will be prepared in manuscript.

WAR DIARY of 43rd Bde RFA
or
~~INTELLIGENCE~~ SUMMARY.
(*Erase heading not required.*)

(119)

Army Form C. 2118.

Hour, Date, Place	Summary of Events and Information	Remarks and references to Appendices
8 — 10 — 15	30 + 40th Batteries night lines the same as last night but	36b + 36c 1/40,000.
7.45 PM.	must be prepared to fire on BOIS HUGO if required.	36c NW 3 and part of I
8.55 PM.	Instructions for attack on 13th Oct	36c SW I 1/10,000.
	1st Division will attack the enemies line from H19c 9.6 to H13a44	
	with the object of.	
	(a) capturing the enemies front line	
	(c) under favourable circumstances establishing themselves in	
	HULLUCH.	
	The main idea of the Artillery operations is a heavy concentration	
	of fire on the portion of the enemies line to be attacked.	
	Bombardment with HE	
	(1) 43rd Bde RFA H13c 4 5 (inclusive) to H 13 a 44	
	(2). as soon as gas is turned on	
	H13a 9.4 (inclusive) — H7c 7 4	
	(3). As soon as the assault is launched houses on both sides	
	of the road from H 13d 2.5 – H 13b 2 2.	

(9 29 6) W4141—463 100,000 9/14 H W V Forms/C. 2118/10

Instructions regarding War Diaries and Intelligence Summaries are contained in F. S. Regs., Part II. and the Staff Manual respectively. Title pages will be prepared in manuscript.

WAR DIARY
or
~~INTELLIGENCE~~ SUMMARY.
(Erase heading not required.)

of 43rd Bde R.F.A.

Army Form C. 2118.

(120)

Hour, Date, Place	Summary of Events and Information	Remarks and references to Appendices
8.10.15.	half an hour after the assault two companies will be pushed forward into HULLUCH	36b + 36c 1/40,000,
	one company will be directed along the road H13c 4.2 to H13d 2.5. and the other along the road H13a 4.2 – H13b 1.2.	36c NW3 and part of I
	left on the line H13b 7.0., H13b 4.3	36c SW I 1/10,000.
	Ammunition expended 141 Lyddite.	O.P.J.
9–10–15.	30th + 40th Batteries night lines the same as last night	
	Ammunition expended 59 Lyddite.	O.P.J.
10–10–15	Lt Hughiston posted to 30th Battery from 43rd AC.	
	Lt Stewart posted to 43rd AC from 30th Battery.	
	night lines the same as last night not to fire unless ordered from this office	
	Ammunition expended Lyddite 24 Shrapnel 14.	O.P.J.

(9 29 6) W4141—463 100,000 9/14 H W V Forms/C. 2118/10

Army Form C. 2118.

Instructions regarding War Diaries and Intelligence Summaries are contained in F. S. Regs., Part II. and the Staff Manual respectively. Title pages will be prepared in manuscript.

WAR DIARY
or
~~INTELLIGENCE~~ SUMMARY.
(*Erase heading not required.*)

of 43rd Bde RFA.

(121)

Hour, Date, Place	Summary of Events and Information	Remarks and references to Appendices
11—10—15.	Batteries were ordered to dump 200 rds per gun at guns at	36b + 36c 1/40,000.
12.15 PM.	once, gun limbers waggons Bde AC and 1st DAC will remain empty.	36c NW 3 and part of I
	Night lines the same as last night	36c SW I 1/10,000.
	Ammunition expended 80 Lydite.	OPJ.
12-10-15. 8.15 AM	Batteries will fire 40 rds per gun today, at German wire and front line trenches (chiefly on wire)	
	30th Battery Trench H13c 4.5 (inclusive) to H13a.4.0.	
	40th Battery Trench H13a.4.0. – H13 a 4.4.	
	Time table for operations tomorrow 13th inst	
	1st Phase 0.10 – 0.20 From zero.	
	Actual time from 12.50 PM – 1.20 PM	

(9 29 6) W4141—463 100,000 9/14 H W V Forms/C. 2118/10

Instructions regarding War Diaries and Intelligence Summaries are contained in F. S. Regs., Part II. and the Staff Manual respectively. Title pages will be prepared in manuscript.

WAR DIARY
or
~~INTELLIGENCE~~ SUMMARY. of 43rd Bde RFA.
(*Erase heading not required.*)

(122)

Army Form C. 2118.

Hour, Date, Place	Summary of Events and Information	Remarks and references to Appendices
12-10-15.	Intense Fire 2 rds per gun per minute with H.E.	36b + 36c 1/40,000.
	H13c 4.5 (incl) - H13a 4.4 50 rds per gun.	36c NW3 and part of I
	<u>2nd Phase.</u> 0.20 - 1.0. 1.20 PM - 2PM.	36c SW1. 1/10,000
	Ordinary fire 1 rd per gun per minute, continued bombardment as soon as gas turned on,	
	H13a 9.4 (incl) H7.c 7.4 30 rds per gun.	
	<u>3rd Phase.</u> 1.0 - 1.15 2PM - 2.15 PM	
	Fire Ordinary	
	As soon as gas is launched.	
	Houses from H13d 2.5 - H13b 2.2. on both sides of road.	
	10 rds per gun.	
	<u>4th Phase.</u> 1.15 - 1.30 2.15 PM - 2.30 PM.	
	Intense.	

(9 29 6) W4141—463 100,000 9/14 H W V Forms/C. 2118/10

Instructions regarding War Diaries and Intelligence Summaries are contained in F. S. Regs., Part II. and the Staff Manual respectively. Title pages will be prepared in manuscript.

WAR DIARY
or
~~INTELLIGENCE~~ SUMMARY.
of 43rd Bde RFA

(*Erase heading not required.*)

Army Form C. 2118.

(123)

Hour, Date, Place	Summary of Events and Information	Remarks and references to Appendices
12 — 10 — 15.	Preparatory to infantry reconnaissance as in previous phase but intense instead of ordinary fire 25 rds per gun.	36b + 36c 1/40,000.
	5th Phase 1.30 – 2.0 2.30 PM – 3 PM	36c NW3 2nd part of I
	Ordinary	36c SW I 1/10,000.
	Covering infantry reconnaissance, lift onto the line H13b7.0 – H13b4.3. 25 rds per gun.	
	6th Phase. 2.0 – 2.30. 3 PM – 3.30 PM	
	Ordinary	
	Lift	
	H13b9.6½ to H13b6.6 20 rds per gun.	
4.40 PM.	No firing tonight between the hours of 7.15 PM to 10.15 PM	
4.50 PM.	during operations tomorrow the only flags carried will be carried to mark the position of bombing parties, these will be red flags are foot square with a white horizontal stripe.	

(9 29 6) W4141—463 100,000 9/14 H W V Forms/C. 2118/10

Instructions regarding War Diaries and Intelligence Summaries are contained in F. S. Regs., Part II. and the Staff Manual respectively. Title pages will be prepared in manuscript.

Army Form C. 2118.

WAR DIARY or ~~INTELLIGENCE~~ SUMMARY. of 43rd Bde RFA

(*Erase heading not required.*)

(124)

Hour, Date, Place	Summary of Events and Information	Remarks and references to Appendices
12—10—15.	Ref. Time table.	36b + 36c. 1/40,000.
	Target for 43rd Bde is houses from H13d 2.5. — H13b 22 on	36c NW 3 and part of I
7.30 PM.	both sides of the road 30 rds per gun.	36c SW1 1/10,000.
	Phase 2 is therefore the same as Phase 3.	
9.20 PM	The question as to whether gas is to be used or not will be decided	
	at 12 noon, tomorrow and definite orders will then be given	
	If gas is not used 4.5 How[itzers] will not lift their fire during	
	phase 2 but will remain on the same targets as in Phase I	
13—10—15	Ammunition expended. 325 Lyddite.	a.p.j.
	30th Battery report that G14a.7.2 is being heavily shelled	
10.20 AM.	by 8.2" How[itzers] from direction of Wingles, shelling stopped 7.30 AM.	
10.30 AM.	Infantry of 47th Div will carry when they advance a yellow	
	disc 18 inches in diameter with a black cross on it, bombers	
	have a similar disc 6 in in diameter.	

(9 29 6) W4141—463 100,000 9/14 H W V Forms/C. 2118/10

Instructions regarding War Diaries and Intelligence Summaries are contained in F. S. Regs., Part II. and the Staff Manual respectively. Title pages will be prepared in manuscript.

WAR DIARY of 43rd Bde RFA
or
~~INTELLIGENCE~~ **SUMMARY.**
(Erase heading not required.)

Army Form C. 2118.

(125)

Hour, Date, Place	Summary of Events and Information	Remarks and references to Appendices
13 — 10 — 15.	1st Div has captured German front line trenches on their	36G + 36C 1/40,000.
2.40 PM.	front	36C NW 3 and part of 1.
3.30 PM.	30th + 40th Batteries H13b.1.7 to H13b14 at once one round per gun per minute until further orders	36CSW I 1/10,000.
5.40 PM.	30th Battery stop firing at 6PM and go onto night lines as follows Western Edge of HULLUCH H13b 4.3 — H13d 4.8 no firing unless ordered.	
5.45 PM	40th Battery stop firing at 6PM and go onto night lines as follows West end of HULLUCH H13d 4.8 — H13d 2.2 no firing unless ordered	
9.10 PM.	Last orders cancelled with reference to night lines 30th Battery Western edge of HULLUCH from H13b4.3 to H13d 2.2. Fire 20 rds per hour	

Instructions regarding War Diaries and Intelligence Summaries are contained in F. S. Regs., Part II. and the Staff Manual respectively. Title pages will be prepared in manuscript.

WAR DIARY or INTELLIGENCE SUMMARY. of 43rd Bde RFA.

(Erase heading not required.)

Army Form C. 2118.

(126)

Hour, Date, Place	Summary of Events and Information	Remarks and references to Appendices
13-10-15	until further orders or until 6 AM infantry are consolidating the line	36b + 36c 1/40,000.
	40th Battery system of trenches H13b1.9 — H13b1.2	36 NW 3 and part of I.
	2 Gunners one 40th the other 30th wounded	36 c SW1 1/10,000.
	Ammunition expended. 2004 Lyddite	a.P.J.
14-10-15		
3.10 AM	Following from 1st DA. 2nd Bde attacking German. trench from H13c4.2 to about H13c4.8 at 4 am there will be not artillery preparation.	
6 AM.	Following from 1st Div 2nd Bde as you cannot deliver attack before daylight it should not take place	
6.40 AM	The night barrage ceased at 6 AM no further orders for firing at present	
	Units will carry out the usual measures for the defence of the line.	

(9 29 6) W4141—463 100,000 9/14 H W V Forms/C. 2118/10

Instructions regarding War Diaries and Intelligence Summaries are contained in F. S. Regs., Part II. and the Staff Manual respectively. Title pages will be prepared in manuscript.

WAR DIARY
or
~~INTELLIGENCE~~ SUMMARY.
(*Erase heading not required.*)

of 43rd Bde RFA.

(127)

Army Form C. 2118.

Hour, Date, Place	Summary of Events and Information	Remarks and references to Appendices
14—10—15.	London Scottish dug a new trench last night from H19c7.7. to H19a6½,3.	36a G4c. 1/40,000.
11.30 AM.	Ammunition expended 30 Lyddite	36c NW3 and part of 1 36c SW1 1/10,000.
5.30 PM.	Night lines the same as before operations no firing unless ordered	a RJ.
15—10—15.	One section of 30th Battery will be relieved by C71 at 7.30PM tonight.	
	One section of 40th Battery will be relieved by B71 at 8.30 tonight.	
5.30 PM	Night lines the same as last night 43rd BAC will be at L7c.18. 40th Battery wagon line at L23d9.1 30th Battery wagon line L29b.27.	
	Ammunition expended. 18 Lyddite	a RJ.
16—10—15. 11PM	Remaining sections of 30th + 40th Batteries to draw out at 4PM if no further orders.	
3PM.	43rd Bde HQ moved out and went to Lapugnoy D13b.1.3.	

(9 29 6) W4141—463 100,000 9/14 H W V Forms/C. 2118/10

Instructions regarding War Diaries and Intelligence Summaries are contained in F. S. Regs., Part II. and the Staff Manual respectively. Title pages will be prepared in manuscript.

WAR DIARY
or
~~INTELLIGENCE~~ SUMMARY
of 43rd Bde RFA.

(Erase heading not required.)

(128)

Army Form C. 2118.

Hour, Date, Place	Summary of Events and Information	Remarks and references to Appendices
16—10—15	30th & 40th Batteries moved out at 4 PM and also moved to Lapugnoy	36 a b & c 1/40000.
	30th Battery D16b3.5. 40th Battery D16a.3.3.	36c NW3 and part of 1. 36c SW1 1/10,000
	Ammunition expended 20 Lyddite	APJ
17-10-15.	Nothing to report.	APJ.
18-10-15.	40th Battery going up into action tonight and will be attached to the Cley Group 47th Divisional Artillery.	APJ.
19—10—15	43rd Bde HQ, ammunition column, to Lières and 30th Battery to Ballery.	
	43rd Bde HQ T18c 2.0.	
	43rd BAC T24a 6.8.	
	30th Battery B5a6.9.	
	1 section BAC going up into action at NOEUX LES MINES	
	40th Battery in action at FOSSE 7. DE BETHUNE.	APJ.

1247 W 3299 200,000 (E) 8/14 J.B.C. & A. Forms/C. 2118/11.

Instructions regarding War Diaries and Intelligence Summaries are contained in F. S. Regs., Part II. and the Staff Manual respectively. Title pages will be prepared in manuscript.

WAR DIARY
or
~~INTELLIGENCE SUMMARY~~ of 43rd Bde RFA.

(Erase heading not required.)

(129)

Army Form C. 2118.

Hour, Date, Place	Summary of Events and Information	Remarks and references to Appendices
20 — 10 — 15.	From today there will be a subalterns ride at 9 o'clock till further orders.	36 a.b.c $\frac{1}{40,000}$ a.P.J. 36c NW 3 and part of I
21 — 10 — 15.	Capt Elder RAMC MO 39th Bde RFA will temporarily take over the 43rd Bde while Captain Rowe is on leave	a.P.J. 36c SW 1 $\frac{1}{10,000}$
22 - 10 - 15.	ADVS 1st Div will give a short lecture on horse management tomorrow 23rd inst at Annes 6 PM.	a.P.J.
23 - 10 - 15.	2nd Lt. C. O. Roberts was transferred to England on 8 - 10 - 15.	a.P.J.
24 - 10 - 15	Nothing to report.	a.P.J.
25 - 10 - 15.	10 Signallers are to proceed from this Bde tomorrow at 7am to go on a course of telephony at 1st Div HQ LABUISSIÈRE for a month.	a.P.J.
26 - 10 - 16	Nothing to report.	a.P.J.
27 - 10 - 15.	10 men from 40th Battery and one section of guns from 30th Battery to go to ~~L~~ LABUISSIÈRE. tomorrow for the review of 4th Corps by the King.	a.P.J.
28 - 10 - 15.	The review at 10.15 AM Colonel Sharp CMG represented the 1st Divisional Artillery	a.P.J.

Instructions regarding War Diaries and Intelligence Summaries are contained in F. S. Regs., Part II. and the Staff Manual respectively. Title pages will be prepared in manuscript.

WAR DIARY
or
INTELLIGENCE SUMMARY
(Erase heading not required.)

(130)

Army Form C. 2118.

Hour, Date, Place	Summary of Events and Information	Remarks and references to Appendices
29-10-15 to 31-10-15	Nothing to report	36 abc 1/40,000 aN.
1-11-15.	Capt E.A. Woods posted to 30th Battery from adj 43rd Bde RFA	36c NW 3 and part of 1.
	Lt H B. Holland posted to adj 43rd Bde RFA from 30th Battery	36c SW 1 1/10,000.
2-11-15 to 4-11-15.	Nothing to report	aN.
5-11-15.	G.O.C. 1st Division will inspect horses of this Brigade tomorrow commencing with 30th Battery at 10.45 am.	
6-11-15.	G.O.C. 1st Division inspected the horses in the morning and made special comment on those of the 43rd Brigade Ammunition Column saying that they were the best he had seen in the 1st Division	aN
7-11-15	2nd Lt MUIRHEAD joined the Brigade and is posted to the 30th Battery.	
8-11-15	Nothing to report	aN.
9-11-15.	Capt J.T. PRICE went to hospital, Capt E.A Woods temporarily ~~posted~~ in command of 30th Battery	aN

Instructions regarding War Diaries and Intelligence Summaries are contained in F. S. Regs., Part II. and the Staff Manual respectively. Title pages will be prepared in manuscript.

WAR DIARY
or
~~INTELLIGENCE SUMMARY~~ 43rd Bde RFA
(131)

(Erase heading not required.)

Army Form C. 2118.

Hour, Date, Place	Summary of Events and Information	Remarks and references to Appendices
10—11—15	Bathing to report.	36b T C 1/40,000
11—11—15	Got orders to move midday the following day to billets in Lapugnoy	36c NW3 and part of 1274. 1/10,000
12—11—15	The Sharp Group formed consisting of of the 30th + 40th Batteries and the 5th Siege Battery.	
	The 40th Battery already in action at G27a 3.1	
	The Remainder of the 1st DA is split up into the Clinton + Scott Groups.	
13—11—15 8.30 AM	HQ 30th Battery and BAC move to LAPUGNOY and take up billets there.	
	HQ D16b 1.3. 30th Battery D16c 6.9 BAC D21b 2.8.	
	The 5th Siege Bty moves one section to its new position at G27 c.26 during the night 13/14	
	Driver O'Neill deserted from BAC	

Instructions regarding War Diaries and Intelligence Summaries are contained in F. S. Regs., Part II. and the Staff Manual respectively. Title pages will be prepared in manuscript.

WAR DIARY
or
~~INTELLIGENCE SUMMARY~~
(Erase heading not required.)

Army Form C. 2118

43rd Bde RFA

(132)

Hour, Date, Place	Summary of Events and Information	Remarks and references to Appendices
14 — 11 — 15	43rd Bde HQ moved to LABEUVRIÈRE to make room for the CRE. 47th Division	36 N W 3 and part 1 2 & 4 $\frac{1}{10,000}$
	5th Siege Battery moves its remaining section in during the night 14/15.	36c $\frac{1}{40,000}$
	30th Battery is handed over to the HINTON Group and 40th Battery to the SCOTT group for the defence of the line. These two groups are given the responsibility for the defence of the line.	
15 — 11 — 15	30th Battery moves up one section to its new Battery position at G 32d 6.7. during the night of the 15/16.	
16 — 11 — 15.	The remainder of the Bde go up into action at 8·30 AM by FOUQUEREUIL, VERQUIN, NOEUX LES MINES, MALINGARBE. The Brigade Ammunition Column goes to Hesdin and the 30th Wagon lines to NOEUX LES MINES. L19c	
	HQ in Les BREBIS amongst the French, taking the place of the ELEY Group.	

Instructions regarding War Diaries and Intelligence Summaries are contained in F. S. Regs., Part II. and the Staff Manual respectively. Title pages will be prepared in manuscript.

WAR DIARY
or
~~INTELLIGENCE SUMMARY~~

(*Erase heading not required.*)

of 43rd Bde RFA

Army Form C. 2118.

(133)

Hour, Date, Place	Summary of Events and Information	Remarks and references to Appendices
16—11—15.	40th Battery wagon line behind the Power Station at MAZINGARBE L29 b central.	36c 1/40,000 36 NW 3 and part 12 4 1/10,000
2 PM.	30th Battery registered PUITS 14 BIS at 2 PM. with two guns	
2.30 PM — 3 PM	5th Siege registered PUITS 14 BIS and H19a 7.8 between 2.30 & 3 PM.	
3 PM	The Germans, evidently annoyed at the shooting of the 5th Siege Battery, retaliated by vigorously shelling the wall, POSEN STREET and our front line near the CHALK PIT WOOD with 5.9" and smaller Howitzers and H E 40th Battery retaliated by shelling the houses in HULLUCH and BENIFONTAINE and PUITS 10 BIS and the new trench in front of the latter, Night lines. 40th Battery (1) Trench Junction H14c9.3 (2) PUITS 13 BIS (3). Road at S End of HULLUCH H13d 2.5.	

1247 W 3299 200,000 (E) 8/14 J.B.C. & A. Forms/C. 2118/11.

Instructions regarding War Diaries and Intelligence Summaries are contained in F. S. Regs., Part II. and the Staff Manual respectively. Title pages will be prepared in manuscript.

WAR DIARY
or
INTELLIGENCE SUMMARY 43rd Bde RFA.
(Erase heading not required.)

(134)

Army Form C. 2118.

Hour, Date, Place	Summary of Events and Information	Remarks and references to Appendices
16—11—15.	(4) Trench junction H 13a 9½.6	36c NW 3 and part 12 4
	(5) " " H 13 b ½.7	
	(6) School House H7 d.7.1	
17—11—15.	30th 40th and 5th Siege bombarded trench immediately North of PUITS 14 BIS.	
	from H25c66 to H25d 0.8 for 5 minutes	
	Front line trench at H19a 7.8. for 3 minutes and H19a.8.0 for 2 minutes	
	The enemy retaliated vigorously by shelling our line, although our artillery replied, it did not do so vigorously enough to stop the Germans.	
	The retaliation line were ordered as follows.	
	30th Battery Trench H25c66 – H25d 9.9.	
	40th Battery 2 sections on HULLUCH	
	1 section PUITS 14 BIS.	
	5th Siege 2 guns on redoubt in H20d 1 gun on H26 b 5.7.	
	1 gun on H14c.6.3	

Instructions regarding War Diaries and Intelligence Summaries are contained in F. S. Regs., Part II. and the Staff Manual respectively. Title pages will be prepared in manuscript.

WAR DIARY
or
~~INTELLIGENCE~~ SUMMARY
(Erase heading not required.)

of 43rd Bde RFA (135)

Army Form C. 2118.

Hour, Date, Place	Summary of Events and Information	Remarks and references to Appendices
17—11—15	Night lines ordered as follows.	30th CRCO 3 and pt 12+4
	30th Battery 2 sections Trench H25c66 — H25d 9.9.	
	1 section PUITS 14 BIS.	
	40th Battery same as last night	
	5th Siege 2 guns on redoubt in H20 d central	
	1 gun H26 b.5.7	
	1 gun H14c 6.3.	
	30th Battery had a premature at about 2.15PM Cpl Lee and	
	Gnr Pixon killed and 2 wounded	
12 AM.	30th Battery registered H25d 0.8 and H19 d.1.8	
4PM	30th Battery registered H26a.1.2	Ammunition expended 244 Lyddite
4.5PM	The Germans are reported by the 30th Battery to have opened.	
	a 5 minutes burst of fire in the direction of the HOHENZOLLERN	
	Redoubt.	
	GOC 1st Division noticed that the enemy seemed to have rather the best of the mornings "strafe"	

1247 W 3299 200,000 (E) 8/14 J.B.C. & A. Forms/C. 2118/11.

Instructions regarding War Diaries and Intelligence Summaries are contained in F. S. Regs., Part II. and the Staff Manual respectively. Title pages will be prepared in manuscript.

WAR DIARY
or
~~INTELLIGENCE SUMMARY~~
(Erase heading not required.)

43rd Bde RFA

(36)

Army Form C. 2118.

Hour, Date, Place	Summary of Events and Information	Remarks and references to Appendices
18 – 11 – 15	<u>30th Battery</u> retaliated on PUITS 14 BIS for enemy shelling	36C NW 3 and part 124
9.3AM	North LOOS with Field guns. The Germans stopped immediately	
11.15AM	<u>30th Battery</u> fired at M11d 9.1 at the request of the French.	
	This was not observed, the firing being off the map	
12.15 PM.	<u>Bombardment</u>. 30th + 40th Batteries 50 rds each.	
	5th Siege 11 rds on Trench at PUITS 14 BIS from H25C.66.–H25d04	
	The Germans retaliated on Loos Pylons and a few heavy shells	
	on the CHALK PIT WOOD. The 30th Battery retaliated on the same	
	target	
12.35 PM	<u>30th Battery</u> fired 20 rounds into the trenches at SE end of	
	the Double Crassier at the request of the French	
1PM	<u>30th Battery</u> got their 5th gun in and registered on PUITS 14 BIS	
1.10PM.	<u>30th Battery</u> fired into PUITS 14 BIS for the enemy shelling the	
	CHALK PIT WOOD	

Instructions regarding War Diaries and Intelligence Summaries are contained in F. S. Regs., Part II. and the Staff Manual respectively. Title pages will be prepared in manuscript.

WAR DIARY
or
~~INTELLIGENCE~~ SUMMARY.
(Erase heading not required.)

of 43rd Bde RFA

(137)

Army Form C. 2118.

Hour, Date, Place	Summary of Events and Information	Remarks and references to Appendices
18-11-15.	40th Battery & 30th Battery 50 rds HE each 5th Regs	36c N W 3 ed feb 12 & 4.
3.20 PM	40 rds on trenches west of HULLUCH from H 13 d 3.9 - H 13d. 2.5	
	The bombardment was good on the whole, but there was an	
	immense proportion of blinds and many very poor bursts	
	The Germans retaliated with a Shrapnel Barrage at 3.25 PM	
	behind our front line in H 24 b & d, extending two or three	
	minutes later to the NE of LOOS	
	The CHALK PIT heavily shelled with Field guns also some	
	5.9 shell in the direction of HAY ALLEY and to the N of it	
	The 30th retaliated by shelling trench N of PUITS 14 BIS and	
	Wood 5. and the 40th Battery put some rounds into HULLUCH	

Instructions regarding War Diaries and Intelligence Summaries are contained in F. S. Regs., Part II. and the Staff Manual respectively. Title pages will be prepared in manuscript.

WAR DIARY
or
INTELLIGENCE SUMMARY.
(*Erase heading not required.*)

of 43rd Bde R F A

(138)

Army Form C. 2118.

Hour, Date, Place	Summary of Events and Information	Remarks and references to Appendices
19 – 11 – 15. 16.15 AM.	30th Battery fire on BOIS HUGO and H 26 central in response to enemy shelling trenches N of LOOS, the enemy appeared to be firing from BOIS HUGO, a light enemy field gun immediately started to shell the PYLONS at LOOS.	36c NW3 and part 12.44.
1 PM – 4 PM.	5th Siege stop the front line trench from H26a 1.2 to H19 a8.0. with good effect as this produced a great outburst of fire from the enemy all along the line	
	40th Battery retaliated on HULLUCH + PUITS14 BIS	
1.45 PM	30th Battery registered the redoubt on HILL 70.	
3.5 PM	Bombardment trench in H25 d 01 – 08. effective enemy replied with heavy shrapnel fire on LOOS 40th Bty replied with fire on PUITS 14 BIS.	

Instructions regarding War Diaries and Intelligence Summaries are contained in F. S. Regs., Part II. and the Staff Manual respectively. Title pages will be prepared in manuscript.

WAR DIARY
or
INTELLIGENCE SUMMARY.
(*Erase heading not required.*)

Of 43rd Bde RFA.

(139)

Army Form C. 2118.

Hour, Date, Place	Summary of Events and Information	Remarks and references to Appendices
19-11-15.	2nd Series H 13d 2.5 - H 13d 22 30th & 40th Batteries. Bombarded	36c NW3 and part 12 & 4.
	the enemy replied on our trenches near the HULLUCH Rd	
3.45 PM	30th Battery fired into BOIS HUGO in retaliation	
1 PM	The French fired into Wood 7 at our request.	
	Ammunition expended 295 Lyddite 1 Shrapnel	A.N.
20-11-15.	30th Battery are ordered to place a Howitzer in the	
	CHALK PIT. For purpose of firing up the LENS - LA BASSEE	
	road.	
	Yesterday Lt Col Sharp CMG went up to reconnaitre with General	
	Cartwright DSO.	
11.55 AM	Bombardment 30th & 40th Batteries Bombarded 5th Siege 40 ...	
	The bombardment was fairly effective and the Germans retaliated	
	with Shrapnel along our front and a barrage from NE of LOOS.	

(9 29 6) W4141—463 100,000 9/14 H W V Forms/C. 2118/10

Instructions regarding War Diaries and Intelligence Summaries are contained in F. S. Regs., Part II. and the Staff Manual respectively. Title pages will be prepared in manuscript.

WAR DIARY
or
~~INTELLIGENCE~~ SUMMARY.
(Erase heading not required.)

Army Form C. 2118.

of 43rd Bde RFA

(140).

Hour, Date, Place	Summary of Events and Information	Remarks and references to Appendices
20 – 11 – 15	to G 30 G 80 and also shelled CHALK PIT WOOD and	36 C N W 3 and part 12 + 4
	POSEN STREET	
11.55 AM	30th retaliated on BOIS HUGO.	
2 PM	Cutting Communication trenches from H13C 83 — H13C 6.3.	
	40th Battery 100 rds 5th Siege 80 rds results very poor	
4.30 PM	all quiet.	
	The following officers posted for 14 days instruction	
	2Lt J.H. HUGHES (to 40th Bty)	
	2Lt C.F WISE. (to 30th Bty)	G.R.
	Ammunition expended 434 Lyddite 1 Shrapnel.	
21 – 11 – 15	Bombardment of H13a 6.4 – 5.4 30th & 40th Batteries 50 rds each and	
2 PM	5th Siege 40 rds effect apparently good.	

Instructions regarding War Diaries and Intelligence Summaries are contained in F. S. Regs., Part II. and the Staff Manual respectively. Title pages will be prepared in manuscript.

WAR DIARY or ~~INTELLIGENCE~~ SUMMARY. of 43rd Bde RFA.

(*Erase heading not required.*)

Army Form C. 2118.

(141)

Hour, Date, Place	Summary of Events and Information	Remarks and references to Appendices
21–11–15	Fire of 5th Siege was answered by 5.9" on POSEN STREET.	36C NW3 and part 1274
2.30 PM	40th Battery retaliated on HULLUCH.	
3 PM	Bombardment of enemies front line from H13a 44 — 26. effect very good, masses of material and bodies were seen thrown into the air	
	The enemy retaliated with 5.9" and Field guns on POSEN ST and HAY ALLEY.	
	40th Bty retaliated on HULLUCH and BENIFONTAINE	
4 PM	all quiet.	
	Ammunition expended. 302 Lyddite	a N
22–11–15.	Very foggy morning no observation possible	
3.45 PM	The bombardment of H25c 55 – 8.4 was carried out although observation was impossible.	

Instructions regarding War Diaries and Intelligence Summaries are contained in F. S. Regs., Part II. and the Staff Manual respectively. Title pages will be prepared in manuscript.

WAR DIARY
or
~~INTELLIGENCE SUMMARY.~~
(Erase heading not required.)

43rd Bde RFA

(142)

Army Form C. 2118.

Hour, Date, Place	Summary of Events and Information	Remarks and references to Appendices
22-11-15.	40th Battery retalliated on HULLUCH for shelling of POSEN ST.	36 c N W 3 and Sheet 1274
3.55PM	30th Battery on BOIS HUGO. Ammunition Expended - 331 lyddite	
23-11-15.	30th Battery retaliated on H25c7½6-87. for enemies shelling	
	North LOOS and trenches there about	
10-15 AM.		
10.35	Bombardment of Trench H25c66 effect appeared good	
	enemy retalliated on POSEN ST. 30th Bty reretaliated on H25d08	
1.45PM.	30th Battery were requested by the French to fire on CITIE	
	JEANNE D'ARC.	
2.15	Bombardment of H13d 2.5-3.9 by 30 & 40th 5th Siege effect	
	exceptionally good	
3PM.	30th Battery fired on a battery M.18a7.7 and trench M5c5.1 at	
	the request of the French. Ammunition expended 48 lyddite.	

(9 29 6) W4141—463 100,000 9/14 H W V Forms/C. 2118/10

Army Form C. 2118.

Instructions regarding War Diaries and Intelligence Summaries are contained in F. S. Regs., Part II. and the Staff Manual respectively. Title pages will be prepared in manuscript.

WAR DIARY of 43rd Bde RFA

or

~~INTELLIGENCE~~ SUMMARY.

(*Erase heading not required.*)

(143)

Hour, Date, Place	Summary of Events and Information	Remarks and references to Appendices
24 – 11 – 15.	30th + 40th Batteries Bombardment Puits 14 Bis Trench	36cNW3 and part 12 + 4
11.45 am.	A. 80 rds each.	
2.15 PM	Bombardment 30th + 40th Batteries Trenches east of HULLUCH	
	from H13d 3.9 – H13d 2.5. 80 rds per gun.	
	Ammunition expended. 364 Lyddite.	O.N.
25 – 11 – 15	Bombardment of H19 a 6.9. – H13 c.5.0. by 30th 40th + 5th Siege	
10.10 AM.	Batteries (100 4.5) – (16 6")	
11.45 AM.	40th Battery retaliated for enemy shelling of HAY ALLEY on	
	HULLUCH.	
12.30 PM	30th Battery fired on CITE ST LAURENT at the request of	C.N.
	the French.	

(9 29 6) W4141—463 100,000 9/14 H W V Forms/C. 2118/10

Army Form C. 2118

WAR DIARY
or
INTELLIGENCE SUMMARY
(Erase heading not required.)

42nd Bde RFA

(144)

Instructions regarding War Diaries and Intelligence Summaries are contained in F. S. Regs., Part II. and the Staff Manual respectively. Title Pages will be prepared in manuscript.

Place	Date	Hour	Summary of Events and Information	Remarks and references to Appendices
	25-11-15	3.15PM	Bombardment of PUITS 14 BIS Trench B. enemy retaliated on Guards CHALK PIT WOOD	36c NW3 + pt 1274
			40th Battery retaliated on HULLUCH.	
			30th Battery reported one premature with the 100 fuze and one man accidentally wounded also that the enemy always retaliated on H25C13. when we shell PUITS 14 BIS, also a mound in construction in H23c Ammunition expended 331 Lyddite	OR
	26-11-15		2/Lt B. F. G. DARKER attached to the 30th Battery from 1st DAC.	
		7.45AM – 1.20PM.	The enemy shelled various points on our front line and all Batteries retaliated 30th Battery on BOIS HUGO H19b 8.4 & PUITS 14 BIS, 40th Battery on HULLUCH 5th Siege on HULLUCH.	
		2PM	Bombardment. by 30th & 5 Siege of enemies trench H19b 84 – H20c4.8.	
			30th Battery report new works E of Redoubt in H20d and H21d Ammunition expended 361 Lyddite	

1875 Wt. W593/826 1,000,000 4/15 J.B.C. & A. A.D.S.S./Forms/C. 2118.

Instructions regarding War Diaries and Intelligence Summaries are contained in F. S. Regs., Part II. and the Staff Manual respectively. Title Pages will be prepared in manuscript.

WAR DIARY
or
~~INTELLIGENCE SUMMARY~~
(Erase heading not required.)

43rd Bde RFA

(145)

Army Form C. 2118

Place	Date	Hour	Summary of Events and Information	Remarks and references to Appendices
	27-11-15.		Bombardment of H25c9.3 – H25d.18. Light too bad for observation	36cNW3 ad[illegible] 24
		8 AM.		
		8.20 AM.	Enemy retaliated on Chalk pit wood 30th Battery shelled BOIS HUGO.	
		11 AM.	40th Battery shelled enemy gun position at Benifontaine	
		2 PM	Bombardment of front line H13c4.2 – H13a4.2 by 40th Battery & 5th Liege	
		8 PM	30th & 5th Liege shelled Chalet HUGO believed to be a HQ.	
			Ammunition expended. 343 Lyddite.	RPJ
	28-11-15.		No 52537 S. Smith J. Perry 43rd BDE HQ died on Nov 15th from horse kick	
		11.30 AM	30th Battery stopped second line trench H20c8.4 – H26b16 & also 5th Liege satisfactory results	
		~~11.30 AM~~	~~30th Battery retaliated 20 rds on PUITS 14 BIS for enemy shelling [illegible] of PUITS 14 BIS.~~	
		~~2 PM~~	~~30th 40th & 5th Liege cutting Com Trench in H13a effect appeared [illegible] enemy retaliated on POSEN STREET.~~	
		3.30 PM	Bombardment of PUITS 14 BIS by all three Batteries enemy retaliated on QUALITY STR	
			Ammunition expended. 316 Lyddite.	RPJ

1875 Wt. W593/826 1,000,000 4/15 J.B.C. & A. A.D.S.S./Forms/C. 2118.

Instructions regarding War Diaries and Intelligence Summaries are contained in F. S. Regs., Part II. and the Staff Manual respectively. Title Pages will be prepared in manuscript.

WAR DIARY
or
~~INTELLIGENCE SUMMARY~~
(Erase heading not required.)

43rd Bde R.F.A.

(146)

Army Form C. [illegible]

Place	Date	Hour	Summary of Events and Information	Remarks and references to Appendices
	29-11-15.		Bombardment of PUITS 14 BIS. by all Batteries light very bad.	36cNW3 ad/ent 1274
		8AM.		
		9.45.	30th Battery fired 40rds at CEMETRBY M18a at the request of the French.	
		2PM	All Batteries cutting communication trench in H13a effect apparent Our enemy retaliated	
			on POSEN STA and LONE TREE AVENUE with 4.2 & 5.9.	aN
			Ammunition expended 488 Lydite	
	30-11-15.	9AM	30th Battery shelled the cemetery at M18a at the request of the French.	
		11 AM	Bombardment of PUITS 14 BIS. Trench B. effect good	
		11.28.	Germans observed working at H25 d.4.8 dispersed on being fired on.	
		2PM	Cutting Communication trenches in H7c. All Batteries	
		2.40	Germans shelled CHALK PIT WOOD with light Field guns from the direction of BOIS HUGO.	
		2.45PM	Ammunition expended. 457 Lydite	aN

1875 Wt. W593/826 1,000,000 4/15 J.B.C. & A. A.D.S.S./Forms/C. 2118.

H.Q. 43rd Bde R.F.A.

Dec.

Vol XII

Instructions regarding War Diaries and Intelligence Summaries are contained in F. S. Regs., Part II. and the Staff Manual respectively. Title Pages will be prepared in manuscript.

WAR DIARY
or
~~INTELLIGENCE SUMMARY~~
(Erase heading not required.)

43rd Bde RFA.

(147)

Army Form C. 2118

Place	Date	Hour	Summary of Events and Information	Remarks and references to Appendices
	1-12-15.	10.40 AM	30th Battery shelled W end of Wood 6 in retaliation for enemy shelling the trenches H of LOOS.	36c NW3 and part 1274
		12 PM	40th Battery put 40 rds in to H13a 3.5 to cut trench a good number of direct hits were obtained but probably little damage was done.	
		1.15 - 3.15 PM	40th Battery cut communication trenches from H7c 11 and H7c17 at their junction with the front line & 5th Siege do the same	
		3.15 PM	A Rapid bombardment is ordered by the 40th, 5th Siege, effect seemed fairly good	
			30th Battery put 33 rounds into the Woods of CITÉ ST AUGUSTE at the request of the French also 10 rds into PUITS 11 for French	
			Ammunition Expended 253 Lyddite	
	2.12.15		40th Battery fired into HULLUCH for retaliation on POSEN ST.	
		8.40 AM	30th Battery fired into BOIS HUGO for retaliation on NORTH LOOS.	
		9.50 AM	5th Siege registered PUITS 14 BIS.	

1875 Wt. W593/826 1,000,000 4/15 J.B.C. & A. A.D.S.S./Forms/C. 2118.

Instructions regarding War Diaries and Intelligence Summaries are contained in F. S. Regs., Part II. and the Staff Manual respectively. Title Pages will be prepared in manuscript.

WAR DIARY
or
~~INTELLIGENCE SUMMARY~~
(Erase heading not required.)

of 43rd Bde RFA

(148)

Army Form C. 2118

Place	Date	Hour	Summary of Events and Information	Remarks and references to Appendices
	2-12-15.		Bombardment of Trench A, practically no retaliation, shells bursting very badly, shooting good	36CNW3 & part 12 & 4
		10AM.	5th Siege reregistered PUITS 13 and trench from H13d 9.3 – H13d 2.5.	
		10.15AM		
		10.40AM	30th Battery fired into woods N of CITÉ ST AUGUSTE at the request of the French	
		12.45PM	40th Battery reregistered the trenches ~~W~~ of HULLUCH	
		2PM	Bombardment. 30th Battery trench H13d 9.3 – 6.5 5th Siege H13d 9.3 – 2.5	
			40th Battery trench H13d 6.5 – 2.5	
			The effect was fair.	
		3.35 PM	30th Battery fired 22 rds into the woods N of CITÉ ST AUGUSTE & FOSSE 11 in	
			retaliation for enemy shelling FOSSE 7 with 5.9. shells coming from direction of FOSSE 11.	aPJ
			Ammunition Expended 474 Lyddite.	
	3-12-15		30th Battery report a direct hit on the gunpit of No 2 gun no damage done. retaliated on	
		11.35 AM	on CITÉ ST AUGUSTE.	

1875 Wt. W593/826 1,000,000 4/15 J.B.C. & A. A.D.S.S./Forms/C. 2118.

Instructions regarding War Diaries and Intelligence Summaries are contained in F. S. Regs., Part II. and the Staff Manual respectively. Title Pages will be prepared in manuscript.

WAR DIARY
or
INTELLIGENCE SUMMARY
(Erase heading not required.)

of 43rd Bde RFA

(149)

Army Form C. 2118

Place	Date	Hour	Summary of Events and Information	Remarks and references to Appendices
		11.50 AM	Germans shelling LOOS 30th Battery retaliated on trenches around PUITS 14 BIS	
		12.40 PM	40th Battery fired into HULLUCH for enemy shelling POSEN ST & HAY ALLEY	
		1 PM to 3 PM	Cutting communication trenches with Howitzer fire at their junction with front line trenches.	
			30th H13 C 4 5. 40th H13 a 3.0. 5th How H13C 4.2	
			general effect very good.	
		3.15 PM	Bombardment as follows.	
			30th Bty H 13 C 44 – 47.	
			40th Bty H13c 47 – H13a 3.0. Time allowed 6 minutes	
			5th How H13c 4.2 – 4.4	
		3.45 PM	The enemy shelled the whole of front line of trenches for ten minutes with Field guns & Howitzers	
			40th Bty retaliated on HULLUCH Observation difficult the whole day on account of a mist. Ammunition expended 196 Lyddite	a.a.l.

1875 Wt. W593/826 1,000,000 4/15 J.B.C. & A. A.D.S.S./Forms/C. 2118.

Instructions regarding War Diaries and Intelligence Summaries are contained in F. S. Regs., Part II. and the Staff Manual respectively. Title Pages will be prepared in manuscript.

WAR DIARY
or
~~INTELLIGENCE~~ SUMMARY
(Erase heading not required.)

of 43rd Bde RFA

(150)

Army Form C. 2118

Place	Date	Hour	Summary of Events and Information	Remarks and references to Appendices
	4-12-15.		Bombardment. 30th Bty & 5th Hows	36c NW3 & parts 2 & 4.
		11 AM.	Trench in BOIS HUGO in H26 a and searched the woods 2 & 3 for 6 minutes. The effect was apparently good.	
		11.30 AM	The Germans started shelling the right Battalion with Field guns & Hows	
			30th Baty retaliated BOIS HUGO & CITE ST AUGUSTE.	
			40th Bty " HULLUCH.	
			5th Hows " TRENCH A.	
		2PM.-3.15	Deliberate Bombardment stepping 2nd line trench H20 c4.8 to H19 b.8.4	
			Firing very good effect poor	
		3.50 PM	30th Bty retaliated on BOIS HUGO & CITE ST AUGUSTE in retaliation for enemy shelling Rt Battalion.	
			5th Hows were shelled in the morning and suffered one casualty 30th + 40th were also shelled but sustained no damage.	

1875 Wt. W593/826 1,000,000 4/15 J.B.C. & A. A.D.S.S./Forms/C. 2118.

Instructions regarding War Diaries and Intelligence Summaries are contained in F. S. Regs., Part II. and the Staff Manual respectively. Title Pages will be prepared in manuscript.

WAR DIARY
or
~~INTELLIGENCE SUMMARY~~
(Erase heading not required.)

Of 43rd Bde RFA.

(151)

Army Form C. 2118

Place	Date	Hour	Summary of Events and Information	Remarks and references to Appendices
	4-12-15		There seemed to be a great deal of railway activity today several trains were seen behind YENDIN & WINGLES also behind HAISNES	36C NW 3 & part 1274
			Ammunition Expended 555 Lyddite	QRJ.
	5-12-15	8.20 AM	30th Bty fired onto the LOOS-LENS Rd in retaliation for the enemy shelling our front line trenches	
		10.20 AM	Germans shelling LENS-BETHUNE Rd. 30th Bty retaliated on BOIS HUGO enemy reretaliated on LOOS PYLONS. 30th Bty reretaliated on CITÉ ST AUGUSTE	
			5th Siege & counter Battery turned H32 b 6.8 - 10.9 - 10.7. H33a 8.7, H33b 3.7 at the request of French. The enemies fire ceased almost immediately.	
		10.35.	30th Bty fired into CITÉ ST AUGUSTE in retaliation for enemy shelling LOOS PYLONS	
		1.15 PM	Bombardment Junctions of com trenches with front line H19d 1.7 and H19.a 9.4	
		3.15 PM	Bombardment. of front line trenches H25 b.9.6 - H19 d.1.7	
			During the day FOSSE 7 shelled heavily 5th Siege had two casualties 40th Bty one wounded premature	
			Ammunition expended. 331 Lyddite.	QRJ.

1875 Wt. W593/826 1,000,000 4/15 J.B.C. & A. A.D.S.S./Forms/C. 2118.

Instructions regarding War Diaries and Intelligence Summaries are contained in F. S. Regs., Part II. and the Staff Manual respectively. Title Pages will be prepared in manuscript.

WAR DIARY
or
~~INTELLIGENCE SUMMARY~~
(Erase heading not required.)

of 43rd Bde RFA.

(152)

Army Form C. 2118

Place	Date	Hour	Summary of Events and Information	Remarks and references to Appendices
	6-12-15.		a working party of 150 men from 1st D.A. required for digging trenches, 10 men from each	36CN63 & part 1274
		4.30 AM	of our Batteries & 1 NCO., this fatigue daily at 4.30 AM till further notice	
		9.56 AM	30th Bty report 5.9 Bty shelling FOSSE 7 located at H14b 8.9.	
		11.15 AM	Bombardment PUITS 14 BIS. TRENCH D enemy retaliated on CHALK PIT ALLEY and along line of Rt Battalion	
		11.15 – 12.15.	40th Bty retaliated on HULLUCH & BENIFONTAINE for retaliation of old German, 1st line and communication trenches	
		12.15 PM	30th Bty & also counter Batteries bombarded German trenches around the E of the DOUBLE CRASSIER at the request of the French	
		1.50 PM	Germans shelled FOSSE 7 with a Bty of 5.9 located accurately by Capt Price RFA	
		3.20 AM	Bombardment 5th Regt & 40th Battery enemy retaliated on 15th Divisional area	
		3PM	40th Bty retaliated on HULLUCH. for enemy firing on trenches E of HULLUCH	
			40th Battery one casualty seriously wounded. Ammunition expended 531 Lyddite	GPW

1875 Wt. W593/826 1,000,000 4/15 J.B.C. & A. A.D.S.S./Forms/C. 2118.

Instructions regarding War Diaries and Intelligence Summaries are contained in F. S. Regs., Part II. and the Staff Manual respectively. Title Pages will be prepared in manuscript.

WAR DIARY
or
~~INTELLIGENCE~~ SUMMARY
(Erase heading not required.)

of 43rd Bde RFA

(153)

Army Form C. 2118

Place	Date	Hour	Summary of Events and Information	Remarks and references to Appendices
	7-12-15		2 Lt Parker absorbed in 30th Battery	36c NW 3 & part 1 2 & 4
			2nd Lt Hughston posted to 1st DAC. 2nd Lt Stewart posted to 30th Battery from BAC	
		8.0 AM	30th Battery shelled the trenches near PUITS 14 BIS. Bombardment effect very bad on account of bad ammunition.	
		10 AM	40th Battery bombarded front line trenches H7c1.2. – G12 d9.9. detonations very bad	
		11.30 AM	Germans shelled BSEN STREET with 4.2 Howitzers 40th Battery retaliated on FRILLED HOUSE.	
		12.15 PM.	30th Bty fired into BOIS HUGO and CITÉ ST ELIE in retaliation for enemy shelling LENS rd.	
		12.20 – 2.20 PM.	5th Siege Billets and vicinity shelled by 4.2	
		1.30 PM	ST AUGUSTE woods bombarded by 30th Bty for enemy shelling LENS Rd	
		2.30 PM	30th & 5th Siege bombarded trench H19a 8.0 – H19a 7.8.	
			Ammunition expended 488 Lyddite	ON.

1875 Wt. W593/826 1,000,000 4/15 J.B.C. & A. A.D.S.S./Forms/C. 2118.

Instructions regarding War Diaries and Intelligence Summaries are contained in F. S. Regs., Part II. and the Staff Manual respectively. Title Pages will be prepared in manuscript.

WAR DIARY
or
~~INTELLIGENCE SUMMARY~~
(Erase heading not required.)

of 43rd Bde R.F.A

(154.)

Army Form C. 2118

Place	Date	Hour	Summary of Events and Information	Remarks and references to Appendices
	8-12-15	8 AM.	40th Battery fired into BENIFONTAINE in retaliation for enemy shelling trenches in G10	36c NW 3 & part 1204
		9.20 AM	Enemy shelling LENS–BETHUNE Road 30th Battery retaliated on Trench S of WOODS	
		10 AM	Bombardment. Have in front line trench H 13c 4 6 and 50 yds N of it. effect much better than usual	
		10.40 AM.	Germans shelling 65 METRE POINT 30th Battery retaliated on ST AUGUSTE WOODS	
		11.15 AM	30th Battery fired into ST AUGUSTE in retaliation for enemy shelling LENS–BETHUNE Road	
		12.10 PM	40th Battery fired into support trenches ~~W~~ of HULLUCH in retaliation of enemy shelling our trenches in front of HULLUCH.	
		1.15 PM.	30th Bty fire on ST AUGUSTE Woods in retaliation for enemy shelling FOSSE 7.	
		2 PM	Bombardment. Have in front line trench H 19 d 0.8 – 50 yds south of it, could not fire all rounds on account of enemies aircraft.	
		4 PM	40th Bty fired into HULLUCH in retaliation for enemy shelling old German front line Ammunition expended 352 Lyddite.	O.R.

1875 Wt. W593/826 1,000,000 4/15 J.B.C. & A. A.D.S.S./Forms/C. 2118.

Instructions regarding War Diaries and Intelligence Summaries are contained in F. S. Regs., Part II. and the Staff Manual respectively. Title Pages will be prepared in manuscript.

WAR DIARY
or
~~INTELLIGENCE SUMMARY~~
(Erase heading not required.)

of 43rd Bde RFA

(155)

Army Form C. 2118

Place	Date	Hour	Summary of Events and Information	Remarks and references to Appendices
	9-12-15		40th Battery fired on the enemies front line trench H13c4.6 and 50yds N of it.	36cNW3 & pt 1274
		2.20 PM.	40th Battery fired in retaliation on German front line H13c4.6 for enemy shelling our front line. Ammunition expended 218 Lyddite	ON.
	10-12-15		Bombardment Blow in front line of trench from H19a80 to 50yds N of it, very effective	
		11.15AM	Enemy retaliated on the front line trench opposite H19a80 and also on POSEN STREET	
		12 noon	40th Battery retaliated on HULLUCH	
		11.25AM	30th Battery fired at Batteries at M18d7.8 & N8c60 at the request of the French	
		2PM.	Bombardment Blow in front line trench from H19a9.3 to 50yds N of it. Fairly effective all Batteries	
		3.30 PM	40th Battery retaliated on HULLUCH. For enemy shelling our front & support trenches of the Left Bde	
			40th Battery had 3 prematures today one man wounded. Ammunition expended 111 Lyddite	ON

1875 Wt. W593/826 1,000,000 4/15 J.B.C. & A. A.D.S.S./Forms/C. 2118.

Instructions regarding War Diaries and Intelligence Summaries are contained in F. S. Regs., Part II. and the Staff Manual respectively. Title Pages will be prepared in manuscript.

WAR DIARY
or
~~INTELLIGENCE~~ SUMMARY
(Erase heading not required.)

of 43rd Bde RFA

(156)

Army Form C. 2118

Place	Date	Hour	Summary of Events and Information	Remarks and references to Appendices
	11-12-15		This evening 30th Bty forward Howitzer goes up into the Chalk PIT.	36CNW3T pub 1284
		11.45	Bombardment H7C11 & 50 yds N of it 40th & 5th Siege result of bombardment was very poor indeed	
		2PM & 3PM	Two short bombardments of 3 minutes each at TRENCH C at PUITS 14 BIS 30th & 5th Siege	
		3.30PM.	at 3.30. a dense column of smoke was observed rising behind the German lines the fire being at FOSSES de LENS this continued till dark.	
			Batteries located by 30th Battery	
		3.30 PM	H26 B33.	
		4.20 PM.	on line between B33C14 and M5d82	
		4.30 PM	3 direct hits by 4.2 How on 30th Battery officers mess latrine demolished, shells coming from LENS.	
			40th Battery had 2 prematures Ammunition expended 280 Lyddite	RN

1875 Wt. W593/826 1,000,000 4/15 J.B.C. & A. A.D.S.S./Forms/C. 2118.

Instructions regarding War Diaries and Intelligence Summaries are contained in F. S. Regs., Part II. and the Staff Manual respectively. Title Pages will be prepared in manuscript.

WAR DIARY
or
~~INTELLIGENCE SUMMARY~~
(Erase heading not required.)

of 43rd Bde RFA

(157)

Army Form C. 2118

Place	Date	Hour	Summary of Events and Information	Remarks and references to Appendices
	12-12-15		2 Lt G Ramsden posted to the 30th Battery from 1st DAC	36c NW 3 & part 12 & 4
		2.15 PM	Bombardment. Raw in front line trench. from H13c 4.5 to 50 yds N of it. 40th Bty & 5th Siege	
			effect of bombardment fairly good	
		3.40 PM	A heavy bombardment all along our front line 30th Battery retaliated on BENIFONTAINE	
			and BOIS HUGO WOODS. 40th Bty retaliated on BENIFONTAINE and on German front line	
			N of HULLUCH	
			40th Battery had two prematures, one gunner severely wounded	
			Ammunition Expended 289 Lyddite 6 Shrapnel	ON
	13-12-15.		Communication established with Howitzers in CHALK PIT WOOD	
			Bombardment Raw in front line trench for 50 yds S of Point H13c 4.2 40th & 5th Siege	
		10 AM.		
		2 PM	Bombardment. Raw in front line trench for 50 yds N of Point H19a 8.0. 30th & 5th Siege effect bad	
			There was slight activity on PUITS 14 BIS during the day	
			Ammunition Expended. 356 Lyddite.	ON

1875 Wt. W593/826 1,000,000 4/15 J.B.C. & A. A.D.S.S./Forms/C. 2118.

Instructions regarding War Diaries and Intelligence Summaries are contained in F. S. Regs., Part II. and the Staff Manual respectively. Title Pages will be prepared in manuscript.

WAR DIARY or ~~INTELLIGENCE SUMMARY~~ of 43rd Bde RFA.

(Erase heading not required.)

Army Form C. 2118

(158)

Place	Date	Hour	Summary of Events and Information	Remarks and references to Appendices
	14-12-15		Trench H13d 2.5 – 5.9 30th Battery effect good	36cNW3 & part 1 2 & 4.
		1.15 – 2 PM	The 5th Siege Bty have limited to 2 rds per gun per day consequently did not fire today at all. Ammunition expended 243 Lyddite	AN
	15-12-15		During the afternoon FOSSE 7 was shelled heavily between the 5th Siege & 40th Bty but during the shelling 3 fell amongst the 40th Battery killing 6 men & wounding 2.	
		11 AM	Bombardment 30th Bty PUITS 14 BIS Trench A effect fair no retaliation. 30th Bty had 3 prematures no casualties. Ammunition expended 197 Lyddite	AN
	16-12-15		Orders came in for CAPT. J. T. PRICE. RFA 30th Bty to proceed to England for service with a new unit	
		3 PM	30th Bty fired 40 rds into ST PIERRE at 3 PM because of a report that an engineers dump was situated there. Ammunition expended 156 Lyddite.	AN

Instructions regarding War Diaries and Intelligence Summaries are contained in F. S. Regs., Part II. and the Staff Manual respectively. Title Pages will be prepared in manuscript.

WAR DIARY
or
INTELLIGENCE SUMMARY
(Erase heading not required.)

43rd Brigade RFA.

(159)

Army Form C. 2118

Place	Date	Hour	Summary of Events and Information	Remarks and references to Appendices
	17-12-15.		In future the Artillery Groups supporting 1st Division Front will be known as Right left and Howitzer Group instead of "HINTON", "SCOTT", and "SHARP" groups.	36c NW 3 & Part 1 2 & 4
		2.5 PM.	30th Battery fired 50 rds unto the trench in H13C as a blind preparatory to the registering of the CHALK PIT Howitzer	
		2.45 PM.	30th Bty fired 40 rds unto FOSSE 11 and the East end of DOUBLE CRASSIER at the request of the French. Ammunition expended 179. Lyddite.	O.R.
	18-12-15		CAPT. J.T. PRICE RFA went to England. Ammunition expended 130 Lyddite	O.R.
	19-12-15.	11 AM	The Howitzer in the CHALK PIT. registered today at 11 AM only 3 shots were necessary.	
			Driver wounded in 40th Battery. Ammunition expended 62 Lyddite.	O.R.

1875 Wt. W593/826 1,000,000 4/15 J.B.C. & A. A.D.S.S./Forms/C. 2118.

Army Form C. 2118

Instructions regarding War Diaries and Intelligence Summaries are contained in F. S. Regs., Part II. and the Staff Manual respectively. Title Pages will be prepared in manuscript.

WAR DIARY
or
~~INTELLIGENCE SUMMARY~~

of 43rd Bde RFA

(Erase heading not required.)

(160)

Place	Date	Hour	Summary of Events and Information	Remarks and references to Appendices
	20-12-15.		N MAROC was heavily shelled at intervals through the day, the 30th Battery retaliated on N 7 d 9.3., CITÉ ST PIERRE, and CITÉ ST JEANNE D'ARC with 70 rds. Ammunition expended 69 Lyddite	36C NW 3 & part 1 2 & 4. ARJ
	21-12-15	10 AM	Bombardment 30th Bty 20 rds on PUITS 14. BIS Trench B effect good	
		4 PM.	North MAROC was very severely shelled with Fieldguns & Howitzers	
	22-12-15		Ammunition expended 131 Lyddite	ARJ
	6	10 PM	LIEUT RITCHIE 40th Bty placed on the sick list from today	
			The CHALK PIT GUN fired 4 rds (one of which was blind) into H13c 4.2 under cover of 30th Bty firing on PUITS 14 BIS Ammunition expended 358 Lyddite.	ARJ
	23-12-15.	2 PM.	30th Battery Bombarded strong points at H25. b. 5.½ . 9½ and H19 d 2½ . 3. at 2 PM 40 rds fired much material thrown up from the latter place Ammunition expended 234 Lyddite	ARJ

1875 Wt. W593/826 1,000,000 4/15 J.B.C. & A. A.D.S.S./Forms/C. 2118.

Army Form C. 2118

WAR DIARY
or
~~INTELLIGENCE SUMMARY~~
(Erase heading not required.)

43rd Bde RFA

(161)

Instructions regarding War Diaries and Intelligence Summaries are contained in F. S. Regs., Part II. and the Staff Manual respectively. Title Pages will be prepared in manuscript.

Place	Date	Hour	Summary of Events and Information	Remarks and references to Appendices
	24-12-15	12-12.4	30th Battery fired on Trench A PUITS 14 BIS, with very good effect much material thrown up. Ammunition expended 285 Lyddite	36C NW 3 & part 12 T 4 arl
	25-12-15		We tried to be as quiet as possible today and there was "set piece". The Germans fired a few rounds from BENIFONTAINE and at midday N. LOOS and S. MAROC were fairly heavily shelled, to which we retaliated. Ammunition expended 216 Lyddite	arl
	26-12-15	2.20 PM	30th Battery fired 60 rounds at strong points H25C $8\frac{1}{2}.4\frac{1}{2}$. H25c 9.2, H25d 1.0 the effect was very good about 10 direct hits being obtained	
		8 PM	The French report that the Germans have cut their own wire about 2000 yds south of our junction with the French that is to say about the DOUBLE CRASSIER, probably in contemplation of an attack. 5th Siege + 40th Bty accordingly laid their night lines as far south as was able 30th Bty night lines FOSS 11 & FOSS 12. Ammunition expended 229 Lyddite	arl

1875 Wt. W593/826 1,000,000 4/15 J.B.C. & A. A.D.S.S./Forms/C. 2118.

Instructions regarding War Diaries and Intelligence Summaries are contained in F. S. Regs., Part II. and the Staff Manual respectively. Title Pages will be prepared in manuscript.

WAR DIARY
or
INTELLIGENCE SUMMARY
(Erase heading not required.)

43rd Bde RFA

(62)

Army Form C. 2118

Place	Date	Hour	Summary of Events and Information	Remarks and references to Appendices
	27-12-15		The "B" (CHALKPIT aun) gun fired 30 rds during the day at the front trench from H13c 5.0 to 4.5 and registered 24 direct hits	36c NW 3 & part 12 & 4
		2 PM.	30th Battery fired 50 rds at the front trench H25c.9.4. and c7.L	
			LIEUT. J. J. DONAGHUE. RFA 40th Bty was severely wounded also 1 gunner	
			2nd LIEUT P. Q. MUIRHEAD was posted from 30th Bty — 40th Bty and 2nd LIEUT L.F. HOANE was posted from 1st DAC to the 30th Bty. Ammunition expended 305 Lyddite	ad.
	28-12-15.		30th Bty bombarded trenches A & B at POITS 14 BIS the effect could not be observed	
		7-7.5. AM.	One gunner wounded in the 40th Bty. Ammunition expended 214 Lyddite	
	29-12-15	11 AM.	"B" gun fired 30 rds into the trench H13c 4.2 – 4.5 with very good effect 20 direct hits were registered, much material thrown up, two Huns thrown into the air, one minus a leg.	ad
		2 PM	30th Battery fired 25 rds at the trench H25c.9.4. effect quite good	

Instructions regarding War Diaries and Intelligence Summaries are contained in F. S. Regs., Part II. and the Staff Manual respectively. Title Pages will be prepared in manuscript.

WAR DIARY
or
~~INTELLIGENCE SUMMARY~~
(Erase heading not required.)

43rd Bde RFA

(163)

Army Form C. 2118

Place	Date	Hour	Summary of Events and Information	Remarks and references to Appendices
	29-12-15		30th Battery fired 15 rds at H25c7.4 on account of bad light, the effect could not	36cNW3T [illegible]
		3.15 PM	be observed. Ammunition expended 22 [illegible] Lyddite	
	30-12-15		"B" gun fired at H13a 4.2 – H13c 4.2 with fairly good effect through the day	[initials]
			20 rds fired 12 hits	
			Both 30th & 5th Siege reported a Battery firing at about H9d 8.8. between 12.30 PM & 1 PM	
		2 PM.	30th Battery bombarded H25c 8½.7 effect very good	
		3 PM	Bombarded H25c 6.5 effect again very good. Ammunition expended 168. Lyddite	[initials]
	31-12-15		"B" gun fired 17 rds on trench H13c 4.2 – 4.5 and registered 14 direct hits	
			Night lines of 40th Battery altered as follows (a) H13d.2.5. (b) H13b.3.0. (c) H13b.1.7. (d). H7c.4.4.	
			on account of recent enemy activity in the North. Ammunition expended 324 Lyddite.	[initials]

1875 Wt. W593/826 1,000,000 4/15 J.B.C. & A. A.D.S.S./Forms/C. 2118.

1914-1916
1ST DIVISION TROOPS

T

43 ~~XLIII.~~ BRIGADE R.F.A.

AUG 1914 - MAY 1916

BROKEN UP

Gds. Divn.
G. S.
WAR DIARY APPENDICES
JUL 1917

1ST DIVISION

H.Q.,
43RD BRIGADE R.F.A.

JAN - MAY 1916

1st Divisional Artillery.

H. Q. 43rd BRIGADE R.F.A. :: JANUARY 1916.

SECRET

WAR DIARY
or
~~INTELLIGENCE SUMMARY~~
(Erase heading not required.)

(180)

0499/576

Date	Hour	Summary of Events and Information	Remarks and references to Appendices
[illegible]-1-16		B gun fired 30 rds and obtained about 15 hits at H.30 a.4.2 – C.4.	
2	12-3pm	30th Battery fired 40 rds at H.25c 5½.7. and H.25a.6.6. shooting was very much affected by the high wind.	Ammunition expended
		MAJOR LONGSTAFF took over command of 30th Battery	224 lyddite
3-1-16.		MAJOR W.C.H. BELL 40th Battery went to a four-days course for senior officers at AIRE.	
		The enemy were very active on our front system of trenches in the morning. "B" gun fired 30 rds at H.32c 4.2 – a.4.2 effect only fair on account of wind.	Ammunition expended
		Most of the enemies firing came from WINGLES	242 lyddite
3-1-16		40th Division relieved tonight by part of the dismounted Cavalry Division	
		[illegible] the enemy retaliated with 5" [illegible]	

Army Form C. 2118

WAR DIARY
or
~~INTELLIGENCE SUMMARY~~

(Erase heading not required.)

Instructions regarding War Diaries and Intelligence Summaries are contained in F. S. Regs., Part II. and the Staff Manual respectively. Title Pages will be prepared in manuscript.

43rd Bde RFA

(181)

124

Place	Date	Hour	Summary of Events and Information	Remarks and references to Appendices
	3-1-16		Enemy shelled our front line of trenches very heavily indeed we retaliated	36 N W 3 T part 1 2 T 4
		1.15-2PM	on their communication trenches in H 19 b Ammunition expended 171 Lyddite	36 C GN 1/40,000
	4-1-16.		Tonight the remainder of the dismounted cavalry Division relieve 47th Div in C sector and half the 47th Division relieve the French in the left sector	
			FOSSE 7 shelled slightly during the morning	
			40th Battery retaliated on communication trenches in H.13.c and Wood 3 CITÉ ST EMILE, PUITS 14 BIS and H31 b 27 Ammunition expended 102 Lyddite	GN
	5-1-16.		Trenches in H.19.c were shelled with 4.2	
		12-12.45	The left hand chimney of METALLURGIQUE works demolished by our 9.2	
			Ammunition expended 155 Lyddite	GN
	6-1-16.		Last night the 47th Div took over the RT sector of the French the 1st Div extended its front down to H 31 c 6.9. on the	

1875 Wt. W593/826 1,000,000 4/15 J.B.C.&A. A.D.S.S./Forms/C.2118.

Army Form C. 2118

125

WAR DIARY

or

~~INTELLIGENCE SUMMARY~~

(Erase heading not required.)

of 43rd Bde R.F.A.

(182)

Instructions regarding War Diaries and Intelligence Summaries are contained in F. S. Regs., Part II. and the Staff Manual respectively. Title Pages will be prepared in manuscript.

Place	Date	Hour	Summary of Events and Information	Remarks and references to Appendices
	6-1-16		Night of the 3rd/4th 2nd Welsh Battalion forms the garrison of LOOS	36 H W 3 & part 12 S 4
		2.15 PM	30th Battery fired 40 rds at the new trench H25 d.5.9 — H25 c.5.1.	36 C
			B gun fired 43 rds and obtained 27 hits on the trench H13 c.4.2. — H13 a.4.2, effect very good. Ammunition expended 231 Lyddite.	O.N. 1/40,000
	7-1-16		A very quiet day, no activity at all observed on our trenches.	
		3 PM	"B" gun fired 11 rds. Ammunition Expended 154 Lyddite.	O.N.
	8-1-16.		Germans very active up to 10.15 AM on communication trenches and shelled LENS RD redoubt.	
	12	30 AM	Batteries round FOSSE 7 shelled with heavy howitzers.	O.N.
	2	15 PM	65 metre point shelled by about 15 - 105 mm.	
			30th Battery fired 40 HE on H25b 5-1. to H25d 5.9. (bombardment). A good deal of material thrown up.	

1875 Wt. W593/826 1,000,000 4/15 J.B.C. & A. A.D.S.S./Forms/C. 2118.

Instructions regarding War Diaries and Intelligence Summaries are contained in F. S. Regs., Part II. and the Staff Manual respectively. Title Pages will be prepared in manuscript.

WAR DIARY
or
~~INTELLIGENCE SUMMARY~~
(Erase heading not required.)

of 43rd Bde RFA

(183)

Army Form C. 2118

126

Place	Date	Hour	Summary of Events and Information	Remarks and references to Appendices
			B gun fired 20 rds on H13a 4 2 – H13c 4 2	36C NW 3 & parts 1 2 & 4
			5th Bage fired 10 HE in retaliation for enemy shelling CHALK PIT Wood with 150 mm	36b & C
			Ammunition expended 91 lyddite.	1/40,000
	9-1-16		A great deal more heavy shell on our front line trenches than usual 5th Bage	ahl
			fired 22 HE & 12 AP shell in retaliation Trenches in G18d & G30d informed	
			that the fire seemed to come from BENIFONTAINE & WINGLES	
		11 AM	There was a burst of fire of all natures over LOOS.	
		1.15 PM	The Germans had a burst of fire of all natures over our front	
			B gun fired 22 rds and had 22 direct hits & 3 blinds.	
			Ammunition expended 140 lyddite	
	10-1-16		Last night 40th Bde & 39th Bde took part in a bombardment preparatory to the RRR [illegible] PUITS 14 BIS	ahl

1577 Wt. W595/826 1,000,000 4/15 J.B.C. & A. A.D.S.S./Forms/C. 2118

Instructions regarding War Diaries and Intelligence Summaries are contained in F. S. Regs., Part II. and the Staff Manual respectively. Title Pages will be prepared in manuscript.

WAR DIARY
or
~~INTELLIGENCE SUMMARY~~
(Erase heading not required.)

43rd Bde R.F.A.

(184)

Army Form C. 2118

127

Place	Date	Hour	Summary of Events and Information	Remarks and references to Appendices
			In future the following nomenclature will be used on the IVth Corps front.	36c N.W. 3 & parts 1 & 4 36b & c 1/40,000
			(a) RIGHT SECTOR for Rt Division frontage.	
			Maroc Section for Rt Bde frontage from M9d 2.6. – M5b 1.5	
			LOOS Section for L Bde frontage M5b 1.5 – H31c 6.9	
			(b) LEFT SECTOR for L Division frontage 14 BIS Section for Rt Bde frontage from H31c 6.9 – H19a 1.8.	
			HULLUCH Section from L. Bde frontage from H19a 1.8 – G12a 9.3	
		1.30 PM	4.5" How fired 22 rds HE in retaliation for 30 rds fired (150 mm) in H20c 4.8 at about 1.30 PM	
			8" gun fired 30 rds 27 hits	
			Ammunition expended 505 Lyddite	
				APJ

1875 Wt. W593/826 1,000,000 4/15 J.B.C. & A. A.D.S.S./Forms/C. 2118.

Instructions regarding War Diaries and Intelligence Summaries are contained in F. S. Regs., Part II. and the Staff Manual respectively. Title Pages will be prepared in manuscript.

WAR DIARY

or

~~INTELLIGENCE SUMMARY~~

(Erase heading not required.)

Army Form C. 2118

43rd Bde RFA

(125)

128

Place	Date	Hour	Summary of Events and Information	Remarks and references to Appendices
	11-1-16		5th Siege engaged H 20 b 2.9. where there is an observation station suspected with 13 HE	36c N W 3 & pt 12 F 4 Ed 4 c 1/40,000
		2.30 PM	B gun fired 30 rds and observed 20 direct hits.	
			Hostile mining is reported to be directed against a point in our front line immediately North of the NORTHERN SAP in H 13 a 0.5 Ammunition expended 133 lyddite	
	12-1-16	1 PM	1st Corps Artillery bombarded the HAIRPIN about 1 PM	a/N
			This morning 30th Battery was ordered to destroy enemy batteries at N 3 c 2.8. F M 18088	
			30th Battery fired on enemy trench mortar at H 19 d 3.3. with very good effect.	
			A heavy hostile minenwerfer (200 lbs) was observed from school house G 3 c 1.4 firing from enemy second line trench about M 4 c 9.8. in the direction of Artillery Row.	
			The actual position of the smoke of discharge was observed, & was completely silenced by the 30th Battery who got 2 direct hits on that part of trench	
			Ammunition expended 364 lyddite	a/N

1875 Wt. W593/826 1,000,000 4/15 J.B.C. & A. A.D.S.S./Forms/C. 2118.

Instructions regarding War Diaries and Intelligence Summaries are contained in F. S. Regs., Part II. and the Staff Manual respectively. Title Pages will be prepared in manuscript.

WAR DIARY
or
~~INTELLIGENCE SUMMARY~~
(Erase heading not required.)

43rd Bde M.G.A. (186)

Army Form C. 2118

Place	Date	Hour	Summary of Events and Information	Remarks and references to Appendices
	13-1-16	9.30 AM	FOSSE 7 was shelled with 8" and the CHALK PIT had about 50 5.9 into it but none touched "B" gun who fired 30 rds during the course of the day	36C.N.W.3 & parts 1, 2 & 4 36 b.T.C. 1/40,000
			Bombardment 30 rds on strong points H 25 c. 9 7 and H 25 c 7 4. Ammunition expended 251 Lyddite	a.N.
	14-1-16	2.15 PM	Bombardment 30th Battery fired on communication trenches H 25 d 5.9 to H 25 b 6.1 40 rds, effect only fair	
		8.30 PM	MAROC shelled at 8.30 PM with 5.9.	
			B Gun fired 30 rds. Ammunition expended 139 Lyddite	
	15-1-16		Enemy fairly quiet except at FOSSE 7 which was shelled at a slow rate of fire all the afternoon with 5.9	a.N.
			"B" Gun fired 20 rds H 13 a 4 2 to H 13 c 4 2 15 direct hits.	
			30th Battery fired at H 25 d 5.9 to H 25 b 5.1 effect good (40 rds)	

1875 Wt. W593/826 1,000,000 4/15 J.B.C. & A. A.D.S.S./Forms/C. 2118.

Instructions regarding War Diaries and Intelligence Summaries are contained in F. S. Regs., Part II. and the Staff Manual respectively. Title Pages will be prepared in manuscript.

WAR DIARY
or
~~INTELLIGENCE SUMMARY~~ 43rd Bde RFA (187)
(Erase heading not required.)

Army Form C. 2118

150

Place	Date	Hour	Summary of Events and Information	Remarks and references to Appendices
		11.30 AM	gun flashes were located at H9d 8.2	36c NW 3 & parts of 36 SW 1-2-4, 36c 1/40,000
			This morning "B" gun was handed over to D73 Bty 15th Division, two guns of	
			the 40th Bty were handed over to the 30th Battery who also receive one gun from D73	
			in exchange for that in the CHALKPIT	
			30th Battery is divided into two 4 gun Batteries positions M2C77 & M2C44	
			under the 15th Div as counterbatteries. Ammunition expended 202 rounds.	
			Capt E.A. WOODS RFA slightly wounded by 5.9 shell, still at duty.	
	16-1-16		Bde marches out of action (less 30th & BAC) to rest billets in LAPUGNOY	
			Wagon lines moved off early afternoon.	
			Our old HQ taken over by Colonel INGHAM. 73rd Bde 15th Div	
			Ammunition expended 67 rounds	

1875 Wt. W593/826 1,000,000 4/15 J.B.C. & A. A.D.S.S./Forms/C. 2118.

Instructions regarding War Diaries and Intelligence Summaries are contained in F. S. Regs., Part II. and the Staff Manual respectively. Title Pages will be prepared in manuscript.

WAR DIARY
or
~~INTELLIGENCE SUMMARY~~
(Erase heading not required.)

43rd Bde R.F.A.

Army Form C. 2118

(188)

151

Place	Date	Hour	Summary of Events and Information	Remarks and references to Appendices
	17-1-16		LT COL F.L. SHARP RFA & LT RITCHIE went on leave	CRJ 36cNW&SE 1/40,000
	18-1-16 to 26-1-16		nothing to report at rest	
	27-1-16		at Rest 30th Bty at S. MAROC had a premature today resulting in 3 wounded	
	28-1-16		LT COL F.L. SHARP CMG RFA returns from leave and assumes command of 15th DA during the absence of Brig. Gen G.N. CARTWRIGHT D.S.O. RFA.	CRJ
	29-1-16 to 31-1-16		at rest nothing to report	CRJ

1875 Wt. W593/826 1,000,000 4/15 J.B.C. & A. A.D.S.S./Forms/C. 2118.

Instructions regarding War Diaries and Intelligence Summaries are contained in F. S. Regs., Part II. and the Staff Manual respectively. Title Pages will be prepared in manuscript.

WAR DIARY
or
~~INTELLIGENCE SUMMARY~~
(Erase heading not required.)

43rd Bde RFA

(189)

Army Form C. 2118

Place	Date	Hour	Summary of Events and Information	Remarks and references to Appendices
	1-2-16.		Brigadier General Cartwright D.S.O. returns from leave and reassumed command of 1st DA	36C NW 3 & parts 1, 2 & 4 36b & c 1/40,000
			3 men 30th Battery wounded by premature	
	2-2-16. to 5-2-16.		at rest nothing to report	O.N. O.N.
	6-2-16		at rest, one section of 30th Battery (30 A) came out under Lt Stewart and billeted in LAPUGNOY.	
	7-2-16.		Brigade Route March, as follows, MARLES - LOZINGHEM - ALLOUAGNE - BURBURE - HORIONVILLE - ECQUEDUQUES - FAUCQUENHEM - LIERES - ST HILAIRE - COTTES - BOURECQ LILLERS - ALLOUAGNE - LAPUGNOY, starting at 7.55 AM and arriving back at our billets at 3PM	O.N. O.N.
	8-2-16.		Capt. J.H. TURNER. RNZA 40th Battery joins the New Zealand contingent in EGYPT.	
	9-2-16		At rest.	O.N.

1875 Wt. W593/826 1,000,000 4/15 J.B.C. & A. A.D.S.S./Forms/C. 2118.

Instructions regarding War Diaries and Intelligence Summaries are contained in F. S. Regs., Part II. and the Staff Manual respectively. Title Pages will be prepared in manuscript.

WAR DIARY
or
INTELLIGENCE SUMMARY
(Erase heading not required.)

43rd Bde R.F.A.

(190)

Army Form C. 2118

Place	Date	Hour	Summary of Events and Information	Remarks and references to Appendices
	10-2-16.		Staff ride for 1st Division Colonel F.L. SHARP C.M.G. went.	36a 36c / 40,000 3rd edition 36C S.C.1 Edition 6.
	11-2-16. to 15-2-16.		at rest.	
	16-2-16		Divisional Artillery starts moving up into action	
			43rd Bde as follows,	
			30th Battery go into position of B.76. Bty RFA at M2d O.6.	
			40th Battery put 4 guns into position of 21st LONDON Bty RFA at M2C.2.1 two guns in position of 22nd LONDON Bty R.F.A. at G B2d½.2.	
			The 43rd Bde AC remains at VERQUIN	
			The 2nd Siege RGA joins the Group tomorrow, when the Colonel takes over the 1st Division Howitzer Group. Position one section M2b 8.9. and one section at L6 a 8.9.	
			Tonight two sections of the 40th Battery and one section of the 30th Battery go up to action. CAPT. E.A. WOODS has been detailed to command a Battery in the 38th Division	AW

Army Form C. 2118

WAR DIARY
or
~~INTELLIGENCE SUMMARY~~ 43rd Bde R.F.A

(Erase heading not required.)

(191)

Instructions regarding War Diaries and Intelligence Summaries are contained in F. S. Regs., Part II. and the Staff Manual respectively. Title Pages will be prepared in manuscript.

Place	Date	Hour	Summary of Events and Information	Remarks and references to Appendices
	17-2-16		Bde HQ move to LES BREBIS at L36c ½.6. and 1st Division take over the defence of the line	36c NW & c $\frac{1}{40,000}$ 36c SW 1 edition 6.
			30th Battery register south of the DOUBLE CRASSIER and 40th Battery North of it	
			O mine was exploded this morning at the EAST end of the copse at about M6c 8.8. and the enemy occupied the crater	
		2PM.	Communication trenches in G33 d 5.0. shelled with 10 rds 4.2	
			30th & 40th Bty registered the guns they have already got in action the remainder of the guns come in tonight. Ammunition expended	
	18-2-16.		Copse Barrage as follows	
			2nd Phase German observation stations and machine gun emplacements between E end of Crassier and the railway junction in M 6d	

1875 Wt. W593/826 1,000,000 4/15 J.B.C. & A. A.D.S.S./Forms/C. 2118.

Instructions regarding War Diaries and Intelligence Summaries are contained in F. S. Regs., Part II. and the Staff Manual respectively. Title Pages will be prepared in manuscript.

WAR DIARY
or
~~INTELLIGENCE SUMMARY~~
(Erase heading not required.)

Army Form C. 2118

43rd Bde R.F.A.

(92)

Place	Date	Hour	Summary of Events and Information	Remarks and references to Appendices
			40th Battery 1 section M5c29. – M5c92.	36 a & 36 c 3rd edition 36 c SW 1 6th Edition
			2 sections M5d 5.5 – M6c 5.5	
			30th Battery 1 section M5c92. – M5d 5.5.	
			2 sections M6c 5.5. – M6b 5.3.	
			Right Group. (1). Eastern half of DOUBLE CRASSIER, (2). German front line system in M5c (3) CALONNE gun German front line trenches opposite the copse	
			Left Group. German front line and support trenches ~~[illegible]~~ north of the Double Crassier.	
			Rate of fire 1 rd per gun per minute	
			Night lines as follows.	
			30th Battery 1 gun M11 a 5.5	
			1 gun M11 a 1.1.	
			1 gun Trenches E of DOUBLE CRASSIER	
			1 gun Trenches round PUITS 11 2 guns tunnels South of DOUBLE CRASSIER	

1875 Wt. W593/826 1,000,000 4/15 J.B.C. & A. A.D.S.S./Forms/C. 2118.

Army Form C. 2118

Instructions regarding War Diaries and Intelligence Summaries are contained in F. S. Regs., Part II. and the Staff Manual respectively. Title Pages will be prepared in manuscript.

WAR DIARY
or
~~INTELLIGENCE SUMMARY~~
(Erase heading not required.)

43rd Bde RFA.

(193)

Place	Date	Hour	Summary of Events and Information	Remarks and references to Appendices
			40th Battery 2 guns enfilading trench in M5C	36a+6c. 1/40,000
			2 guns opposite Harts Crater	36cSCI
			2 guns opposite Harrison's Crater	6 edition 1/10,000
			2nd Siege Tunnels in railway to PUITS 16.	
			CAPT. E. A. WOODS departed to 38th Division. Ammunition expended 175 Lyddite	
	19-2-16.		42 Battery shelled the GRENAY Rd. in M1d & M2c from the direction of LENS	AM.
		2 PM	the same battery shelled trenches in M5C	
		2.3PM to 4PM	30th & 40th Batteries completed their registrations	
		11AM - 5.15PM	30th Battery bombarded the southern half of HARTS CRATER at the rate of 3 rds per hour	
		5.15-7.15	one round every 5 minutes.	
		11AM - 4.30PM	40th Battery bombarded the southern half of HARRISON's crater at the rate of 3 rds per hour, this rate was increased to 6 rds per hour and the area bombarded spread over the whole of the CRATER, on the infantry	

1875 Wt. W593/826 1,000,000 4/15 J.B.C. & A. A.D.S.S./Forms/C. 2118.

Instructions regarding War Diaries and Intelligence Summaries are contained in F. S. Regs., Part II. and the Staff Manual respectively. Title Pages will be prepared in manuscript.

WAR DIARY
or
~~INTELLIGENCE SUMMARY~~
(Erase heading not required.)

43rd Bde RFA.

(94)

Army Form C. 2118

Place	Date	Hour	Summary of Events and Information	Remarks and references to Appendices
			having cleared out of the trenches opposite.	36a NW&C 1/40000 3rd edition
		5.15 PM.	At the request of Brig General Davies 3rd Infantry Bde the rate of fire was increased to 12 rds per hour till 7.15 PM	36cSW1 6th edition 1/10,000 ORD
		7.30 PM.	At 7.30 the 1st Bat Scots G. took HARRISON'S crater. Ammunition expended 262 lyddite	
	20-2-16		Hostile Artillery was more active today, they shelled BULLY GRENAY, S. MAROC, from the direction of LENS and also kept up a continuous fire on Harrisons Crater. 30th Battery fired on HART'S crater; and 40th Battery on HARRISON'S Crater, this was kept up all day one round every ten minutes	
			A small trench mortar and 4.5" How offensive was carried out against the apex of the triangle at M5C2.9 between 2.30 PM and 5 PM. The 4.5 Howitzer fire was undertaken by 40th Battery	
			Programme of offensive	
			4.30 PM. 4.5 Howitzers concentrated their fire just inside the apex of the triangle and fired 30 rds deliberate over about ½ an hour	

1875 Wt. W593/826 1,000,000 4/15 J.B.C. & A. A.D.S.S./Forms/C. 2118.

Instructions regarding War Diaries and Intelligence Summaries are contained in F. S. Regs., Part II. and the Staff Manual respectively. Title Pages will be prepared in manuscript.

WAR DIARY
or
~~INTELLIGENCE SUMMARY~~
(Erase heading not required.)

43rd Bde RFA.

(195)

Army Form C. 2118

Place	Date	Hour	Summary of Events and Information	Remarks and references to Appendices
			To enable them to do this our trenches were cleared from SAP J. to the Junction of 2nd + 3rd Inf Bdes. at M5c 4.7. Ammunition Expended 208 Lyddite.	36a + b + c 1/40,000. 3rd Edition AN
	21-2-16.		at 9.15 AM minnenwerfers were engaged as follows,	36c S.W.1 6th Edition 1/10,000.
			M4d 1.3. 30th Battery 12 rounds.	
			M5c 4.5. 40th Battery 20 rds.	
			The GOC 1st Division was very pleased with the work done by the 40th Battery on the 21st inst, in firing at the apex of the triangle and directs that at least 20 rounds per day be steered into the same locality in retaliation or otherwise in future.	
		9PM	40th Battery fired about 70 rounds into M6c 7.3.	
			one gun of the 51st Battery and one howitzer of the 40th Battery were today put into LOOS under the Howitzer Group. LT. A. PROBART JONES in charge, these guns are so placed as to enfilade the trench from M5c 2.9. to M4d 8.4. the guns were successfully got in. Ammunition expended 432 Lyddite.	AN

Instructions regarding War Diaries and Intelligence Summaries are contained in F. S. Regs., Part II. and the Staff Manual respectively. Title Pages will be prepared in manuscript.

WAR DIARY
or
~~INTELLIGENCE SUMMARY~~
(Erase heading not required.)

Army Form C. 2118

43rd Bde RFA

(196)

Place	Date	Hour	Summary of Events and Information	Remarks and references to Appendices
	22-2-16		a fairly busy day, the enemy shelled Maroc Grenay & Fosse 7	36a b. & c 3rd edition 1/40,000 36c SW1 6th Edition 1/10,000
		1PM	Soon after 1PM we received intimation from DA that the French had authoritative information that the enemy intended to attack south of our line near Souchez, the bombardment to commence at 2PM and the attack to be at 5PM.	
		2.15PM.	at 2.15PM the French report that they captured 2 prisoners who declared that there would be an attack between 2.30 and 3PM on their front.	
		3.25PM.	at 3.25 PM very heavy shelling round SOUCHEZ & VIMY was reported	
		4.30PM	intimation was received that the enemy were occupying the NE end of HARTS crater. The 1st Infantry Bde, therefore cleared the trenches from 4.30 PM. till 7PM and 30th Bty fired at the rate of 30 rds per hour	
			Ammunition Expended. 200 Lyddite.	GN
	23-2-16		The enemy shelled GRENAY FOSSE 7 with 4.2 How. during the morning	
			Ammunition Expended 403. Lyddite	GN

Instructions regarding War Diaries and Intelligence Summaries are contained in F. S. Regs., Part II. and the Staff Manual respectively. Title Pages will be prepared in manuscript.

WAR DIARY
or
~~INTELLIGENCE SUMMARY~~

(Erase heading not required.)

43rd Bde RFA

(197)

Army Form C. 2118.

Place	Date	Hour	Summary of Events and Information	Remarks and references to Appendices
	24-2-16.		The French having had a slight reverse at VERDUN leave has been stopped.	36a b c 3rd edition 1/40,000
		11.40 AM	4.2 Hows fired 20 rds on West end of Double Crassier	36c SW1 6th edition 1/10,000
			All night lines were checked and the houses in M11c were registered. Ammunition expended 149 [illegible]	
	25-2-16.		Hostile artillery was not very active.	
			A suspected mine shaft about 70 yds beyond our barricade on the northern arm of the Double Crassier at M4d 5.6 was registered and bombarded	
		7PM	A small operation took place with the object of capturing HARTS. Crater the tasks of the batteries were as follows.	
			<u>30th Battery</u> front line trenches M6c 9.8 – M6b 4.1.	
			<u>40th Battery</u> Front " " M6c 9.8 - M6c.0.5.	
			<u>2nd Hwz Battery</u> M6b 4.1. — M6b 3.3.	
			The diary of the operation is as follows.	

1875 Wt. W593/826 1,000,000 4/15 J.B.C. & A. A.D.S.S./Forms/C. 2118.

Instructions regarding War Diaries and Intelligence Summaries are contained in F. S. Regs., Part II. and the Staff Manual respectively. Title Pages will be prepared in manuscript.

WAR DIARY
or
~~INTELLIGENCE~~ SUMMARY
(Erase heading not required.)

43rd Bde RFA.

Army Form C. 2118

(193)

Place	Date	Hour	Summary of Events and Information	Remarks and references to Appendices
		7PM	2 mines exploded under Harts Crater by 10173 Tunnelling company, the whole Division artillery open fire	36a b&c 3rd Ed. 1/40,000 36c SW 1 6th Ed. 1/10,000
		7.20PM.	ordered to increase fire to Btty fire 5 secs for 2 minutes and then return to Btty fire 10 secs.	
		8.24PM.	cease firing E of LOOS - PUITS 12. rd, 40th Battery continue	
		9.5PM	cease firing	
			net result a small post was established on the N.W. corner of Harts Crater. Ammunition expended 139 Lyddite.	
	26-2-16		A fairly quiet day Ammunition expended 1327 Lyddite.	
	27-2-16.		There was a good deal of activity North of the DOUBLE CRASSIER between LOOS. and MAROC, a regular bombardment seemed to be in progress.	
		11AM.	We fired 30 rds at the German front line between the craters at the request of the inf and again at 12.15 AM	

Instructions regarding War Diaries and Intelligence Summaries are contained in F. S. Regs., Part II. and the Staff Manual respectively. Title Pages will be prepared in manuscript.

WAR DIARY
or
~~INTELLIGENCE SUMMARY~~
(Erase heading not required.)

43rd Bde RFA

(199)

Army Form C. 2118

Place	Date	Hour	Summary of Events and Information	Remarks and references to Appendices
		12.45.	Fired 30 rds at the mine shaft on DOUBLE CRASSIER (northern arm) at about M4d 5.5½	36 a b & c. 3rd Ed. 1/40,000.
		2.3PM	registered the tunnel mouth at M5c 4.1 and shelled it at the request of B. General Thullier comdg 2nd Brigade.	36c SW1 6th Ed 1/10,000.
		4.35PM	Fired 27 rds in the apex of the triangle M5c 2.9.	
		5.15PM.	Fired 17 rds. on E end of Double Crassier	
		6PM.	12 rds fired on front line trench from M6c 9.7. – M6b 5.3.	
			2nd Heavy Bty registered M6c 2.4½ – M6c 9.7½. Ammunition expended 167 Lyddite. Shr	
	28-2-16		Fired 16 rds at the trenches opposite HARTS. Crater at 1.33AM and again at 4-30 AM at the request of the infantry communication was established this evening with the Left Battalion Left Bde at LOOS M6a 2.8.	
			Hostile Artillery was more active today a minenwerfer was located at about M10 c 6.6½.	

1875 Wt. W593/826 1,000,000 4/15 J.B.C. & A. A.D.S.S./Forms/C. 2118.

Instructions regarding War Diaries and Intelligence Summaries are contained in F. S. Regs., Part II. and the Staff Manual respectively. Title Pages will be prepared in manuscript.

WAR DIARY
or
INTELLIGENCE SUMMARY
(Erase heading not required.)

Army Form C. 2118

43rd Bde RFA

(200)

Place	Date	Hour	Summary of Events and Information	Remarks and references to Appendices
		4 PM	We exploded a small mine at the Double Crassier at 4 PM. and the Right Group	36 c N.W. 3rd Ed. 1/40,000
			followed it up with some shrapnel, this drew forth much reprisal from the enemy, which	36 c S.W. 1 6th Ed.
			we retaliated	1/10,000.
			The two guns called the LOOS TWINS were registered in 7 rds	
			LT MUIRHEAD returned from course today. Ammunition 336 Lyddite AM	
	29-2-16		A new system of communication with the infantry in the event of trench mortaring has	
			been established on the receipt of message MINNIE HART. or MINNIE Harrison, the	
			40th Battery will immediately fire 12 rds rapidly in the trenches opposite the crater	
			indicated	
			during the morning the enemy shelled the wagon line at FOSSE 2 with a 6" gun.	
			30th Battery 2 killed & 4 wounded. Ammunition expended. 204 Lyddite AM.	

1875 Wt. W593/826 1,000,000 4/15 J.B.C. & A. A.D.S.S./Forms/C. 2118.

SECRET

Instructions regarding War Diaries and Intelligence Summaries are contained in F. S. Regs., Part II. and the Staff Manual respectively. Title Pages will be prepared in manuscript.

WAR DIARY
or
~~INTELLIGENCE SUMMARY~~
(Erase heading not required.)

of 43rd Bde RFA

Army Form C. 2118

(201)

Place	Date	Hour	Summary of Events and Information	Remarks and references to Appendices
	1-3-16		4" gun obtained a direct hit on Group H.Q doing no damage on O.P. a Dropers post on the embankment at M10d 1.5. hit 4 times and the roof of it displaced. Ammunition expended 543 Lydite.	36 a l & c $\frac{1}{40,000}$. 3rd Edition 36 c S.W.1 $\frac{1}{10,000}$ Edition 6.
	2-3-16		Throughout the day heavy shells were fired between Loos Enclosure and the copse.	
			40th Battery fired one round ~~on separate~~ hour at the mineshaft on the Double Crassier at M4b 5½.5.	
			The Division on our left successfully exploded 3 mines under HOHENZOLLERN this evening and occupied the mine system. Ammunition expended. 489. Lydite.	
	3-3-16.		3rd Inf Bde relieves the 1st Inf Bde in the Maroc sector tonight.	
			2nd Siege Battery fired 12 rnds between our front line and the enemys at M10c 0.8½	

1875 Wt. W593/826 1,000,000 4/15 J.B.C. & A. A.D.S.S./Forms/C. 2118.

Army Form C. 2118

WAR DIARY
or
INTELLIGENCE SUMMARY
(Erase heading not required.)

of 43rd Bde RFA

(202)

Instructions regarding War Diaries and Intelligence Summaries are contained in F. S. Regs., Part II. and the Staff Manual respectively. Title Pages will be prepared in manuscript.

Place	Date	Hour	Summary of Events and Information	Remarks and references to Appendices
			as ordered in order that holes might be made to conceal machine gunners who are to be there to prevent the enemy coming too close, as we are digging a Russian sap there	36 c NW / 40,000 3rd Edition. 36c SW 1 / 10,000. Edition 6.
		10 AM.	this morning the 1st Division exchanged from the IV Corps to the 1st Corps.	
			Ammunition expended. 302 Lyddite.	AM.
	4-3-16.		Very quiet day except between 5 & 5.30 PM. when about 50 rds. 4.2 from the direction of CITE ST EDOUARD fell on the Hanau Rd by Artillery Row.	
			Ammunition expended. 462 Lyddite.	AM
	5-3-16		An aeroplane dropped 3 bombs on S. MAROC at 11.30 AM.	
			The signal box at M 6 b 3.4½ has disappeared. Ammunition expended 484 Lyddite. The LOOS towers fired 25 rds 4.5" 23 direct hits obtained on western face of Triangle	AM

1875 Wt. W593/826 1,000,000 4/15 J.B.C. & A. A.D.S.S./Forms/C. 2118.

Instructions regarding War Diaries and Intelligence Summaries are contained in F. S. Regs., Part II. and the Staff Manual respectively. Title Pages will be prepared in manuscript.

WAR DIARY
or
INTELLIGENCE SUMMARY
(Erase heading not required.)

of 43rd Bde RFA.

Army Form C. 2118

(203)

Place	Date	Hour	Summary of Events and Information	Remarks and references to Appendices
	6-3-16.		40th Battery fired 40 rds at the front line trench in M6c as ordered in Artillery bombardment.	36a 6+c 1/40,000. 3rd Edition
		4PM	We exploded a small camouflet on the Nathan Arm of the Double Crassier.	36c SW1 1/10,000 6th Edition
			40th Battery fired on the minestaft and were congratulated by General Pavies 3rd Inf Bde on their excellent shooting.	
			There was an inordinately large amount of MINNIE calls during the day about 300 rds being fired in all. Ammunition expended. 63 Lyddite.	JN
	7-3-16.		O 4.2 How. Battery fired 4 rds at our trenches at the N.W. end of Double Crassier	
		11.30	We fired 24 rds. at the minestaft crater on the Double Crassier	
			2nd Sieg Battery fired 28 HE and AP on the machine gun emplacement at M4c 6.1½ the series appeared effective 10 hits Ammunition Expended 307 Lyddite	

Instructions regarding War Diaries and Intelligence Summaries are contained in F. S. Regs., Part II. and the Staff Manual respectively. Title Pages will be prepared in manuscript.

WAR DIARY

or

~~INTELLIGENCE SUMMARY~~

(Erase heading not required.)

of 43rd Bde RFA.

(204)

Army Form C. 2118

Place	Date	Hour	Summary of Events and Information	Remarks and references to Appendices
	8-3-16.	9-30-10.30	The enemy fired about 200 5.9 Howitzer shells into Wigan and in the afternoon 3 PM to 4. about 100 rds	36c G+C 1/40,000. 3rd Edition
			Loos twins fired 29 rds and claimed 23 direct hits. Ammunition expended. 273 Lyddite.	36c S.W.1 1/10,000. Edition 6.
	9-3-16.		A large trench mortar was firing all day but owing to bad light it was impossible to locate it. Ammunition expended 125 Lyddite.	aR
	10-3-16.		A fairly quiet day. 60 5.9 was fired on the end of the Double Crassier in the afternoon.	
		4PM-5.30	3 minenwerfers shelled the end of the Double Crassier and the trenches north of it. We retaliated on the trenches S of the Crassier.	
			The trench M10a 6.1 – 6.3 was bombarded (27 rds) by order at 9.45 AM.	
			A minenwerfer was seen to fire from M10b7.8. but light was very bad and observation difficult. 5 hits were obtained on trench near it. Ammunition expended. 78 Lyddite.	aR

Instructions regarding War Diaries and Intelligence Summaries are contained in F. S. Regs., Part II. and the Staff Manual respectively. Title Pages will be prepared in manuscript.

WAR DIARY
or
~~INTELLIGENCE SUMMARY~~

(Erase heading not required.)

of 43rd Bde R.F.A.

Army Form C. 2118

(205).

Place	Date	Hour	Summary of Events and Information	Remarks and references to Appendices
	11-3-16.		40th Battery bombarded the front German trench in M6c by order	36c6+c 1/40,000. 3rd Edition
		1 P.M.	A machine gun emplacement reported at M6c 2½.6. by the Black Watch was engaged by 40th Battery	36cSW1 1/10,000. 6th Edition
		3.45	A minnenwerfer shot at the trenches of 1st Bn 1st Bde from near PUITS 16 at the request of the MUNSTERS Ammunition expended 154 lyddite	A.W.
	12-3-16.		At midday today an order came into force restricting the ammunition expenditure as follows	
			43rd Bde 550 per week.	
			2nd Siege Section 30 per week.	
			The LOOS towers 20 rds 4.5 and 14 HE & shrapnel for 18 pr	
			The west end of Double Crassier was shelled very heavily all day long	
			2nd Siege Battery fired 7 HE and 7 A.P. on the mineshaft at M4d 2½.4 obtained 5 direct hits. about 20 bombs were dropped in NOEUX-LES-MINES	Ammunition expended 307 lyddite A.W.

Instructions regarding War Diaries and Intelligence Summaries are contained in F. S. Regs., Part II. and the Staff Manual respectively. Title Pages will be prepared in manuscript.

WAR DIARY
or
~~INTELLIGENCE SUMMARY~~ of 43rd Bde RFA
(Erase heading not required.)

Army Form C. 2118

(206)

Place	Date	Hour	Summary of Events and Information	Remarks and references to Appendices
	13-3-16.		The 9.2 bombarded the mineshaft on the western end of the Double Crassier at 12 noon.	36c b+c.
			which caused a great deal of retaliation from the Hun,	1/40,000.
			Minnenwerfers were located and strafed at M10b 6.8½, M11a ½.9½.	3rd Edition
			The lone gun at CALONNE was put in the night before last, it is under the 54th Battery	36c SW1
			and fired 5 rds in registration. Ammunition expended 234 lyddite.	1/10,000 Edition 6.
	14-3-16.		FOSSE 6. shelled intermittently all day, one gun of 111th Battery (60 pr) knocked out.	
			The mine buildings got strafed badly also. Ammunition expended 31 lyddite.	
	15-3-16.		The 2nd Inf Bde relieved the 3rd Inf Bde. in the Maroc sector tonight.	
			Two large minnenwerfers firing on the Double Crassier at 8.45 AM. were accurately	
			located at M11a ½.9½. and M10b 3½.9.	
			German sentries were seen at their posts all day, two working parties at M6c.9.8. and M4d 5.3. located. Ammunition expended 80 lyddite	

1875 Wt. W593/826 1,000,000 4/15 J.B.C. & A. A.D.S.S./Forms/C. 2118.

Instructions regarding War Diaries and Intelligence Summaries are contained in F. S. Regs., Part II. and the Staff Manual respectively. Title Pages will be prepared in manuscript.

WAR DIARY
or
~~INTELLIGENCE SUMMARY~~
(Erase heading not required.)

of 43rd Bde R.F.A.

(207)

Army Form C. 2118

Place	Date	Hour	Summary of Events and Information	Remarks and references to Appendices
	16.3-16.	6 AM	We exploded four large mines under the Southern arm of Double Crassier, thus materially altering its appearance	36c b+c 1/40,000. 3rd Edition
			Sgt Pidcock Bde. Am. Col. received a commission as 2nd Lt.	36c S.W.1 1/10,000. Edition 6
			Minenwerfer located at M10b 9.4½. M10b. 2.5½. & M11a ½ . 9½.	
			A very heavy minenwerfer or aerial torpedo fired 6 rds on trenches in M4d..	
			Ammunition expended 43 Lyddite.	
	17.3-16.		Leave reports a fairly quiet day on the whole.	DW
		2.30-3.30	A 5.9 How fired about 100 rds on the Eastern edge of the South arm of Double Crassier	
			2nd Siege Battery retaliated with 9 H.E. & 11 A.P. Ammunition expended 64 Lyddite.	
	18.3-16.	1 PM	At the urgent request of the Black Watch we fired 40 rds on the Front line trench at the South end of Loos Crassier	AH

Instructions regarding War Diaries and Intelligence Summaries are contained in F. S. Regs., Part II. and the Staff Manual respectively. Title Pages will be prepared in manuscript.

WAR DIARY
or
~~INTELLIGENCE SUMMARY~~
(Erase heading not required.)

of 43rd Bde RFA

(208)

Army Form C. 2118

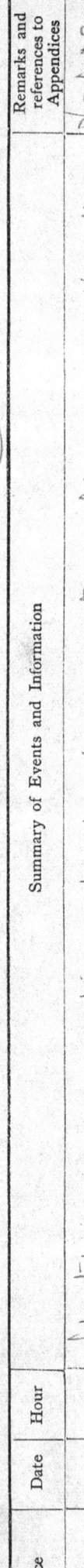

Place	Date	Hour	Summary of Events and Information	Remarks and references to Appendices
			White tapes were seen marking the site of a new trench between M4d 2½ . 3½.	36 a b & c
			M 4d 8 . 3½. Ammunition expended 15 Lyddite.	1/40,000. 3rd Edition.
	19-3-16		a good deal of shelling of LOOS with Heavy Artillery,	36 c S.W. 1
			the minnenwerfer at M11a ½ . 9½. fired on the trenches N of the Double Crassier	1/10,000. 6th Edition
			These were eventually silenced by 30th Battery.	
			a sniper was seen firing from M4c.7.1, an officer was observing for him through Field glasses	
			Ammunition expended 99 Lyddite.	
	20-3-16			O.N.
		7.30	a German mine was blown up near the W end of the Double Crassier, German field	
			guns & minnenwerfer fired at once. very little rifle & machine gun fire, all quiet in 20 minutes	
			Loos Crassier got shelled off and on all day	
			Ammunition expended 53 Lyddite	O.N.

1875 Wt. W593/826 1,000,000 4/15 J.B.C. & A. A.D.S.S./Forms/C. 2118.

Instructions regarding War Diaries and Intelligence Summaries are contained in F. S. Regs., Part II. and the Staff Manual respectively. Title Pages will be prepared in manuscript.

WAR DIARY
or
~~INTELLIGENCE SUMMARY~~
(Erase heading not required.)

of 43rd Bde RFA

(209)

Army Form C. 2118

Place	Date	Hour	Summary of Events and Information	Remarks and references to Appendices
	21-3-16.		The only apparent effect of the German mine yesterday is that 20 yds of the Faulkner Arm of the Double Crassier. having subsided about 5 yds. and also improving the view from PUTNEY HILL.. Ammunition expended 72 Lyddite	36 c 6 & c 1/40,000. 3rd Edition 36c SW1 1/10,000 6th Edition a.H.
	22-3-16		~~Hostile~~ Artillery normal Five germans watched one of their own dogs playing between their front line and their wire at M10 a. 77 Ammunition expended. 37 Lyddite.	a.N.
	23-3-16.		our front line in M4d & 5c was shelled heavily during the day 30th Battery retaliated on various points in M5c - 6b - 10d. Ammunition expended 16 Lyddite	a.N.
	24-3-16		30th Battery silenced a minnenwerfer firing from M11 a ½. 9½. We exploded a mine at 12 noon at M4d 7½. 4 on the Northern arm of the Double Crassier. Ammunition expended. 50 Lyddite.	a.b.
	25-3-16.		Our trenches North of Double Crassier was shelled with 4.2 How during the day 30th Battery O.P. shelled with 77mm during the morning	

1875 Wt. W593/826 1,000,000 4/15 J.B.C. & A. A.D.S.S./Forms/C. 2118.

Instructions regarding War Diaries and Intelligence Summaries are contained in F. S. Regs., Part II. and the Staff Manual respectively. Title Pages will be prepared in manuscript.

WAR DIARY
or
~~INTELLIGENCE~~ SUMMARY
(Erase heading not required.)

of 43rd Bde R.F.A

(210)

Army Form C. 2118

Place	Date	Hour	Summary of Events and Information	Remarks and references to Appendices
			30th Battery fired at a notice board in the enemies 2nd line at M10 a. 9½. 4½. Ammunition expended 27 Lyddite.	36 a.b.c.d. 1/40,000. 3rd Edition
	26-3-16.		The Loos Howr fired 6 rds at M5c 1.8 and a bomb store was believed to have been exploded	36c S.W. 1/10,000. 6th Edition.
			The enemy shelled SIEGE 11 all the morning with 4.2	
			30th Battery strafed all located minnenwerfer positions during the morning	
			Ammunition expended 110 Lyddite.	C.H.
	27-3-16.		Quiet day enemy again shelled SIEGE 11.	
			40th Battery retaliated on front line on the LOOS CRASSIER	
			Major Bole went sick to Base.	
			30th Battery received three new guns belonging to 16th DA. in return for three in workshops	
			Ammunition expended. 42 Lyddite.	C.H.
	28-3-16.		Enemy again shelled SIEGE 11 in the morning. Clock on LENS Church has altered time from 9.14 to 9.0. Ammunition expended. 45 Lyddite	

1875 Wt. W593/826 1,000,000 4/15 J.B.C. & A. A.D.S.S./Forms/C. 2118.

Instructions regarding War Diaries and Intelligence Summaries are contained in F. S. Regs., Part II. and the Staff Manual respectively. Title Pages will be prepared in manuscript.

WAR DIARY
or
~~INTELLIGENCE SUMMARY~~
(Erase heading not required.)

of 43rd Bde RFA.

(211)

Army Form C. 2118

Place	Date	Hour	Summary of Events and Information	Remarks and references to Appendices
	29-3-16.		A string of two box huts were observed 17° R of Right spire of ST PIERRE church from G33d2½.2	36c b & c 1/40,000 3rd Edition
		12.30 PM.	LOOS Twins fired 6 from aadguns 8 direct hits obtained. Ammunition expended 30 Lyddite	36c SW1 1/10,000 6th edition.
				AN.
	30-3-16.		BULLY-GRENAY & LES BREBIS were shelled with 5.9 during the morning	
			a great deal of movement was observed in the enemies trenches,	
			30th Battery fired on a party of Ten men who were carrying planks up the communication trench	
			to the support line at M10 a 9½.7.	
			Sentries were seen at 11 different places in their front line South of the DOUBLE CRASSIER	
			Ammunition expended 96. Lyddite.	
	31-3-16		The 30th Battery registered the newfacing Battery portion at M2a8.1	AN.
			The enemy shelled the Craters with about 100 5.9 in the morning doing very little damage	
			We retaliated vigourously on their front & support line opposite the Craters.	
			Ammunition expended. 126 Lyddite.	AN.

1875 Wt. W593/826 1,000,000 4/15 J.B.C. & A. A.D.S.S./Forms/C. 2118.

1.

43 Bar. R.F.A.

Vol XVI

Instructions regarding War Diaries and Intelligence Summaries are contained in F. S. Regs., Part II. and the Staff Manual respectively. Title Pages will be prepared in manuscript.

HEADQUARTERS 43rd BRIGADE, R.F.A.

WAR DIARY or ~~INTELLIGENCE SUMMARY~~ of 43rd Bde R.F.A.

(Erase heading not required.)

SECRET

212

Army Form C. 2118

Place	Date	Hour	Summary of Events and Information	Remarks and references to Appendices
	1-4-16.		The Germans were fairly active again today, especially on the craters	36a 6 & c / 40,000 3rd Ed
			a 150 mm Battery fired at FOSSE most of the day. Ammunition expended 185 HE	36c SW1 / 10,000 6th Ed
	2-4-16.		Hostile Artillery very active all day	a.N.
			54th Battery at GRENAY was heavily shelled during the morning	
			The Germans fired about 400 rds of 5.9 on the CRATERS during the day	
			One of the batteries was located by MAJOR BURKE as firing from 50° L of the right spire	
			of ST PIERRE Church, viewed from G33 d 2½.2. Ammunition expended 93 HE.	a.N.
	3-4-16.		The enemy did a great deal of work in getting their front line South of the DOUBLE CRASSIER clean.	
			minenwerfers were located at M11 a ½.9½. & M10 b 2½.6 Ammunition expended 249 HE.	a.N.
	4-4-16.		A very quiet day a few rounds were fired into LOOS, a small minenwerfer was seen at	
			M10 b 2½.5. Ammunition expended 107 HE.	a.N.

1875 Wt. W593/826 1,000,000 4/15 J.B.C. & A. A.D.S.S./Forms/C. 2118.

Instructions regarding War Diaries and Intelligence Summaries are contained in F. S. Regs., Part II. and the Staff Manual respectively. Title Pages will be prepared in manuscript.

WAR DIARY
or
~~INTELLIGENCE SUMMARY~~
(Erase heading not required.)

43rd Bde RFA

(213)

Army Form C. 2118

Place	Date	Hour	Summary of Events and Information	Remarks and references to Appendices
	5-4-16.		a very quiet & dull day. Ammunition expended 36 HE. a.N.	36c NW3 1/40000 3rd Ed
	6-4-16.	12.6AM	The enemy sprung a mine in M6b 9.7 by dawn they had wired it and dug a communication trench to it. New wire appeared near the snipers house. Ammunition expended 83 HE. a.N.	36c SW1 1/10000 6th Ed
	7-4-16		Fairly active day north of the DOUBLE CRASSIER. 40th Battery had a premature wounding one gunner, who subsequently died. Points were registered by the 2nd Siege & 30th Batteries in the 23rd Division Area in case of hostile attack there. Ammunition expended 106 HE. a.N.	
	8-4-16		a 4.2 Battery fired about 30 rounds at the 117th Battery & 111 Heavy Battery. 8" Hows fired into Fosse des Mines on and off all the morning. a.N.	
		9.15 PM	Great artillery activity north of LOOS CRASSIER. Ammunition expended. 154 HE. a.N.	

1875 Wt. W593/826 1,000,000 4/15 J.B.C. & A. A.D.S.S./Forms/C. 2118.

Instructions regarding War Diaries and Intelligence Summaries are contained in F. S. Regs., Part II. and the Staff Manual respectively. Title Pages will be prepared in manuscript.

WAR DIARY
or
~~INTELLIGENCE SUMMARY~~
(Erase heading not required.)

of 43rd Bde RFA

(214)

Army Form C. 2118

Place	Date	Hour	Summary of Events and Information	Remarks and references to Appendices
	9-4-16.		A Fairly quiet day.	36a b + c 1/40,000 3rd Ed
		3PM	Three Germans were seen dressed in Khaki	36c SW1 1/10,000 6th Ed
		8PM	We sprung a mine on the Southern Arm of the DOUBLE CRASSIER	
			The enemy were not much alarmed and retaliated very feebly Ammunition expended 144 HE.	
	10-4-16.	4.30PM	The 68th Bde 23rd Div. on our right indulged in a feint attack at 4.30 PM today, using smoke bombs, it was very successful and the Hun manned his front line, so it is hoped that some were killed by our artillery fire.	
			Working parties seen on H12C70 as usual Ammunition expended 55 HE.	
	11-4-16.	2PM	We exploded a mine on the Northern arm of Double Crassier at 2 PM today, this brought forth remarkably quick retaliation	
			Two Balloons were up in LENS most of the day long	
			Ammunition expended 111 HE	

1875 Wt. W593/826 1,000,000 4/15 J.B.C. & A. A.D.S.S./Forms/C. 2118.

Army Form C. 2118

Instructions regarding War Diaries and Intelligence Summaries are contained in F. S. Regs., Part II. and the Staff Manual respectively. Title Pages will be prepared in manuscript.

WAR DIARY
or
INTELLIGENCE SUMMARY

(Erase heading not required.)

of 43rd Bde RFA

(215)

Place	Date	Hour	Summary of Events and Information	Remarks and references to Appendices
	12-4-16.		The weather very bad indeed	36 c & t c. 1/40,000 3rd Ed
		7.50.	about 50 77mm fell into LOOS	
	6-6.30PM		25 rds 77mm on South Maroc	36 c SW1 1/10,000 6th Ed
			Working Parties on Hill 70 seen as usual in the early morning	
	13-4-16.		8" shelled FOSSE 3. from the direction of ST AUGUSTE during the morning Ammunition Expended 75 HE	
			There were a good many shells on SIEGE & T11 during the day. 30th Battery OP hit 3 times during the day. Ammunition expended 10 HE.	
	14-4-16.		Trenches between the Craters shelled heavily in the morning with various kinds of shells	
		9.0PM	The enemy put a mine up. on the Southern arm of DOUBLE CRASSIER	
			2nd Siege engaged a minnenwerfer and obtained a direct hit on it	
			The north Pylon of the TOWER BRIDGE LOOS knocked down by 5.9's	
			30th Battery OP. again hit. Ammunition expended . 59 HE	

1875 Wt. W593/826 1,000,000 4/15 J.B.C. & A. A.D.S.S./Forms/C. 2118.

Instructions regarding War Diaries and Intelligence Summaries are contained in F. S. Regs., Part II. and the Staff Manual respectively. Title Pages will be prepared in manuscript.

WAR DIARY
or
~~INTELLIGENCE SUMMARY~~
(Erase heading not required.)

of 43rd Bde MFA

(216)

Army Form C. 2118

Place	Date	Hour	Summary of Events and Information	Remarks and references to Appendices
	15-4-16.		South MAROC heavily shelled during the early morning	36 a b & c 1/40,000 3rd Ed
		11.30 AM.	LOOS. was heavily shelled near the remaining Pylon.	36cSW1
			A few large minnenwerfer seen to fire from M10 b 7.9. Ammunition expended 77 HE. a.N.	1/10,000 6th Ed.
	16-4-16.		Two large minnenwerfer seen to fire from M10 b 7.9 worried the Gloucester Regt much,	
			30th Battery fired at them,	
		3.30 PM	The remaining LOOS Pylon brought down by 5.9, thus effacing the most conspicuous landmark of the countryside	
			The 111th Heavy Battery was again heavily shelled between 4.30PM & 5.15PM by 4.2 How Bty	
			Ammunition Expended 138 HE.	
	17-4-16.		South MAROC again shelled with 77 mm in the morning a.N	
			40th Battery had a great many turning HART calls during the day.	
			The 2nd Siege fired 50 AP at the SNIPERS House at the request of LEFT Group 15 direct hits	
			Ammunition expended 51 HE a.N	

1875 Wt. W593/826 1,000,000 4/15 J.B.C. & A. A.D.S.S./Forms/C. 2118.

Instructions regarding War Diaries and Intelligence Summaries are contained in F. S. Regs., Part II. and the Staff Manual respectively. Title Pages will be prepared in manuscript.

WAR DIARY
or
INTELLIGENCE SUMMARY
(Erase heading not required.)

of 43rd Bde RFA.

Army Form C. 2118

(217)

Place	Date	Hour	Summary of Events and Information	Remarks and references to Appendices
	18-4-16		A fairly quiet day. We sprung a mine between the two craters, it failed to make a crater, it being most probable that it did some damage to the enemies galleries. Ammunition expended 34 HE.	36c NW 1/40,000 3rd Ed. 36c SW 1 1/10,000 6th Ed
	19-4-16.		Enemy active at intervals but for the most part very quiet. Ammunition expended 85 HE.	
	20-4-16.		Quiet day, not nearly so many working parties observed on HILL 70 in the morning. Ammunition expended. 41 HE.	
	21-4-16.		A clear day resulting in greatly renewed activity everywhere. 4 Balloons 2 unusually close observed today. NOEUX-LES-MINES again shelled with 8" during the morning, LES BREBIS also shelled with 4.2 Hows. Capt J.T. PRICE who used to command 30th Battery was killed at VERMELLES this morning. Ammunition expended. 97 HE	

Instructions regarding War Diaries and Intelligence Summaries are contained in F. S. Regs., Part II. and the Staff Manual respectively. Title Pages will be prepared in manuscript.

WAR DIARY
or
INTELLIGENCE SUMMARY
(Erase heading not required.)

43rd Bde MFA

(218).

Army Form C. 2118

Place	Date	Hour	Summary of Events and Information	Remarks and references to Appendices
	22-4-16.		Rained all day very bad for observation. Ammunition expended 87 HE. aN	36 c S.W. 1/40,000 3rd Ed
	23-4-16.		A Quiet day in the trenches but very lively further back.	36c SW1 1/10,000 6th Ed
			LES BREBIS and FOSSE 6 shelled most of the morning.	
			30th Battery had one premature wounding a gunner. Ammunition expended 133 HE.	
			CAPT AITKEN 30th Battery slightly hit by a piece of 8" at FOSSE 2 de Loeuvs. aN	
	24-4-16		LT. COL. MACNAGHTEN D.S.O. having gone as CRA 15th Division LT COL F.L. SHARP C.M.G. has gone	
			as OC. 39th Bde RFA. temporarily and MAJOR LONGSTAFF D.S.O RFA takes over temporary command	
			of the Howitzer Group.	
			The 43rd Bde is shortly to be disbanded	
		4-5 PM	The enemy shelled our trenches in M9b + M4c heavily. Ammunition expended. 70 HE. aN	
	25-4-16.		The interpreter slightly wounded by a bit of 8", his horse was hit with it while he was riding &	
			was killed on the spot. South Maroc again heavily shelled with 77 & 4.2 during the morning	

Instructions regarding War Diaries and Intelligence Summaries are contained in F. S. Regs., Part II. and the Staff Manual respectively. Title Pages will be prepared in manuscript.

WAR DIARY
or
~~INTELLIGENCE SUMMARY~~
(Erase heading not required.)

of 43rd Bde RFA

(219)

Army Form C. 2118

Place	Date	Hour	Summary of Events and Information	Remarks and references to Appendices
			2nd Siege fired 10 HE + 7 AP at M6c 0.4 by order of 1st Div at suspected mineshaft	36 a & c 1/40,000 3rd Ed
		4.10 PM.	We blew up a camouflet on the Southern arm of Double Crassier	36c SW1 1/10,000 6th Ed
		8.40 PM	our 18 Prs on the right sector started a heavy bombardment, keeping it up for about half an hour	
			This drew a certain amount of retaliation at about M4c Ammunition expended 53 HE	
	26-4-16.		South Maroc again shelled with 77 mm & 4.2 How 30th Battery OP hit again	
			Ammunition expended 48 HE	
	27-4-16	5 AM.	There was a heavy bombardment on our front and also the 16th Division on our left	O.N.
			This turned out to be the accompaniment of 4 small enemy attacks,	
			The Germans captured the Chalk Pit in H 35 central, but we blew up the Howitzer there, in case the Germans should get hold of it	
			The enemy were driven out about half an hour later	

Army Form C. 2118

Instructions regarding War Diaries and Intelligence Summaries are contained in F. S. Regs., Part II. and the Staff Manual respectively. Title Pages will be prepared in manuscript.

WAR DIARY
or
~~INTELLIGENCE SUMMARY~~

(Erase heading not required.)

of 43rd Bde RFA

(220)

Place	Date	Hour	Summary of Events and Information	Remarks and references to Appendices
			During the morning the 40th Battery fired 55 rounds on an SOS L Rt L Bde.	36c NW & C 1/40,000 3rd Ed
			30th & 40th Waggon lines at FOSSE 2 DE NOEUX again shelled with 8".	36c SW1 1/10,000 6th Ed
			Ammunition expended. 133 HE GN	
	28-4-16.		LOOS shelled with 5.9 & 4.2 Hows. in the early morning.	
		9AM	The enemy began cutting our wire by the LENS BETHUNE at about 9AM	
			LES BREBIS shelled with 4.2 during the morning.	
		8.50PM	In the evening at 8.50PM a cutting expedition by the 1st Northants was organised. The Artillery part of the expedition was eminently successful. The infantry only succeeded in obtaining one German prisoner and they did not manage to get him over alive, about 20 of the enemy were killed in their trenches by our Artillery fire. No identifications were brought back, which was unfortunate as the whole raison d'être of the performance was to collect prisoners. Ammunition expended 133 HE GN	

1875 Wt. W593/826 1,000,000 4/15 I.B.C. & A. A.D.S.S./Forms/C. 2118.

Army Form C. 2118

Instructions regarding War Diaries and Intelligence Summaries are contained in F. S. Regs., Part II. and the Staff Manual respectively. Title Pages will be prepared in manuscript.

WAR DIARY
or
INTELLIGENCE SUMMARY
of 43rd Bde RFA

(Erase heading not required.)

(221)

Place	Date	Hour	Summary of Events and Information	Remarks and references to Appendices
	29-4-16.	4am-6	Great artillery activity on the PUITS 14 BIS & HULLUCH sectors accompanied by gas, the gas drifted over MAZINGARBE & MAROC, at MAROC it was strong enough to warrant 30th Battery putting on their gas helmets. Ammunition expended 718 HE.	36a&c 1/40,000 3rd Ed 36cSW1 1/10,000 6th Ed
	30-4-16.		There was considerable activity all day on the trenches in M5d, 5.9's falling there most of the morning. AN	
			A large & heavy minnenwerfer was active on M5d 7.7. in the morning and was strafed with 4.2 How & 6" How. It appeared to be firing from the vicinity of M6c 4.2. Ammunition expended 75 HE. AN	

1875 Wt. W593/826 1,000,000 4/15 J.B.C. & A. A.D.S.S./Forms/C. 2118.

Officer I/c,
Adjutant-General's Office at the Base.

Herewith War Diary of the 43rd Brigade R.F.A. for period 1st to 22nd May 1916.

The 43rd Brigade ceases to exist as such on the latter date please.

Lt.R.F.A.
Adjut.43rd Brigade R.F.A.

22.5.16.

Instructions regarding War Diaries and Intelligence Summaries are contained in F. S. Regs., Part II. and the Staff Manual respectively. Title Pages will be prepared in manuscript.

WAR DIARY
or
INTELLIGENCE SUMMARY
(Erase heading not required.)

of 43rd Bde R.F.A.

(222)

Vol 17

Army Form C. 2118

Place	Date	Hour	Summary of Events and Information	Remarks and references to Appendices
	1-5-16.		A quiet day except for some shelling of M4c and M9b	36 a 6 & c
			Major Bell rejoined 40th Battery. Ammunition Expended 166 HE	1/40,000 3rd Edition
	2-5-16.		A very quiet day all day.	36 S W1
			South Maroc & SIEGE II shelled fairly heavily. Ammunition Expended 45 HE	1/10,000 6th Edition
	3-5-16.		8.30 PM we exploded one large and one small mine on the Southern arm of Double Crassier	
			followed by a raiding party. Ammunition expended 47 HE	
	4-5-16		gas cylinders reported to have been observed going into the enemy trenches in	
			the triangle in M.4.d. & M.5.c.	
			2nd Siege engaged suspected mineshaft at M4c 8¾.5. an effective shoot as could	
			be seen. Ammunition expended. 91 HE	
	5-5-16.		The enemy were very active all day on our trenches west of the Double Crassier	
			with 5.9". Ammunition expended. 75 HE	

Instructions regarding War Diaries and Intelligence Summaries are contained in F. S. Regs., Part II. and the Staff Manual respectively. Title Pages will be prepared in manuscript.

WAR DIARY
or
~~INTELLIGENCE SUMMARY~~
(Erase heading not required.)

of 43rd Bde RFA.

(223)

Army Form C. 2118

Place	Date	Hour	Summary of Events and Information	Remarks and references to Appendices
	6-5-16.		Lt. COL. F. L. SHARP. CMG. RFA. definitely posted to 39th Bde RFA dating from 25-4-16	36c b & c 1/40,000 3rd Edition
		4PM.	a quiet day there was a burst of fire on M4b central at 4PM with 5.9"	36c SW1 1/10,000 6th Edition.
			a Trench Mortar was seen firing from M10b 2.5.60.	
			Ammunition expended. 68 HE	
			A.N.	
	7-5-16.		Quiet except for considerable shelling with all nature of shells round the Western ~~face~~ end of Double Crassier, to which we retaliated. Ammunition expended. 75 HE A.N.	
	8-5-16		very quiet day, there was nothing but a little desultory shooting throughout the day	
			Ammunition expended. 23 HE A.N.	
	9-5-16		A very quiet day, a little desultory shelling by 77 mm on the W. end of DOUBLE CRASSIER Ammunition expended. 49 HE	
			A.N.	

1875 Wt. W593/826 1,000,000 4/15 J.B.C. & A. A.D.S.S./Forms/C. 2118.

Army Form C. 2118

WAR DIARY
or
INTELLIGENCE SUMMARY
(Erase heading not required.)

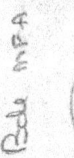

of 43rd Bde MFA

(224)

Instructions regarding War Diaries and Intelligence Summaries are contained in F. S. Regs., Part II. and the Staff Manual respectively. Title Pages will be prepared in manuscript.

Place	Date	Hour	Summary of Events and Information	Remarks and references to Appendices
	10-5-16		a quiet day except for the usual shelling of the W end of Double Crassier with 77 mm & 105 mm,	36 a b & c $\frac{1}{40,000}$ 3rd Ed
			Loos gun fired 6 rds at W face of the triangle. Ammunition expended 69 HE a.h.	36 c S.W.1. $\frac{1}{10,000}$ 6th Edition
	11-5-16.		Hostile Artillery very active indeed, in the morning SIEGE 11 and the trenches N of the Crassier were heavily shelled with 5.9" ~~Ammunition 105 HE~~	
		10.40-12.40	The trenches by the Copse were very heavily shelled by 5.9" from BENIFONTAINE	
			There was very considerable hostile shelling between 4 & 6 PM, the main battle seemed to be taking place by the HOHENZOLLERN REDOUBT and the line N. MAROC Grenay & Les Brebis appeared to be just on the edge of the hostile Barrage	
			Ammunition expended. 105 HE a.h.	
	12-5-16.		Quiet day after yesterday excitement Ammunition expended 113 HE a.h.	
	13-5-16.		Very dull & quiet & misty day 2nd Siege Bty fired 50 HE. at the German	

1875 Wt. W593/826 1,000,000 4/15 J.B.C. & A. A.D.S.S./Forms/C. 2118.

Instructions regarding War Diaries and Intelligence Summaries are contained in F. S. Regs., Part II. and the Staff Manual respectively. Title Pages will be prepared in manuscript.

WAR DIARY
or
~~INTELLIGENCE~~ SUMMARY
(Erase heading not required.)

of 43rd Bde RFA

(225)

Army Form C. 2118.

Place	Date	Hour	Summary of Events and Information	Remarks and references to Appendices
			trench running from M 6 b 9.4. to N1a 0.5 in conjunction with 9.2" in an organised bombardment 16 hits were obtained. Ammn: 24 HE	36 a b + c 1/40,000 3rd Edition
	14-5-16		a quiet day about dusk Loos and Loos Crassier was heavily shelled This culminated with a short intense bombardment which brought an S.O.S call from the Sussex who are the Left Bt Left Bde. Ammunition expended 73 HE	36c SW1 1/10,000 6th Edition
	15-5-16.		Very misty day & very bad for observation Practically no shelling Ammunition expended 186 HE	
	May 16 to May 22		43rd Brigade in process of being dissolved. 38th + 40th Btes formed into 3 Batteries called D25, D26 + D39 respectively Bde H.Q. + BAC dispersed + broken up. WA	

1875 Wt. W593/826 1,000,000 4/15 J.B.C. & A. A.D.S.S./Forms/C. 2118.

1st Division

40th Battery R.F.A.

From 4th August. To 30th Sept. 1914

996

121
~~1082~~
1096

40th Battery R F A XLIII rd Bde

1st ~~3rd~~ Division

Vols: I & II 4.8.309

Instructions regarding War Diaries and Intelligence Summaries are contained in F. S. Regs., Part II. and the Staff Manual respectively. Title pages will be prepared in manuscript.

WAR DIARY
or
INTELLIGENCE SUMMARY.
(Erase heading not required.)

Army Form C. 2118.

Hour, Date, Place	Summary of Events and Information	Remarks and references to Appendices
1914. DEEPCUT. August 4th 6.30pm	Order received to mobilize	
" August 5th	1st day of mobilization - Progress normal.	
" August 6th	2nd day of mobilization - — do —	
	21 horses arrived from Reserve Brigade Glasgow for the Battery.	
	Captain C. E. G. Woollcombe-Adams arrived from Reserve Brigade, Exeter to replace Captain W. S. Chambers posted to 1st Divl Arty. Staff.	
August 7th	39 R.F.A and 3 A.S.C. Reservists arrived from Newcastle on Tyne, many had been 48 and 60 hours without food. Many were <u>not</u> completely equipped. This necessitated re-opening the Clothing Ledger which had been closed. In other circumstances this might cause a serious delay. - Progress Normal	

Instructions regarding War Diaries and Intelligence Summaries are contained in F. S. Regs., Part II. and the Staff Manual respectively. Title pages will be prepared in manuscript.

WAR DIARY
or
INTELLIGENCE SUMMARY.
(Erase heading not required.)

Army Form C. 2118.

Hour, Date, Place	Summary of Events and Information	Remarks and references to Appendices
DEEPCUT. 8-8-14 to 16-8-14	Mobilization of the Battery progressed normally and was practically ready on the 8th day actual, although mobilization actually commenced on Wednesday the 5th orders were received that Sunday the 9th was to be considered the first day of mobilization after the 8th day some horses were changed with the Remount Department and some men were changed with those of Base Details – The Battery went out for training on three mornings and the Brigade on Saturday the 15th August. Battery Sergeant Major posted to Base Details on the 14th.	
DEEPCUT 16-8-1914.	Right Half Battery left Barracks at 4.30 am and entrained at FARNBOROUGH STATION, taking 45 minutes although one hour and nine minutes were	

(9 29 6) W 3332—1107 100,000 10/13 H W V Forms/C. 2118/10.

Instructions regarding War Diaries and Intelligence Summaries are contained in F.S. Regs., Part II. and the Staff Manual respectively. Title pages will be prepared in manuscript.

WAR DIARY
or
INTELLIGENCE SUMMARY.
(Erase heading not required.)

Army Form C. 2118.

Hour, Date, Place	Summary of Events and Information	Remarks and references to Appendices
16-8-14 (continued)	allowed. Train ~~—~~ started punctually at 6.34 am. The Left Half Battery followed an hour later.	
	On arrival at Southampton the Battery embarked on "SS "City of Chester" all horses had to be slung in which took about 2½ hours, sailed at 1.0. oclock, came alongside at Boulogne at 8.0. am 17-8-14, and at once	
17-8-14. (continued)	commenced disembarking, marched out to Rest Camp (No 4) at Pont Fleuret, 1st Section arriving at 12.30 pm.	
19-8-14 Boulogne	Left Rest Camp at 6.45. am, entrained Boulogne Station at 8.15. am completed 9.40. am Left at 12.15 pm via Abbeville, AMIENS, ARRAS to the controlling station BUSIGNY 10.30 pm	

(9 29 6) W 3332—1107 100,000 10/13 H W V Forms/C. 2118/10.

Instructions regarding War Diaries and Intelligence Summaries are contained in F.S. Regs., Part II. and the Staff Manual respectively. Title pages will be prepared in manuscript.

WAR DIARY
or
INTELLIGENCE SUMMARY.
(Erase heading not required.)

Army Form C. 2118.

Hour, Date, Place	Summary of Events and Information	Remarks and references to Appendices
~~18~~ 19-8-1914 (continued)	~~He~~ Sent on to WASSIGNY 12 MN. detrained in the dark (1½ hours) marched ¾ mile to bivouac.	
WASSIGNY. 20-8-1914.	Marched 6.15 am to billets at MALASSISSE about 6 miles.	
MALASSISSE. FRIDAY. 21st August 1914.	Marched out of billets 8.15. am. with rest of 43rd Brigade R.F.A. to DOMPIERE. (12 miles) and went into billets at 1.30. pm.	
DOMPIERRE . Sat 22nd	Marched out of DOMPIERE at 4.30 am. Joined up with rest of 1st Division and proceeded via DOULER & MAUBERGE and halted 2 miles N. of Town. Marched on to go into billets at VIEUX RENG but owing to alarm of proximity of enemy took up a position of readiness. After dark marched on to CROIX LES ROUVEROY and bivouacked there.	
CROIX LES ROUVEROY. Sunday 23rd	Took up a position of observation at 7 AM. At 5pm moved forward at speed to extricate 70th Battery which was being shelled by German Howitzers. Unable to locate hostile guns and returned to bivouac at dark	

(9 29 6) W 3332—1107 100,000 10/13 H W V Forms/C. 2118/10.

Instructions regarding War Diaries and Intelligence Summaries are contained in F. S. Regs., Part II. and the Staff Manual respectively. Title pages will be prepared in manuscript.

WAR DIARY
or
INTELLIGENCE SUMMARY.
(Erase heading not required.)

Army Form C. 2118.

Hour, Date, Place	Summary of Events and Information	Remarks and references to Appendices
CROIX LES ROUVEROY Monday 24th Aug	At 1.30 am 1 section detached to HAUTAIN in support of infantry. At dawn remainder of battery occupied position of observation. till general retirement at 11am on VILLERS SIRE NICOLE where 2 positions were taken up with the whole of the 1st D.A. Dug in both places. Fired at evening squadrons at extreme range (4 rds) they scattered. Marched 5pm retired via BETTIGNY to bivouac at FEIGNIES	
FEIGNIES Tue 25 Aug.	Battery on rear guard with II Inf Brigade. Column 2½ hrs late at clearing village. Marched via HAUTMONT - MONCEAU TO TAISNIERE G.S. wagons to MARBAIX where they stampeded with the rest of the supply column. Day of alarms. Situation apparently critical	
TAISNIERES Wed 26th	Marched at 6.30 am. but did not clear village for about 2 hours, to ~~to~~ MARBAIX ~~LE GRAND FAYT~~. Fighting going on ~~all~~ on the N. & West. Moved to LE GRAND FAYT, but on arrival there 1.45pm a general retirement ordered at 2 P.M. Roads badly blocked, they were narrow and slippery. Halted at LA GOELLE for an hour, then on through to FESMY to OISY. Rain all night & no water for horses	
OISY. Thurs 27th	Marched via ETREUX - GUISE to BERNOT. Came into action several times to cover retirement of rear guard but did not fire. Battery ordered to take up a covering position S W of GUISE to cover retirement. Hot rear guard action took place in the evening. battery ordered back to N of GUISE but order cancelled before getting there. Very hard day for the horses. long march on in the dark to Bernot.	
~~BERNOT~~ ~~Fri. 28th~~		

(9 29 6) W 3332—1107 100,000 10/13 H W V Forms/C. 2118/10.

Instructions regarding War Diaries and Intelligence Summaries are contained in F. S. Regs., Part II. and the Staff Manual respectively. Title pages will be prepared in manuscript.

WAR DIARY
or
INTELLIGENCE SUMMARY.
(Erase heading not required.)

Army Form C. 2118.

Hour, Date, Place	Summary of Events and Information	Remarks and references to Appendices
BERNOT 28. VIII. 14	Marched 4.30 AM. via RIBEMONT – LA FERTE to ST GOBIN arriving 10 PM. Came into action near BRISSY but did not shoot – battery in readiness to cover retirement and later to support Scots Greys & XII Lancers fighting W. across the River.	
ST. GOBIN 29. VIII. 14	Day of Rest. Busy day!	
ST. GOBAIN 30. VIII. 14	Left 4 am. and marched to PINON. Long very hot march partly through forest. Bivouacked in PINON ~~[illegible]~~ CHATEAU 6.30 pm. Bought 3 horses at ~~[illegible]~~ DANIZY	
PINON 31. VIII. 14	Moved off at 4.30 A.M. through SOISSONS to bivouac at LARAPERIE at 8.30 pm. Hard march.	
LARAPERIE (near SOISSONS) 1. IX. 14	Left 5.30 AM. and went into bivouac at MAROLLES Bridge. Moved out 11 pm. to allow bridge to be blown up remaining on road side ready to march at 1 AM.	
MAROLLES 2. IX. 14	continued night march arriving MEAUX 5.30 AM.	
MEAUX 3. IX. 14. Thurs	Marched 4 am. via VARREDDES – GERMIGNY – SAMMERON to bivouac ~~at~~ near JOUARRE. Halted nearly all day east of SAMMERON and got to bivouac after dark as usual. Rear guard slightly engaged.	
1		

Instructions regarding War Diaries and Intelligence Summaries are contained in F. S. Regs., Part II. and the Staff Manual respectively. Title pages will be prepared in manuscript.

WAR DIARY
or
INTELLIGENCE SUMMARY.

(Erase heading not required.)

Army Form C. 2118.

Hour, Date, Place	Summary of Events and Information	Remarks and references to Appendices
LE GRAND GLAIRET 4-IX-14 Fri.	Moved with I Division to billets in COULOMMIERS a 9 ~~mod~~ mile march. Got in early. Rested horses & men Refitting as much as possible.	
COULOMMIERS. 5-IX-14. Saturday	In position of observation 2 miles S.W. of COULOMMIERS. deeply entrenched – left position at dawn and marched with Division to billets at ROZNY 10.30. am – No contact with enemy.	
ROZNY 6-IX-14. Sunday	Battery ready to move off at 7.30. am after various orders during the night remained in reserve at ROZNY till 1.30 pm when ordered forward towards VOINSLES under Lt. Col. Cunliffe-Owen commanding 26th Brigade R.F.A. – Ordered to occupy a position East of VOINSLES to cover the advance of the 3rd and 5th Cavalry Brigades from South on to VOUDNOY – VOUDNOY found unoccupied. The Division then moved forward to occupy the line LE PLESSIS – ANDNOY. At dusk Battery rejoined 43rd Brigade R.F.A. and bivouacked South of VOUDNOY	

(9 29 6) W 3332—1107 100,000 10/13 H W V Forms/C. 2118/10.

Instructions regarding War Diaries and Intelligence Summaries are contained in F. S. Regs., Part II. and the Staff Manual respectively. Title pages will be prepared in manuscript.

WAR DIARY
or
INTELLIGENCE SUMMARY.
(Erase heading not required.)

Army Form C. 21[illegible].

Hour, Date, Place	Summary of Events and Information	Remarks and references to Appendices
VOUDNOY. 7-IX-14. Monday	Marched 3.45 am joined Advanced Guard under General Balfin but just after starting order came to stand fast till 7.0 am – 8.30 am marched with Advanced Guard to Ammillis and St. Eloi the latter was held by German Cavalry after our own Cavalry and Cyclists had passed through but they did not remain long – From AMILLES marched N.E. to FALEYS where a small engagement was in progress between British Cavalry Brigade and enemy but the enemy retired before Battery was required. Continued march via CHOISY to JOUY-SUR-MORIN arriving there at 7 pm billetted there. Village was occupied by enemy on arrival of advanced Guard.	
JOUY-SUR-MORIN. 8-IX-14. Tuesday.	Battery rejoined its own Brigade and marched at 7.30 am via JARIEL to CHAMPMARTIN a portion of the Column in front between LES CROCHETS and CELLOT was shelled by a German Battery from MONTSLAGIEL – The Battery came into action with orders to fire due NORTH at 4.300 yards no observing station could be found – The German Battery retired before it had been found – Battery then ordered to join 39th Bde near GRAND MARCHE but before finding Colonel ~~Cleary~~ CAREY the G.O.C. 1st Division ordered Battery to come into action and shell road about BOUSSIERE –	

(9 29 6) W 3332—1107 100,000 10/13 H W V Forms/C. 2118/10.

Army Form C. 21[illegible]

Instructions regarding War Diaries and Intelligence Summaries are contained in F. S. Regs., Part II. and the Staff Manual respectively. Title pages will be prepared in manuscript.

WAR DIARY
or
INTELLIGENCE SUMMARY.

(*Erase heading not required.*)

Hour, Date, Place	Summary of Events and Information	Remarks and references to Appendices
JOUY-SUR-MORIN. 8-IX-14 Tuesday (continued)	came into action at 2.30 pm near TRETORIE saw Germans retiring but they were all out of range and it was impossible to advance nearer. Battery was already amongst the II Division then, at 3.30 pm moved to SABLONNIERS halted ½ hour. Thunderstorm, thence marched in rear of 2nd Infantry Brigade to X road 1 mile North of HONDEVILLIER, bivouacked there for night – Sound of heavy fighting from N.E.	
HONDEVILLIERS 9-IX-14 Wednesday.	Left bivouack at 4.0 am with remainder of Brigade to join Advanced Guard of 3rd Infantry Brigade & 39th Bde. R.F.A. to force the passage of the MARNE at NOGENT, on approaching the River 54th Battery detached to 2nd Inf. Brigade, remainder of Brigade marched N.E. across country to CHEVANCE but by the time they had reached there the cavalry had crossed the river without opposition. The Battery then continued its march with long halts of uncertain duration and finally bivouacked at BEAUREPAIRE FARM 2½ miles N. of CHARLY – Germans reported entrenched 4 miles ahead.	

(9 29 6) W 3332—1107 100,000 10/13 H W V Forms/C. 2118/10.

Instructions regarding War Diaries and Intelligence Summaries are contained in F. S. Regs., Part II. and the Staff Manual respectively. Title pages will be prepared in manuscript.

WAR DIARY
or
INTELLIGENCE SUMMARY.
(Erase heading not required.)

Army Form C. 2118.

Hour, Date, Place	Summary of Events and Information	Remarks and references to Appendices
~~9-IX-14. (continued)~~ BEAUREPAIRE 10-IX-14. Thursday.	Left BEAUREPAIRE at 6. am marching at head of main body via THIOLET - LUCY - TORCY to COURCHAMPS the II Division being about 2 miles on our left at COURCHAMPS joined advanced Guard. II Division heavily engaged on our left. Battery thrust hurriedly into a bad position into action against a retreating column about MONNES - Reconnoitring officer had found a very good position but his report was not awaited, after shelling column at 5000 yds Germans commenced shelling Infantry occupying ridge 3500 yds to N. the Northampton Regt. immediately commenced to ~~retreat~~, and being mis-taken for advancing Germans were shelled by R.F.A away to right. Battery then ordered to search behind the ridge evacuated for hostile Guns - the retirement of Northampton Regt. now joined by Sussex Regt. became a flight and a rabble passed through observation and Battery drawing heavy fire on to both and breaking up Battery Telephone Wire - All this time Battery was under heavy fire from hostile Howitzer Battery firing high explosive shell, but luckily they did not do much damage.	

(9 29 6) W 3332—1107 100,000 10/13 H W V Forms/C. 2118/10.

Army Form C. 2118.

Instructions regarding War Diaries and Intelligence Summaries are contained in F. S. Regs., Part II. and the Staff Manual respectively. Title pages will be prepared in manuscript.

WAR DIARY
or
INTELLIGENCE SUMMARY.
(Erase heading not required.)

Hour, Date, Place	Summary of Events and Information	Remarks and references to Appendices
10-XI-14 (continued)	1 officer & 2 men slightly wounded - at Observing Station 2 men wounded - At one time there were practically no troops between Battery and Germans but 60th Rifles were then sent forward to replace the Northampton Regt. - Battery continued searching hostile artillery until ordered to shell the village of PRIEZ reported full of Germans - Order questioned 3 times before being acted on but the order was definite and peremptory. A few shell were then fired into or near the village - It was afterwards discovered that the village only contained our stragglers and wounded, on advance of 60th Rifles enemy withdrew to a position ½ S. of RASSY but enemy's retreating columns were visible but were out of range - Battery remained till dark to cover further advance of Infantry and bivouacked on ground.	
RASSY 11-XI-14 Friday	Battery marched at 6.0 am at head of main body to COINCY and billetted there, very wet day.	
COINCY 12-XI-14 Saturday	Battery marched with III Inf Brigade in adv guard arrived COINCY. - and billetted there. Marched 6 am. with A.G. Took up a position of observation ½ mile E. of MONT NOTRE DAME overlooking river VESLE alongside a French battery - but did not shoot	

(9 29 6) W 3332—1107 100,000 10/13 H W V Forms/C. 2118/10.

Instructions regarding War Diaries and Intelligence Summaries are contained in F. S. Regs., Part II. and the Staff Manual respectively. Title pages will be prepared in manuscript.

Army Form C. 2118.

WAR DIARY
or
INTELLIGENCE SUMMARY.
(Erase heading not required.)

Hour, Date, Place	Summary of Events and Information	Remarks and references to Appendices
BAZOUCHES 13.IX.14 Sunday	Marched 7am. via PARS - VAUXCÉRÉ - Batteries of Brigade in readiness 1 Mile N. of L in LONGUEVAL. Moved on and crossed bridge over AISNE at BOURG about 3.P.M trotted on PARGNAN. Remained there in readiness and then bivouacked there	
PARGNAN. 14.IX.14 Mon	Marched at dawn. Position of observation near Tour de PAISSY in morning. 10am. ordered on to ARBRE de PAISSY. Ordered into action near cross roads N. of Arbre de PAISSY. Several splendid targets seen but before battery got into action, urgent order came to move to CHIVY valley to meet a German counter attack. [Started along track as ordered but found it impossible, got back on track, then trotted east via PAISSY - MOULINS and VENDRESSE.] Came into action south of Mt. FAUCON. Counter attack had already been repulsed by 46th and 113th Batteries R.F.A. Shelled small parties of enemy and searched for German Guns. Remained in same position at nightfall. Major Maddocks slightly wounded but fit for duty.	

Instructions regarding War Diaries and Intelligence Summaries are contained in F. S. Regs., Part II. and the Staff Manual respectively. Title pages will be prepared in manuscript.

WAR DIARY
or
INTELLIGENCE SUMMARY.
(Erase heading not required.)

Army Form C. 2118

Hour, Date, Place	Summary of Events and Information	Remarks and references to Appendices
Mt. FAUCON. Tuesday 15-9-14.	Came under orders of Colonel Carey comdg 29th Brigade R.F.A. remained in action in same place all day, engaged many targets, parties of infantry trenches and searching for guns. 113th and 46th Batteries heavily shelled all day not far from 40th Battery R.F.A., so shifted Battery to a more covered position 200x further East.	Right Section ordered to top of the hill to join a section of 115th Battery but on arrival there the place was untenable owing to heavy shell fire having in the meantime been opened on it, Section lost 4 horses, 1 gun was abandoned there till nightfall, 115th Battery has several casualties including their Comdg Officer
Mt FAUCON. Wednesday 16-9-14.	Same as 15th instant.	
– do – Thursday 17-9-14.	Ordered to another position on top of Mt GOURTONNE Pt. 175 moved to it in afternoon gained nothing in view and lost 2000x range.	
MT GOURTONNE. Thursday 17-9-14 to Wednesday 30-9-14.	Battery remained in same position during this period, was well dug in and well covered from aeroplane observation and was never located by enemy. Observation station was moved twice, finally to the Northern point of the hill, fired on an average 250 rounds per day till 29th instant, when orders came to economize ammunition, average then reduced to under 100 a day.	

(9 29 6) W 3332—1107 100,000 10/13 H W V Forms/C. 2118/10.

Army Form C. 2118

Instructions regarding War Diaries and Intelligence Summaries are contained in F. S. Regs., Part II. and the Staff Manual respectively. Title pages will be prepared in manuscript.

WAR DIARY
or
INTELLIGENCE SUMMARY.
(Erase heading not required.)

[26th? RFB].

Hour, Date, Place	Summary of Events and Information	Remarks and references to Appendices
MT GOURTONNE, Thursday 17-9-14 to Wednesday 30-9-14. continued	On the the Germans attacked our position, Battery fired 667 rounds, having to engage advancing lines of Germans across an area unswept by 18 prs. The Battery 1st line wagons and horses were placed at a farm on the S.E. side of the hill, but even there they were not safe from occasional shells and during this period 5 men were wounded and a few horses killed. On the 30th a shell hit observation station 1 man slightly wounded.	
30 Sept 1914	W Maddock Major Cmdg 10th Battery R.F.A.	

(9 29 6) W 3332—1107 100,000 10/13 H W V Forms/C. 2118/10.

1st Division

54th Battery R.F.A.

From 4th August To 30th Nov. 1914

nil for [illegible]

a96

57th Battery RFA.

121/2489

1st Division

XLIIIrd Bde

Vols I. II & VII.

4.8 — 1.11.14.

57th Battery, R.F.A.

August to November 1914.

(4.8.14 to 1.11.14)

Date 1914	Hour	Place	Summary of events & information	Remarks & Reference to Appendices
4.8	8 pm	Deepcut	orders to mobilize received	
5.8 – 15.8			} mobilization proceeding	
16.8			Embark at S'hampton – on F.S. Turcoman.	
17.8			arrive BOULOGNE. 11 pm.	
18.8			disembarked march to rest camp –	
19.8			entrain for BUSIGNY.	
20.8			arrive WASSIGNY. march to MOULIN LOINTAIN. billet there.	
21.8			march to DOMPIERRE and billet at Chateau HUGEMONT.	

14

Date	Hour	Place	Summary of events & information	Remarks & References to Appendices
22.8.			march through MAUBEUGE and bivouac at ROUVEROY le CROIX.	
23.8.		ROUVEROY le Croix.	in action in observation till evening when sent for to assist in retirement of 2 batteries from GIVRY RIDGE when got into action too dark to recognise where the German fire was coming from.	
24.8.			retire to FEIGNIES. through BETTIGNIES.	
25.8.			retire through HAUTMONT ~~....~~ to TAISNIERES	
26.8			retire to OISY.	
27.8			retire to BERNOT & ?GUISE	
28.8			retire to ST GOBAIN.	

Date	Hour	Place	Summary of events and information	Remarks and References to Appendices
Aug 29.		St GOBAIN	Rested. men & horses very tired	
30.	3 am		marched via BRANCOURT to PINON	Major Deshon went sick.
31	4 am		marched via SOISSON to CHAUDUN	very hot
1 Sept	3:30 am		Marched via VILLERS-COTTERETS where 5th Cav Bde were engaging enemy to La Ferte Millon, Bty was in rear guard pressed by enemy.	horses tired men very sleepy
2	1 am		marched to MEAUX, bridges at la Ferte Millon blown up. In observation in rear guard at MAY-EN-MULTIEN	Gr Hunter missing on 30th. Gnr Dear & Bullin missing on 2nd Sept
3	4 am		marched via VARREDES and St JEAN to JOUARRE	
4	4 am		Took up position of readiness overlooking bridge over R. MARNE at LA FERTE, retired to COULOMMIERS in rear guard	
5	4.15 am		Marched to ROZOY	Destroyed 1 horse

16

Date	Hour	Place	Summary of Events & information	Remarks & References to Appendices
6	10am	ROZOY	left ROZOY, in action at 2pm. against enemy's concealed batt'y – Batty under shell fire while advancing to action no casualties continued advance 5pm reaching VAUDOY 8pm.	
7.	4:30am	VAUDOY.	advance to CHOISY Major Deshon returned	
8.	4 am	CHOISY.	marched to bivouac – 2 mi N of HONDEVILLIERS French army fighting at nightfall on R flank	
9.	4am	HONDEVILLIERS	marched via SAULCHERY to crossing of MARNE bivouaced with cavalry Dn at BEAUREPAIRE FARM.	

Date	Hour	Place	Summary of Events and Information	Remarks and References to Appendices
10	5am.	BEAUREPAIR FARM.	on German heels— brought into action with speed to find our infantry retiring— searched ~~slope~~ behind slope at 4500–4700 for enemy's battery which ceased firing but reopened. Infantry advance recommenced battery limbered up advanced to RAZY? ridge opened on enemy's column. battery fired on [illegible]— limbered up advanced to position 2 mi N W of PRIEZ to engage	Infantry in retiring drew fire on to the battery's observing station. [illegible] Lindsay RA who was standing 20 yards behind battery observing station was killed—

Date	Hour	Place	Summary of events & information	Remarks & Reference to Appendices
Sept			enemy in CHOUIY village set village on fire with Lyddite and rooted the Germans out of it - Casualties 1 man Gr RAYNER wounded 1 horse wounded -	Sept 11. omitted - adv to VAUXCERE
12	4 am		advanced and crossed R. Aisne after fight for passage. bivouac Oeilly	
13.	4 am		advanced to TOUR DE PAISSY Inf. advanced & captured ridge on CHEMIN DES DAMES Bty came into action 300 yds behind firing line under cover German firing line 1200 yds away & 900 from O.P.	

Date	Hour	Place	Summary of events & information	Remarks & References to Appendices
			Bty remained in action here 4 days. During that engaged following targets, factory 2500, Searching for invisible Heavy Hows. Machine guns at 900. Convoy at 5000. Searching fire on German retirement at 1400 which was effective.	
14			Same position & objectives as 13th.	
15.			do do do. Major Deslon severely wounded Dr Brew slightly. O.P. had to be abandoned owing to enfilade gun fire & machine guns	
16			Same position & objectives	
17			Mr Rait Kerr observed from Inf trenches on to factory. Centre & left Searching fire onto Inf trenches	

Date	Hour	Place	Summary of events & information	Remarks & Reference to Appendices
	1pm		French on right beaten back. Battery retired to next ridge & supported Queen's counter attack by searching fire – bivouac JUMGNY.	
18			In action at PAISSY engaging factory ridge 3500 – Bivouac Jumigny, very wet night, stood to arms 1 am – till dawn	
19			In action at PAISSY, same objective. Bty located by aeroplane, under shell fire soon after, bivouac Caves in PAISSY close to position	
20			Bty position moved slightly & dug in under natural banks, very heavy shell fire all day – Gr Mason killed Gr White dangerously wounded, Dr Hogben slightly –	

Date	Time	Place	Summary of events & information	Remarks & Reference to Appendices
21		PAISSY	Action at PAISSY, heavy shell fire all day, same objectives, Casualties Sgt Tanner wounded 12 horses killed – Major Edwards joined	
22			As previous day – No casualties	
23			Action same place – One gun on factory, one gun on German observation station remaining 4 guns searching & sweeping for German battery – Line found from results of Aeroplane observation as communicated from 10th D.A. Br Whitby wounded in leg.	

Date	Hour	Place	Summary of events & Information	Remarks & Reference to Appendices
24.		PAISSY	As yesterday, further searching & sweeping for German batteries with corrections received as the result of Aeroplane Observation.	
25.		"	Same position as yesterday — same objectives. 2nd Lt. Bond. killed.	
26		"	Right half battery withdrawn to a more covered position. At 8/45 there was a strong German counter attack on our left. Battery fired a few rounds — Germans retired behind crest. Searching & sweeping for German battery — corrections received from results of Aeroplane observations. Fires laid out, guns remained fully manned — in view of possible attack after dusk.	Gnr Miller — Killed " Davis — Wounded " Beale — " — Dr Gay — admitted to Hosp. (Fever). 4 horses — Killed.

23

Date	Hour	Place	Summary of events & Information	Remarks & Reference to Appendices
27.		THISSY.	Action same place. Same objectives during day. German attack about 12 midnight on our right front which was repulsed. Battery objective:– German battery at 3500.	
28		"	Action same place. Battery engaged during day 3 batteries, a trench and a machine gun. The position of these objectives were obtained from the map and engaged by searching & sweeping except the machine gun, the fire on which was observed by the B.C. from a forward Observation Post. Mr Duncan went into the Infantry fire trench during the morning and gained some most useful information as regards position of targets, etc. Continued P.T.O.	

Date	Hour	Place	Summary of Events & Information	Remarks & References
28 Contd.		PAISSY.	German Attack took place about midnight but was repulsed –. Battery objectives – Machine Gun and trenches. Ranges 3100 3200 3400 3500 } 2nd "C"	
29		"	Same position & objectives as yesterday.	
30		"	Action same place – same objectives.	
1/10/14		"	Same as previous day.	
2/10/14		"	— Ditto —	
3 "		"	— Ditto —.	
4 "		"	Action same place. Lt:-Duncan went into Infantry fire trench P. T. O	

Date	Hour	Place	Summary of events & Information	Remarks & References to Appendices
4th Contd.		PAISSY.	I acted as Forward Observing Officer, observing fire from the battery on German trenches, observation post, and flashes of a battery and an advanced section of guns with excellent results.	Ranges. Trench – 3025, Battery – 2225 [redacted], Adv. Section. 3000.
5th		"	Action at same position – Lt Duncan again working in the fire trenches as forward observing officer.	
6th:		"	Same as preceding day	
7 "		"	Ditto	
8 "		"	— " —	
9 "		"	— " —	
10 "		"	— " —	
11 "		"	— " —	

Date	Hour	Place	Summary of events & information	Remarks & reference to Appendices
12/10/14		PAISSY.	Same as 11th October 1914	
13 "		"	— Ditto —	
14 "		"		
~~15~~ "		"		
15 "		"	In action same place, engaging the same objectives.	
"	5-0 Pm	"	Orders received to withdraw from present position. Battery relieved by the ___ Battery French Artillery.	
	6-0 Pm	"	Battery moved by march route in the direction of NEVILLY. ~~[illegible]~~ ~~Bivouacked~~ at BOURG for about 3 hours.	
			16th. Contd P.T.O	

Date	Hour	Place	Summary of events & information	Remarks & Reference to Appendices
16th.	11/30 Pm	BOURG	Continued march and stopped for about 5 hours at MURET. at which place the battery arrived at 8/45 Am. 16th.	
~~17th~~, 16th	2-0 Pm	MURET	Battery marched via DROIZY to NEUILLY-SUR-FRONT. arriving at the latter place at 6.0 Pm when entrainment was commenced at once and carried out successfully - without a hitch ?	
~~17th~~. 16th	9-15 Pm	NEUILLY-SUR-FRONT.	In the train until arrival at SAINT OMER. at 1-30 Pm 18th. The battery detrained and	
18th.	2-0 Pm	SAINT OMER.	proceeded in the direction of CASSEL. Bivouac - BALLINCHOVE.	

Date	Hour	Place	Summary of events & information	Remarks & reference to Appendices
19th		BALLINCHOVE	Rest in Bivouac.	
20th	4-0 Am	"	March to POPERINGHE and billeted there for the night.	
21st	4-0 Am	POPERINGHE	Advanced to PILKEM via ELVERDINGHE - In reserve all day.	
21st	6-0 Pm		Advanced about 1 mile N and took up position in action for the night. Objectives - Two bridges Ranges 4100 - 3500.	
22nd	4-0 Am	PILKEM	In Action same place. O.P. in church of BIXSCHOOTE. Retired about 200 yards and shelled enemies position. Withdrew to Bivouac near PILKEM.	Sgt. Sims - wounded severely by Rifle fire, whilst in the forward position.

30

Date	Hour	Place	Summary of events & information	Remarks & References to Appendices
23rd	4-0 Am	1 Mile N.W of PILKEM	Took up a new position about 1 Mile to the N.W. of PILKEM. Lt. Duncan – as Forward Observing Officer – went into the infantry fire trench. Battery shelled German trenches practically all day. The Infantry reported that our fire was of great assistance to them in their advance. A number of Germans killed by our shells were found in the trenches – Range 1850 yards. The battery was under Rifle fire most of the day and for about ½ time a very heavy shell fire. Remained in position all night.	Br Woods wounded in upper arm by shrap. 1 Horse killed & 2 wounded.

Date	Time	Place	Summary of events & information	Remarks & Reference to Appendices
24th.	5-0 Am	1 Mile N.W of PILKEM.	In action in same place. Lt: Raie then in Infantry fire trench (Forward Observing Officer).	
	9-0 pm	"	Relieved by French & marched to ~~GHELVELT.~~ YPRES	
25th.		~~GHELVELT~~ YPRES	Rested whole day.	
26th.	6 am.	~~GHELVELT~~ YPRES	Marched to GHELVELT & came into action.	
27th.		GHELVELT	In action same place - battery under heavy fire whole day. Lt. Duncan in Infantry fire trench as F.O.O.	

Date	Hr.	Place	Summary of events & information	Remarks & Reference to Appendices
28th		GHELVELT	In action same place battery still under heavy fire – Lt. Rait Kerr in Infantry fire trench as F.O.O.	
29th.		GHELVELT	In action same place until 3 pm. battery forced to retire owing to position becoming unsafe – came into action at WESTHOEK. Gnr. Broadbrook & Gordon slightly wounded. Wagon line shelled by German heavy guns. 3 horses killed.	

Date	Hour	Place	Summary of events & information	Remarks & Reference to Appendices
30 .d.		WESTHOEK	In action same place. Lt. Duncan with "E" Gun went forward to assist Infantry at barricade. Battery shelled with German Heavy Guns.	
31 st.		— " —	In action same place under heavy shell fire. Lts. Raitt, Steel & Duncan went forward with two guns.	
1st. Nov.		— " —	In action same place. Battery & wagon line heavily shelled by German heavy guns.	

P.T.O.

nil

a96

121/2650

57th Batty: R.F.A.

— 1st Division

Vol III. 1–30.11.14

57th Battery, R.F.A. November 1914.

Date	Hour	Place	Summary of events & information	Remarks & Reference to Appendices
1st Nov		WESTHOEK near YPRES	In action same place. Battery and wagon line heavily shelled by Heavy Howitzers –	

100

Date	Hour	Place	Summary of events & information	Remarks & References to Appendices
1st	Nov.	WESTHOEK	Casualties:- Killed Gr. Wilson, Dr. Simmonds Dr. Yates, Dr. Kavanagh Wounded. Gr. McLeod, Br. Millbanks S.S. Wood, Dr. Botting Dr. Mott, Dr. Rose Dr. Stewart, Dr. Buckley Dr. Whitmarsh	
2nd		WESTHOEK	In action same place - Strong German attacks all day which were all repulsed with heavy losses - Lt. Rait-Kerr with Right Section with 2nd & 4th Infantry Brigades.	37

Date	Hour	Place	Summary of events & information	Remarks & Reference to Appendices
3rd		WESTHOEK	In action same place, enemy shelling heavy all day, several attacks were made by the enemy but were repulsed. Right section detached.	
4th			×Reported about 1 a m that Germans had broken through our lines ~~so we moved 8?~~ got the ammo up ~~400 yds back~~, we had intended to move in any case as the enemy had the range to our guns, ~~so that to move~~. We came into action in some bushes or undergrowth, about 400 yds back.	×afterwards ascertained to have been a German Spy.

38

Date	Hour	Place	Summary of events & information	Remarks & Reference to Appendices
4th Con		WESTHoek	Heavy shell dropped just over No 2 Gun (D Sub) killing Cpl Norris, Gr Cousins and wounding A/Br Clark, " Doggett, Gr O'Boyle	
5th		WESTHoek	Withdrawn from this position about 2 a.m. marched to about ½ mile NORTH of DICKEBUSH, where we billetted for the night. Lt Duncan ~~[illegible]~~ with one gun with 2nd Infantry Brigade was left there (near VELDHOEK)	BSM Edwards joins 46th Bty ~~[illegible]~~ Lt W F Duncan wounded.

Date	Hour	Place	Summary of events & information	Remarks & Reference to Appendices
6th Nov		HAZEBROUCK	marched and billetted here Lieut Rait KERR relieved Mr Duncan.	
7th Nov.		—"—	Resting - Br. Hogg who is with gun in trenches killed.	
8th		—"—	Resting	
9th		—"—	—"—	
10th		—"—	—"—	"B" detachment sent ~~the 3rd [illegible]~~ with guns in infantry trenches.
11th		—"—	—"—	
12th	6 am	Hazebrouck	marched with 96 th. Bde. & billeted near ~~[illegible]~~ VLAMERTINGHE we hear that the following casualties had occurred with detached sub section. (A) Lieut. W.C. Rait Kerr - killed Bdr. Jackson, Br. Tierney & Br. Emmerson wounded &	

Date	Hour	Place	Summary of events & information	Remarks & Reference to Appendices
			Cosgrove/Gurman missing	2Lt Abraham posted vice, Capt Rait left missing.
13th.		NR. ER. VLAMERTINGE	Marched to ~~Castle~~ BELLEWAARDE FARM via YPRES & came into action about 6pm – raining nearly the whole day – vehicles stuck in several places.	
14th.		HOOGE ~~[illegible]~~	In action same place – ground in very bad state – vehicles moved with difficulty – Mr. Rose S.J. wounded during night in wagon line.	
15th.		HOOGE ~~[illegible]~~	In action same place – 3 wagons sent back to A.C. Detachment with gun in trenches relieved by "A" Sub.	

Date	Hour	Place	Summary of events & information	Remarks & Reference to Appendices
23rd		MERRIS	Resting.	
24th		"	As above	
25th		"	as above	
26th	2.0. p.m.	ESTAIRES	marched to this neighbourhood to join 8th Division and billetted in the neighbourhood.	
27th	"	"	reconnoitred position for four guns which was occupied at night by two guns, two being kept ready to join 33rd Bde. R.F.A. about two miles. S.W.	
28th	"	"	reposted lines with section in action and section proceeded as above to join 33rd Bde. R.F.A.	
29th		"	Registered points in enemy's lines. Detached Section did not fire	45

Date	Hour	Place	Summary of events & information	Remarks & Reference to Appendices
16th		BELLEWAARDE (HOOGE)	In action same place	
17th		VLAMERTIGNE	Marched to billets at dusk. Centre sect. left in action near HOOGE 3 more days.	
18th		MERRIS	Bivouacked to rest.	
19th		"	As above.	
20th		"	As above.	
21st.		"	As above.	
22nd		"	As above.	

44

Date	Hour	Place	Summary of events & information	Remarks & Reference to Appendices
30th Nov.	—	ESTAIRES.	In action same place quiet day —	

F W Robinson
Major
57th Battery RFA

47

www.ingramcontent.com/pod-product-compliance
Lightning Source LLC
Chambersburg PA
CBHW080916230426
43668CB00014B/2139